THE
NUTRITIONAL
COST of
PRESCRIPTION
DRUGS

Ross Pelton, R.Ph.
James B. LaValle, R.Ph.

Morton Publishing Company
925 West Kenyon Avenue, Unit 12
Englewood, CO 80110
phone: 1-303-761-4805
fax: 1-303-762-9923
http://www.morton-pub.com

This is a Perspective book.

We think that books should be organized and designed for easy use and reference and we have made every effort to make sure this one is. We hope you enjoy it.

Dennis Hogan, Publisher
Perspective Books / Morton Publishing

First Edition
Copyright © 2000 by Morton Publishing Company

Printed in the United States of America.

00 01 02 03 04 / 9 8 7 6 5 4 3 2 1

CONTENTS

Contents

FOREWORD

Over the last decade or more, there's been much more emphasis and publicity given to good diet, as well as the use of vitamins and minerals as important tools for staying well. But despite our best efforts to stay healthy, prescription or non-prescription drugs may be necessary from time to time. For some of us, circumstances necessitate the continuous use of one or more drugs.

Until now, there have been almost no easily accessible resources available that tell us about the interactions between prescription drugs and nutrients. The "warnings" we occasionally receive about vitamin or mineral use from drug prescribers are often overly broad or not well supported. Even worse, many of us have come to realize that "warnings" about drugs and nutrients from government agencies are just as likely to be reliable as any other government pronouncement.

That's why *The Nutritional Cost of Prescription Drugs* is a uniquely valuable book. Ross Pelton and James LaValle have assembled in one place all the *reliable, documented* information the "average" prescription drug user might need to both avoid hazardous drug-nutrient interactions and take necessary nutritional measures to correct drug-induced nutritional deficiencies. Even better, what follows can serve as a easily-understandable "primer" on the uses of each of the vitamins and minerals.

Now that you have this uniquely valuable resource, why not show it to your doctor? You might also mention that there is a "professional" version* available in an easy-to-use "handbook" form!

Jonathan V. Wright, MD
Medical Director, Tahoma Clinic
Kent, Washington

A graduate of Harvard University and the University of Michigan Medical School, Dr. Wright has been in the practice of nutritional and natural medicine at the Tahoma Clinic in Kent, Washington since 1973. His several books (including the recent best-selling Natural Hormone Replacement for Women over 45*) have sold over 750,000 copies. He and Alan R. Gaby, M.D., teach nationally respected seminars in nutritional medicine for health care professionals.* — RP & JL

* *The Drug-Induced Nutrient Depletion Handbook 1999–2000* by Ross Pelton, James B. LaValle, Ernest B. Hawkins, Daniel L. Krinsky. Lexi-Comp Inc.

INTRODUCTION

The Nutritional Cost of Prescription Drugs discusses the health problems that can develop when people take drugs that cause their bodies to lose nutrients. The medical name for this is *drug-induced nutrient depletion,* and it has recently become a "hot" new health topic. Although some "hot" new topics are fads that come and go, drug-induced nutrient depletion is not a fad. Instead, it is moving to center stage, because it is a topic of vital significance to both health professionals and the general public. The information in this book is designed to teach the millions of people who need to take medications regularly how to maintain good nutrition while using prescription drugs.

Studies documenting that many commonly prescribed drugs cause the depletion of one or more nutrients have been appearing in the peer-reviewed scientific literature for decades. Unfortunately, this information has not received the publicity and attention it deserves, until now.

This book addresses over 1,000 drugs that can cause the depletion of nutrients in humans. Most of the major categories of drugs cause nutrient depletions (e.g., oral contraceptives, antacids, antibiotics, cardiovascular drugs, etc.). In the 34th annual survey of the top 200 drugs dispensed in the U.S., 11 of the top 20 drugs prescribed in 1998 were drugs for which studies showed potential nutrient depletions.[1] This is a problem that affects millions of people.

Many of the side effects from drugs may actually be due to nutrient depletions that are caused by the drugs, when taken over time. Now that this information has been brought to light, it seems that health professionals have a professional responsibility to become knowledgeable about drug-induced nutrient depletions so that they can counsel patients and customers accordingly. However, doctors and pharmacists are often too busy to spend extra time with each individual patient. That is why this book is really designed to put this information into your hands — the general public. In the end, your health is your responsibility.

HOW TO USE THIS BOOK

This book has been organized and cross-referenced so readers can easily locate information about drugs, nutrients, and the health problems associated with specific nutrient losses. It is organized into the following sections:

Part I: Quick Reference Chart

This section presents in a chart format an overview of the drugs that cause the loss of nutrients.

Part II: Drugs and Their Effects on Nutrition

This section provides a more detailed discussion of the drugs that cause nutrient losses and the potential health problems that can develop from these losses. It also provides information on a drug or drug category's sales, prescription volume, and ranking in the United States for 1998 (based on the annual survey of prescription drugs conducted by IMS Health as reported in *Pharmacy Times*[2]).

Part III: Nutrient Reviews

Each nutrient is profiled in detail in this section. It includes a list of the generic names of drugs that can deplete that nutrient (the brand names of drugs are listed only in the Alphabetical Index). It also summarizes the symptoms and causes of nutrient depletion to help you determine if your symptoms or health problems might be related to a deficiency of that nutrient. The reviews also contain an overview of each nutrient, information about the nutrient's biological functions and effects, side effects and toxicity, dosages, and dietary sources.

Part IV: Index

Drugs in the Index are listed by their *generic name only*. If you know the brand name but not the generic name of a drug, you can find the generic name in the alphabetical *Brand Names/Generic Names* list that follows the Index. This list provides the generic name for each brand name. Each drug listing in the Index provides page numbers for both the discussion of the drug or drug group and the *Nutrient Review* for each nutrient depleted by it. The scientific basis for this, which is explained below, is also listed in the index for each drug that causes nutrient depletions.

THE SCIENTIFIC BASIS FOR THIS BOOK

Each generic drug listed in the alphabetical index contains a notation called the *Scientific Basis*, abbreviated as "SB." This notation explains the scientific basis (or reason) for a drug's inclusion in this book according to one or more of the following four categories.

SB #1 is the most common rationale for including a drug in this book. SB #1 indicates that the *scientific studies reporting a nutrient depletion(s)* were conducted using this specific drug.

SB #2 indicates that *studies from drugs in the same pharmacological class have reported nutrient depletions.* For example, assume that no studies have reported that drug X has depleted any nutrients. However, if studies have reported that other drugs in the same pharmacological class have caused nutrient depletions, it can be assumed that drug X could deplete the same nutrients. This frequently happens when other drug companies come out with a version of a drug in a class of drugs with documented nutrient depletions, which have already been on the market for some time.

SB #3 refers to *a drug that works the same way as another drug that is known to cause a nutrient depletion.* (Note: The technical description of this is that both drugs have the same mechanism of action.)

SB #4 is for *drugs where there is inferred or indirect evidence of depletion based on disruption of physiological processes.* An example of this is when chemotherapy drugs or antibiotics disrupt the normal functioning of the gastrointestinal tract.

THE LIMITATIONS OF THIS BOOK

It would be virtually impossible to track down every single study that has been published on the wide range of drugs we discuss in this book. However, we feel that we have succeeded in locating most of the studies that have been published on drug-induced nutrient depletions, and we have attempted to provide a level of balance by factoring in negative or conflicting studies where they exist. The majority of our database research was conducted on Medline, which we feel contains most recognized medical journals.

For space and cost reasons, a listing of the scientific studies we researched is not included as part of this book. However, information on how to access that list as well as abstracts of the studies can be found at the publisher's web site: www.morton-pub.com/html/nutritionalcost.html. Our primary goal in this is to show health professionals and the general public that a large and credible body of scientific research exists that has reported and documented drug-induced nutrient depletions.

We are not suggesting that drug-induced nutrient deficiencies are the source of peoples' medical problems. Conditions such as high stress, environmental pollution, poor diets, and many other factors can contribute to health problems. However, when people take medications that create additional nutrient losses, it may be the proverbial straw that breaks the camel's back. Nutrient depletions can have a negative effect on digestion, metabolism, detoxification, and other aspects of metabolic function, and ultimately disrupt an individual's immune system and overall health.

The problem of drug-induced nutrient depletions is probably much larger and more widespread than reported in this book. In many cases, a drug's effect on various nutrients has simply not been studied yet. It is difficult to get funding for such studies, but hopefully the evidence presented in this book will stimulate more research in this area and require this type of testing before approval of a new drug. Gaining insight into nutrient depletions that are caused by drugs may lead us to being able to reduce symptoms and side effects allowing for improved quality of care.

A MESSAGE ABOUT HEALTH

A number of years ago I saw one of Ashleigh Brilliant's humorous postcards that stated, "Life is the only game in which the object of the game is to learn the rules."[3] That little statement made a strong impression on me, because I felt it made a serious statement about health and life. When you purchase a new car or any other piece of expensive equipment, you are given a detailed operating manual that tells you how to care for the equipment, keep it running smoothly, and trouble-shoot problems. However, we come into life with this amazingly complex, wonderful machine called the human body that has no operating manual. And unfortunately, many people don't think to take care of it until it starts to break down. If we learn some of the simple, basic fundamental rules of health, it will ultimately make the "Game of Life" much longer and more enjoyable.

Since their inception many years ago, standards such as Recommended Dietary Allowance (RDAs) have been promoted as nutrient guidelines that meet the needs of most healthy individuals. In fact, though they are adequate to prevent outright nutritional deficiency diseases such as scurvy, beriberi, and pellagra, they are not designed for optimal health. The line drawn below represents what we will refer to as the **Health LifeLine**, going from death on the one end to optimal health and wellness at the other end. The RDAs are sufficient to prevent most people from getting these severe nutritional deficiency diseases, which fall on the Health Line about where you see the X.

Optimal
Death_____X_____Health
HEALTH LIFELINE

Does it make sense to consume just enough nutrients to keep you slightly beyond the X point on the Health LifeLine? Some health professionals refer to the RDAs as the *minimum wage of nutrition*. It is important to realize that RDAs have nothing to do with optimal health and wellness. In most cases, nutrient intakes necessary for optimal health are greater than the RDAs. Don't be satisfied with minimal health. Aim for optimal health.

THE SAFETY OF NUTRITIONAL SUPPLEMENTS

In the past decade there have been hundreds, perhaps thousands, of studies published that report that doses of nutrients higher than the RDAs provide significant health benefits. Unfortunately, it has traditionally taken decades for such research to filter down through health professionals to the general public. A good example is the work of Dr. Kilmer McCully who began publishing studies in 1969 that showed that elevated blood homocysteine was a major risk factor to cardiovascular disease. At the time, tremendous amounts of research dollars and large professional egos were committed to the cholesterol hypothesis. It has taken almost 30 years for Dr. McCully's message to get heard, but we now know that additional levels of folic acid, vitamin B_6, and vitamin B_{12} will lower elevated homocysteine levels. Taking levels of three B vitamins at levels above the RDA (costing only pennies per day) may be one of the most effective ways to decrease your risk of cardiovascular disease.

The issue of safety usually comes up when nutritional supplement recommendations above the RDA are suggested. However, the margin of error with most nutrients is much broader than it is with prescription drugs. A case in point is the recent study published in the *Journal of the American Medical Association* titled "Incidence of Adverse Drug Reactions in Hospitalized Patients: a meta-analysis of prospective studies."[4] The authors of this study report that in 1994, an estimated 2,216,000 hospitalized patients experienced a serious adverse drug reaction and in the same year an estimated 106,000 hospitalized patients died, not from mistakes, but from what was believed to be the correct use of those medications. If outpatient drug-related deaths were considered, the figure would undoubtedly be much higher. This study implies that deaths related to the correct use of medications may rank among the leading causes of death in the United States.

Statistics compiled from the American Association of Poison Control Centers over a period of eight years also make a powerful statement. These statistics recorded the number of deaths reported at Poison Control Centers from prescription drugs, non-prescription drugs, and nutrients from 1987 through 1994.[5] During this eight year period, there were 4,065 deaths from all drugs (prescription and non-prescription) compared to 5 deaths from nutrients (one was later determined to have been an error).

These studies suggest that drugs represent a much greater risk than nutritional supplements. However, the improper use of nutrients can also cause problems. For example, vitamin D and iron are the two nutrients that can cause health problems if consumed in excessive quantities over time. Also, vitamin A and vitamin E, which are fat-soluble and the trace mineral selenium are examples of nutrients that can produce toxic effects when taken in excess. Still, individuals would have to use gross negligence over an extended period of time in order to create a problem with these nutrients. In general, the diseases developed, money lost, and the pain, suffering, and death that occur in individuals who do not ingest sufficient levels of nutrients for optimal health and wellness are much more significant compared to the occasional incidence of a toxic overdose of a nutrient.

In her book *New Passages*, Gail Sheehy notes that the aging process for health conscious baby boomers is quite different than for previous generations.[6] Our parents made plans for or actually retired between the ages of 55 and 65. At this age, Ms. Sheehy states that health conscious baby boomers can consider themselves "in the infancy of their second adulthood." A healthy extension of both quantity and quality of life is available to everyone.

The judicious use of optimal levels of nutritional supplements along with a healthy diet and life style enables most individuals to have a great deal of control over their own immune system and their own aging process. These are choices and decisions that every person can make for himself or herself that will have enormous impact on your health, quality of life, and how long you will live. As Albert Szent-Gyorgy, the discoverer of vitamin C, stated: "Active supplements are the least expensive, most effective health insurance you can buy."

For many people, the term *nutritional supplement* means vitamins. In reality, a lack of minerals is equally if not more problematic than a deficiency of vitamins. This is because most huge factory farming organizations use chemical fertilizers that do not include trace minerals. Thus, the commercial food supply is experiencing a continual decline in trace minerals, which are essential nutrients. This is why you should take nutritional supplements that contain a wide range of both vitamins and minerals.

There is a considerable range in nutritional supplement programs. Some products provide higher than RDA dosage levels in a one-tablet-daily formulation. However, the dosage recommendation for many high potency nutritional supplements entails taking several tablets daily. This can provide the additional benefit of maintaining a more even blood level of nutrients throughout the day, which in turn may increase antioxidant protection and help to slow down the aging process.

Greater stress, more environmental pollutants, poorer nutritional content of much food, and medications that cause the loss of nutrients all point to the need today to take well-formulated high potency multivitamin/mineral supplements. At the very least, it is essential to consider taking the nutrients known to be depleted by medications being taken. There are a variety of companies that provide nutrition-specific formulas for classes of drugs that deplete nutrients. However, check their formulas against the chart in this book to assure proper nutrient replacement.

At Natural Health Resources, our goal is to provide health education products and services that will enable and empower millions of Americans to have healthier, happier, longer lives. We hope this book helps many of you along this path.

Ross Pelton, Jim LaValle
Natural Health Resources

NOTES

1 34th Annual Survey of Top 200 Drugs by IMS Health, *Pharmacy Times* (April 1999) : pp. 16-42.
2 34th Annual Survey of Top 200 Drugs by IMS Health, *Pharmacy Times* (April 1999) : pp. 16-42.
3 A. Brilliant, *Pot-Shot #1409*, Brilliant Enterprises, Santa Barbara, California.
4 J. Lazarou, et al., "Incidence of adverse drug reactions in hospitalized patients: a meta-analysis of prospective studies," *JAMA* 1998 Apr 15, 279(15):1200-5.
5 Information supplied by Donald Loomis. Original data from the American Association of Poison Control Centers. Statistics first published in the *American Journal of Emergency Medicine*.
6 G. Sheehy, *New Passages* (New York: Random House, 1995)

The Quick Reference Guide To Nutrient Losses

Drug	Nutrient Losses	Potential Health Problems
ANTACIDS		
Magnesium & Aluminum Antacids	Calcium Phosphorus Folic acid	Osteoporosis, heart & blood pressure problems, tooth decay Skeletal problems and anxiety or nervousness Birth defects, cervical dysplasia, anemia, heart disease, cancer risk
Sodium Bicarbonate Alka-Seltzer®, baking soda	Potassium Folic acid	Irregular heartbeat, muscle weakness, fatigue, edema Birth defects, cervical dysplasia, anemia, heart disease, cancer risk
ANTIBIOTICS		
Antibiotics, General Aminoglycosides, Cephalosporins Fluoroquinolones, Macrolides, Penicillins, Tetracyclines, etc.	B vitamins Vitamin K	Short term depletion affects are minimal but failure to re-inoculate the GI tract with beneficial bacteria, also known as probiotics, often results in dysbiosis, which causes gas, bloating, decreases the digestion & absorption of nutrients, and also may lead to a variety of other health problems. Everyone, from infants to the elderly are urged to take probiotics (containing acidophilus and bifidus bacteria) twice daily with meals for 2 weeks following a course of antibiotics.
Tetracyclines	Calcium Magnesium Iron Vitamin B_6 Zinc	Osteoporosis, heart & blood pressure irregularities, tooth decay Cardiovascular problems, asthma, osteoporosis, cramps, PMS Slow wound healing, fatigue, anemia Depression, sleep disturbance, increased cardiovascular disease risk Weak immunity, wound healing, sense of smell/taste, sexual dysfunction
Tuberculosis drugs Rifampin	Vitamin B_6 Vitamin D	Anemia, tiredness, weakness, increased cardiovascular disease risk Osteoporosis, muscle weakness, hearing loss

Drug	Nutrients	Problems
Isoniazid, INH	Vitamin B_3 Vitamin D	Skin, gastrointestinal and nervous system problems Osteoporosis, muscle weakness, hearing loss
Ethambutol	Calcium Zinc Copper	Osteoporosis, heart & blood pressure irregularities, tooth decay Weak immunity, wound healing, sense of smell/taste, & sexual dysfunction Anemia, fatigue, cardiovascular and connective tissue problems
Aminoglycosides Neomycin, Amikacin, Gentamicin, Kanamycin, Neomycin, Streptomycin, Tobramycin	Fat, Nitrogen, Iron Potassium, Calcium Magnesium, Vitamin A Sodium, Vitamin B_{12} Carotenoids	Minimal problems with short-term use
Trimethoprim Bactrim®, Septra® Proloprim®, Trimpex®	Folic Acid	Minimal problems with short-term use
Penicillins	Potassium	Irregular heart beat, muscle weakness, fatigue, edema
ANTICONVULSANTS		
Phenobarbital & Barbiturates	Vitamin D Calcium Folic Acid Vitamin K Biotin	Osteoporosis, muscle weakness, hearing loss Osteoporosis, heart & blood pressure irregularities, tooth decay Birth defects, cervical dysplasia, anemia, heart disease, cancer risk Blood clotting and skeletal problems Hair loss, depression, cardiac irregularities, dermatitis

Drug	Nutrient Losses	Potential Health Problems
ANTICONVULSANTS (cont.)		
Phenytoin (Dilantin®)	Vitamin D	Osteoporosis, muscle weakness, hearing loss
	Calcium	Osteoporosis, heart & blood pressure irregularities, tooth decay
	Folic Acid	Birth defects, cervical dysplasia, anemia, heart disease, cancer risk
	Vitamin K	Blood coagulation and skeletal problems
	Vitamin B_{12}	Anemia, tiredness, weakness, increased cardiovascular disease risk
	Vitamin B_1	Depression, irritability, memory loss, muscle weakness, edema
	Biotin	Hair loss, depression, cardiac irregularities, dermatitis
Carbamazepine (Tegretol®)	Folic Acid	Birth defects, cervical dysplasia, anemia, heart disease, cancer risk
	Vitamin D	Osteoporosis, muscle weakness, hearing loss
	Biotin	Hair loss, depression, cardiac irregularities, dermatitis
Primidone (Mysoline®)	Folic Acid	Birth defects, cervical dysplasia, anemia, heart disease, cancer risk
	Biotin	Hair loss, depression, cardiac irregularities, dermatitis
Valproic acid (Depakane® Depakote®, Depacon®)	Folic Acid	Birth defects, cervical dysplasia, anemia, heart disease, cancer risk
	Carnitine	Muscle weakness, cramps, fatigue
	Copper	Anemia, fatigue, cardiovascular and connective tissue problems
	Selenium	Lower immunity, reduced antioxidant protection
	Zinc	Weak immunity, wound healing, sense of smell/taste, sexual dysfunction
ANTI-DIABETIC DRUGS		
Sulfonylureas Acetohexamine (Dymelor®) Glyburide (Micronase®/Glynase®/DiaBeta®) Tolazamide (Tolinase®)	Coenzyme Q_{10}	Various cardiovascular problems, weak immune system, low energy

Biguanides
Metformin (Glucophage®)

Nutrient	Effect
Coenzyme Q_{10}	Various cardiovascular problems, weak immune system, low energy
Vitamin B_{12}	Anemia, tiredness, weakness, increased cardiovascular disease risk
Folic Acid	Birth defects, cervical dysplasia, anemia, heart disease, cancer risk

ANTI-FUNGAL DRUGS
Amphotericin B

Nutrient	Effect
Calcium	Osteoporosis, heart & blood pressure irregularities, tooth decay
Magnesium	Cardiovascular problems, asthma, osteoporosis, cramps, PMS
Potassium	Irregular heart beat, muscle weakness, fatigue, edema
Sodium	Muscle weakness, memory loss, dehydration

ANTIHISTAMINES
Hydroxyzine
(Atarax®, Vistaril® and others)

Nutrient	Effect
Melatonin	Insomnia, increase cancer risk, increased free radical aging damage

ANTI-INFLAMMATORY DRUGS
Corticosteroids
Prednisone
Methylprednisolone (Medrol®)
Triamcinolone (Aristocort®)
Dexamethasone (Decadron®)

Nutrient	Effect
Calcium	Osteoporosis, heart & blood pressure irregularities, tooth decay
Vitamin D	Osteoporosis, muscle weakness, hearing loss
Potassium	Irregular heartbeat, muscle weakness, fatigue, edema
Magnesium	Cardiovascular problems, asthma, osteoporosis, cramps, PMS
Zinc	Weak immunity, wound healing, sense of smell/taste, & sexual dysfunction
Vitamin C	Lowered immune system, easy bruising, poor wound healing
Vitamin B_6	Depression, sleep disturbance, increased cardiovascular disease risk
Vitamin B_{12}	Anemia, tiredness, weakness, increased cardiovascular disease risk
Folic Acid	Birth defects, cervical dysplasia, anemia, cardiovascular disease
Selenium	Lower immunity, reduced antioxidant protection
Chromium	Elevated blood sugar, cholesterol & triglycerides, diabetes risk

Drug	Nutrient Losses	Potential Health Problems
ANTI-INFLAMMATORY DRUGS (cont.)		
Sulfasalazine (Azulfidine®)	Folic Acid	Birth defects, cervical dysplasia, anemia, cardiovascular disease
Indomethacin (Indocin®)	Folic Acid	Birth defects, cervical dysplasia, anemia, cardiovascular disease
	Iron	Anemia, weakness, fatigue, hair loss, brittle nails
Other NSAIDS Ibuprofen (Motrin®), Sulindac (Clinoril®), Mefenamic Acid (Ponstel®), Piroxicam (Feldene®), Salsalate (Disalcid®), Naproxen (Naprosyn®), and others.	Folic Acid	Birth defects, cervical dysplasia, anemia, cardiovascular disease
Aspirin & Salicylates	Vitamin C	Lowered immune system, easy bruising, poor wound healing
	Calcium	Osteoporosis, heart & blood pressure irregularities, tooth decay
	Folic Acid	Birth defects, cervical dysplasia, anemia, cardiovascular disease
	Iron	Anemia, weakness, fatigue, hair loss, brittle nails
	Potassium	Irregular heartbeat, muscle weakness, fatigue, edema
	Sodium	Muscle weakness, memory loss, dehydration
	Vitamin B$_5$	Fatigue, listlessness, and possible problems with skin, liver, and nerves
ANTI-PARKINSONIAN DRUG		
Levodopa	Potassium	Irregular heartbeat, muscle weakness, fatigue, edema
	SAMe	Important for synthesis of many compounds and detoxification reactions
	Vitamin B$_6$	Depression, sleep disturbance, increased cardiovascular disease risk

ANTI-PROTOZOAL DRUG

Pentamidine	Magnesium	Cardiovascular problems, asthma, osteoporosis, cramps, PMS

ANTIVIRAL AGENTS

Zidovudine (Retrovir®, AZT and other related drugs)	Carnitine	Increased blood lipids, abnormal liver function & glucose control
	Copper	Anemia, fatigue, cardiovascular and connective tissue problems
	Zinc	Weak immunity, wound healing, sense of smell/taste, & sexual dysfunction
	Vitamin B_{12}	Anemia, tiredness, weakness, increased cardiovascular disease risk
Foscarnet	Calcium	Osteoporosis, heart & blood pressure irregularities, tooth decay
	Magnesium	Cardiovascular problems, asthma, osteoporosis, cramps, PMS
	Potassium	Irregular heartbeat, muscle weakness, fatigue, edema

ANXIOLYTIC (ANTI-ANXIETY) DRUGS

Diazepam (Valium®), Alprazolam (Xanax®)	Melatonin	Insomnia, increased cancer risk, increased free radical aging damage

BRONCHODILATORS

Theophylline-containing drugs	Vitamin B_6	Depression, sleep disturbance, increased cardiovascular disease risk
Beta₂ Adrenergic Agonists Albuterol (Aire® Proventil® Ventolin®, Volmax®) Terbutaline (Brethaire®, Brethine®, Bricanyl®)	Potassium	Irregular heartbeat, muscle weakness, fatigue, edema

CANCER CHEMOTHERAPY

	Many nutrients can be depleted.	Multiple problems can develop including inflammation or damage to cells lining the GI tract, disruption of beneficial intestinal bacteria, nausea and vomiting, loss of appetite and inhibition of detoxification mechanisms, which can lead to multiple nutrient depletions.

Drug	Nutrient Losses	Potential Health Problems
CARDIOVASCULAR DRUGS		
Hydralazine-containing vasodilators	Vitamin B_6 Coenzyme Q_{10}	Anemia, tiredness, weakness, increased cardiovascular disease risk Various cardiovascular problems, weak immune system, low energy
Loop Diuretics Furosemide (Lasix®) Bumetanide (Bumex®) Ethacrynic acid (Edecrin®)	Calcium Magnesium Potassium Vitamin B_1 Vitamin B_6 Vitamin C Sodium Zinc	Osteoporosis, heart & blood pressure irregularities, tooth decay Cardiovascular problems, asthma, osteoporosis, cramps, PMS Irregular heartbeat, muscle weakness, fatigue, edema Depression, irritability, memory loss, muscle weakness, edema Depression, sleep disturbance, increased cardiovascular disease risk Lowered immune system, easy bruising, poor wound healing Muscle weakness, dehydration, memory problems, loss of appetite Weak immunity, wound healing, sense of smell/taste, & sexual dysfunction
Thiazide Diuretics Hydrochlorothiazied (HCTZ) Methyclothiazide (Enduron®) Chlorothiazide (Diuril®) Indapamide (Lozol®) Metolazone (Zaroxolyn®) Chlorthalidone (Hygroton®), and others	Magnesium Potassium Zinc Coenzyme Q_{10} Sodium	Cardiovascular problems, asthma, osteoporosis, cramps, PMS Irregular heartbeat, muscle weakness, fatigue, edema Weak immunity, wound healing, sense of smell/taste, & sexual dysfunction Various cardiovascular problems, weak immune system, low energy Muscle weakness, dehydration, memory problems, loss of appetite
Potassium-sparing diuretics Dyazide®, Maxzide®, Triamterene (Dyrenium®)	Calcium Folic Acid Zinc	Osteoporosis, heart & blood pressure irregularities, tooth decay Birth defects, cervical dysplasia, anemia, cardiovascular disease Weak immunity, wound healing, sense of smell/taste, sexual dysfunction

Drug	Nutrient	Symptoms
Centrally-Acting Antihypertensives Clonidine (Catapres®) Methyldopa (Aldomet®)	Coenzyme Q_{10}	Various cardiovascular problems, weak immune system, low energy
ACE Inhibitors Captopril (Capoten®) Enalapril (Vasotec®) Fosinopril (Monopril®) Lisinopril (Prinovil®) Quinapril (Accupril®) Ramipril (Altace®) Trandolapril (Mavik®)	Sodium Zinc	Weak depletion; sodium supplementation or replacement is not warranted unless advised by a physician Only documented in captopril and enalapril: Slow wound healing, loss of sense of smell & taste, lower immunity & sexual dysfunction
Cardiac Glycosides Digoxin (Lanoxin®)	Vitamin B_1 Calcium Magnesium Phosphorus	Depression, irritability, memory loss, muscle weakness, edema Osteoporosis, heart & blood pressure irregularities, tooth decay Cardiovascular problems, asthma, osteoporosis, cramps, PMS Weakness, low energy, skeletal problems
Beta-blockers Propranolol (Inderal®) Sotolol (Betapace®), Nadolol (Corgard®), Atenolol (Tenormin®), Acebutolol (Sectral®), Metoprolol (Lopressor®), Timolol (Blocadren®), ...and others.	Coenzyme Q_{10} Melatonin	Various cardiovascular problems, weak immune system, low energy Insomnia, increased cancer risk, increased free radical aging damage
Calcium Channel Blockers Nifedipine (Adalat®, Procardia®) Verapamil (Calan®, Covera®-HS, Isoptin®, Verelan®)	Potassium	Irregular heartbeat, muscle weakness, fatigue, edema

Drug	Nutrient Losses	Potential Health Problems
CHOLESTEROL LOWERING DRUGS		
HMG-CoA Reductase Inhibitors	Coenzyme Q_{10}	Various cardiovascular problems, weak immune system, low energy
Lovostatin (Mevacor®), Simvastatin (Zocor®), Cerivastatin (Baycol®), Fluvastatin (Lescol®), Pravastatin (Pravacol®), Atorvastatin (Lipitor®).		
Gemfibrozil (Lopid®)	Coenzyme Q_{10}	Various cardiovascular problems, weak immune system, low energy
	Vitamin E	Heart disease risk, weak immune system, increased free radical damage
The "fibrates"		
Clofibrate (Atromid-S®)	Copper	Anemia, fatigue, elevated cholesterol, connective tissue problems
	Vitamin B_{12}	Anemia, tiredness, weakness, increased cardiovascular disease risk
Fenofibrate (TriCor®)	Vitamin E	Heart disease risk, weak immune system, increased free radical damage
	Zinc	Weak immunity, wound healing, sense of smell/taste, sexual dysfunction
Bile Acid Sequestrants	Vitamins A, D, E, K,	Proceed to individual nutrient monographs
Cholestyramine (Questran®)	B_{12}, Beta-carotene, Ca, Mg, Zn, Fe, Fat, Folic acid, Phosphorus	
Colestipol (Colestid®)	Vitamins A, D, E, B_{12},	Proceed to individual nutrient monographs
	Beta-carotene, folic acid, iron	
ELECTROLYTE REPLACEMENT		
Potassium Chloride (Timed Release)	Vitamin B_{12}	Anemia, tiredness, weakness, increased cardiovascular disease risk
Micro-K®, Slow-K®		
FEMALE HORMONES		
Estrogen Replacement (ERT) &	Vitamin B_6	Depression, sleep disturbance, increased cardiovascular disease risk
Hormone Replacement (HRT)	Magnesium	Cardiovascular problems, asthma, osteoporosis, cramps, PMS

Drug	Nutrient	Effects of Loss
Oral Contraceptives	Folic acid	Birth defects, cervical dysplasia, anemia, cardiovascular disease
	Vitamin B_1	Depression, irritability, memory loss, muscle weakness, edema
	Vitamin B_2	Problems with skin, eyes, mucous membranes and nerves
	Vitamin B_3	Cracked, scaly skin, swollen tongue, diarrhea
	Vitamin B_6	Depression, sleep disturbances, increased cardiovascular disease risk
	Vitamin B_{12}	Anemia, tiredness, weakness, increased cardiovascular disease risk
	Vitamin C	Lowered immune system, easy bruising, poor wound healing
	Magnesium	Cardiovascular problems, asthma, osteoporosis, cramps, PMS
	Selenium	Lower immunity, reduced antioxidant protection
	Zinc	Weak immunity, wound healing, sense of smell/taste, & sexual dysfunction
GOUT MEDICATIONS		
Colchicine, Col-benemid®	Vitamin B_{12}	Anemia, tiredness, weakness, increased cardiovascular disease risk
	Calcium	Osteoporosis, heart & blood pressure irregularities, tooth decay
	Sodium	Muscle weakness, dehydration, loss of appetite, poor concentration
	Phosphorus	Weakness, low energy, skeletal problems
	Potassium	Irregular heartbeat, muscle weakness, fatigue, edema
	Beta-carotene	Lower immunity, reduced antioxidant protection
LAXATIVES		
Mineral oil Agoral®, Haley's M-O®	Vit. A, D, E, K, and Beta-carotene	Multiple problems associated with depletion of fat-soluble nutrients
	Calcium	Osteoporosis, heart & blood pressure irregularities, tooth decay
	Phosphorus	Weakness, low energy, skeletal problems
Sodium Phosphate enema Fleet® enema	Calcium	Osteoporosis, heart & blood pressure irregularities, tooth decay
	Magnesium	Cardiovascular problems, asthma, osteoporosis, cramps, PMS

Drug	Nutrient Losses	Potential Health Problems
LAXATIVES (cont.)		
Bisacodyl Bisac-Evac®, Bisacodyl Unisers®, Bisco-Lax®, Carter's Little Pills®, Clysodrast®, Dacodyl®, Deficol®, Dulcolax®, Feen-A-Mint®, Fleet® Laxative	Potassium	Irregular heartbeat, muscle weakness, fatigue, edema
PSYCHOTHERAPEUTIC MEDICATIONS		
Tricyclic Antidepressants Amitriptyline (Elavil®) Desipramine (Norpramin®) Nortriptyline (Aventyl®, Pamelor®) Doxepin (Sinequan®), Imipramine (Tofranil®), and others	Coenzyme Q_{10} Vitamin B_2	Various cardiovascular problems, weak immune system, low energy Problems with skin, eyes, mucous membranes and nerves
Major Tranquilizers Chlorpromazine (Thorazine®) Thioridazine (Mellaril®) Fluphenazine (Permitil®, Prolixin®) Mesoridazine (Serentil®), and others	Coenzyme Q_{10} Vitamin B_2 Melatonin	Various cardiovascular problems, weak immune system, low energy Problems with skin, eyes, mucous membranes and nerves Insomnia, increased cancer risk, increased free radical aging damage
Monoamine Oxidase Inhibitors Phenelzine (Nardil®)	Vitamin B_6	Depression, sleep disturbance, increased cardiovascular disease risk
Haloperidol (Haldol®)	Melatonin Vitamin E	Insomnia, increased cancer risk, increased free radical aging damage Depression, sleep disturbance, increased cardiovascular disease risk
Lithium Eskalith®, Lithobid®, Lithonate®, Lithotabs®	Inositol	Excessive urination and excessive thirst
STEROIDS (ANABOLIC) Stanozolol (Winstrol®)	Iron	Anemia, weakness, fatigue, hair loss, brittle nails

THYROID MEDICATIONS

Medication	Nutrient	Effects
Levothyroxine (Levothroid®, Levoxyl® Synthroid®, and others)	Iron	Anemia, weakness, fatigue, hair loss, brittle nails

ULCER MEDICATIONS

Medication	Nutrient	Effects
H-2 Receptor Antagonists Cimetidine (Tagamet®) Famotidine (Pepcid®) Nizatidine (Axid®) Ranitidine (Zantac®)	Vitamin B$_{12}$	Anemia, tiredness, weakness, increased cardiovascular disease risk
	Folic Acid	Birth defects, cervical dysplasia, anemia, cardiovascular disease
	Vitamin D	Osteoporosis, muscle weakness, hearing loss
	Calcium	Osteoporosis, heart & blood pressure irregularities, tooth decay
	Iron	Anemia, weakness, fatigue, hair loss, brittle nails
	Zinc	Weak immunity, wound healing, sense of smell/taste, & sexual dysfunction
	Protein	Potential amino acid deficiencies
Proton Pump Inhibitors Lansoprazole (Prevacid®) Omeprazole (Prilosec®)	Vitamin B$_{12}$	Anemia, tiredness, weakness, increased cardiovascular disease risk
	Protein	Potential amino acid deficiencies

MISCELLANEOUS

Medication	Nutrient	Effects
Methotrexate	Folic Acid	Birth defects, cervical dysplasia, anemia, cardiovascular disease
Penicillamine	Vitamin B$_6$	Depression, sleep disturbance, increased cardiovascular disease risk
	Magnesium	Cardiovascular problems, asthma, osteoporosis, cramps, PMS
	Copper	Anemia, fatigue, elevated cholesterol, connective tissue problems
	Zinc	Weak immunity, wound healing, sense of smell/taste, & sexual dysfunction
EDTA	Calcium	Osteoporosis, heart & blood pressure irregularities, tooth decay
Ritodrine	Calcium	Osteoporosis, heart & blood pressure irregularities, tooth decay
	Potassium	Irregular heartbeat, muscle weakness, fatigue, edema

ANTACIDS

Antacids are of two primary types — those containing magnesium and aluminum salts and those that contain sodium bicarbonate.

MAGNESIUM/ALUMINUM HYDROXIDE ANTACIDS

Many over-the-counter antacids contain a combination of magnesium and aluminum salts. The aluminum in these products can bind with phosphate in the intestinal tract, preventing absorption and resulting in lower levels of phosphate in the blood. To compensate for this loss, the body begins to release both phosphate and calcium from skeletal stores in the bones. Excess calcium eventually is lost through the urine. Making the gastrointestinal tract less acidic also inhibits the absorption of folic acid.

Magnesium/aluminum hydroxide-containing antacids deplete calcium, phosphate, and folic acid.

❑ **Calcium depletion:** Insufficient calcium can result in the development of skeletal problems such as *osteoporosis* and *osteomalacia*. Osteoporosis refers to porous, brittle bones that break easily. Osteomalacia is a disease characterized by a gradual softening and bending of the bones with varying severity of pain. Calcium deficiency can also cause high blood pressure, muscle cramps, heart palpitations, tooth decay, back and leg pains, insomnia, and nervous disorders.

❑ **Phosphate depletion:** A deficiency in phosphate can result in skeletal problems, as well as anxiety or nervousness. People who occasionally use magnesium/aluminum antacids are not likely to be affected by the above mentioned problems. Nevertheless, many people (especially the elderly) use these products regularly to alleviate symptoms, and frequent use can lead to problems.

❑ **Folic acid depletion:** A deficiency of folic acid can cause anemia, birth defects, cervical dysplasia, elevated homocysteine, headache, fatigue, depression, hair loss, anorexia, insomnia, diarrhea, nausea, and increased infections. Recent research indicates that folic acid deficiency is also associated with an increased risk of developing breast cancer and colorectal cancer. For a more detailed description of folic acid deficiency problems, proceed to pages 78–80.

SODIUM BICARBONATE ANTACIDS

Sodium bicarbonate-containing antacids deplete potassium and folic acid.

❑ **Potassium depletion:** Short-term or occasional use of sodium bicarbonate antacids is not likely to cause health problems. Many people (especially the elderly), however, use these products regularly to alleviate the symptoms of indigestion. Frequent use of sodium bicarbonate antacids can cause potassium depletion. Symptoms associated with potassium depletion include irregular heartbeat, poor reflexes, muscle weakness, fatigue, continuous thirst, edema, constipation, dizziness, mental confusion, and nervous disorders.

❑ Folic acid deficiency can cause anemia, birth defects, cervical dysplasia, elevated homocysteine, headache, fatigue, depression, hair loss, anorexia, insomnia, diarrhea, nausea, and increased infections. Recent research indicates that folic acid deficiency is also associated with an increased risk of developing breast cancer and colorectal cancer. For a more detailed description of folic acid deficiency problems, proceed to pages 78–80.

ANTI-ANXIETY AGENTS: BENZODIAZEPINES

In 1998, *benzodiazepines*, which represents the primary class of anti-anxiety medications, comprised the 11th largest category of prescription drugs, accounting for over 62,474,000 prescriptions written that year.

DIAZEPAM AND ALPRAZOLAM

> **The benzodiazepines diazepam and alprazolam deplete melatonin.**

Melatonin is the brain hormone that triggers or induces sleep. A deficiency of melatonin results in insomnia and related sleep problems. Insomnia can lead to many other problems, including depression, poor performance at work, and an increase in accidents. Melatonin is also an important *antioxidant*, so a depletion of melatonin could result in greater *free radical* damage and an acceleration of the aging process. Finally, numerous studies have associated low levels of melatonin with an increased incidence of breast cancer.

ANTIBIOTICS

This general introductory section refers to the effects that virtually all antibiotics have on nutrient depletions and the overall health of the gastrointestinal tract. The ensuing discussion refers to the effects of the following classes of antibiotics: penicillins, cephalosporins, fluoroquinolones, macrolides, aminoglycosides, and sulfonamides.

Antibiotics cause the depletion of B vitamins and vitamin K. If the beneficial bacteria in the intestinal tract are not replaced following a course of antibiotics, a condition known as *dysbiosis* can develop, which can cause additional nutrient depletions.

Advancements in technology over the past several decades have produced quantum leaps in our understanding of the many important health benefits that the "friendly" bacteria in the human intestinal tract provide. Scientists have discovered that intestinal bacteria are intimately involved in functions such as digesting and absorbing nutrients, producing vitamins, preventing various forms of cancer, detoxifying pollutants, and metabolizing cholesterol. The beneficial bacteria also provide resistance to infections and control and influence our *immune system*.

The use of antibiotics has grown enormously over the last few decades. Throughout the 1990s, doctors in the United States have written from 200 to 250 million prescriptions for antibiotics each year. Although the discovery and use of antibiotics has been a boost to the health and longevity of people in the 20th century, this widespread use has had some serious health consequences.

One of the main problems associated with the use of antibiotics is that they disrupt the normal balance of bacteria in the intestinal tract. Unfortunately, antibiotics kill the beneficial bacteria along with the pathological species. If an individual does not reinoculate the intestinal tract with beneficial bacteria, other organisms have the opportunity to grow and proliferate. This can result in a variety of health problems, both mental and physical. The term dysbiosis refers to health problems that are caused by a disruption of the normal microflora in the intestinal tract.

After receiving a prescription for antibiotics, the person should take large doses of the beneficial bacteria twice daily with meals for approximately 2 weeks to rebuild and restore the population of "friendly" bacteria in the intestinal tract. The most common of the beneficial bacteria are *Lactobacillus acidophilus* (or *L. acidophilus*) and *bifidobacteria bifidus* (or bifidus). Products containing these beneficial bacteria are called *probiotics*.

The use of antibiotics can cause nutrient depletions via three different mechanisms:

1. The friendly bacteria normally manufacture a wide variety of vitamins in the intestinal tract. Antibiotics kill off the beneficial bacteria, which effectively stops the production of these vitamins, which include vitamin B_1 (thiamin), vitamin B_2 (riboflavin), vitamin B_3 (niacin), vitamin B_5 (pantothenic acid), vitamin B_6 (pyridoxine), vitamin B_{12} (cobalamin), biotin, inositol, and vitamin K.

3. The friendly bacteria produce a wide range of *enzymes* that aid in the digestion and absorption of nutrients. When antibiotics kill off the beneficial bacteria, digestion suffers and fewer nutrients are absorbed.

4. If probiotics are not consumed following a course of antibiotics, unfavorable organisms are likely to grow, which can create additional health problems For example, candida yeast organisms can proliferate and secrete toxins into the body.

Scientists have not yet been able to design studies that are able to determine the amount of nutritional effect provided by the vitamins produced by the beneficial bacteria in our bodies. Still, numerous studies and clinical observations indicate that many people develop significant health problems arising from an imbalance of the bacterial flora in the gastrointestinal tract following the use of antibiotics.

Bacterial imbalance in the intestinal tract can cause a wide range of symptoms and problems throughout the body. Frequently, a person has symptoms in a part of the body far removed from the intestines and does not realize that the problem stems from toxins produced by unfavorable bacteria in the intestinal tract. Symptoms or disorders that can be caused by dysbiosis include acne, diarrhea, constipation, PMS, hormonal problems, easy bruising, candida yeast infections, chronic vaginal and bladder infections, food allergies, bad breath, *osteoporosis*, anemia, anxiety, B-vitamin deficiency, general malabsorption, and nutrient depletion.

The beneficial intestinal bacteria also manufacture vitamin K, a nutrient that regulates blood-clotting mechanisms and calcium deposition into the bone matrix. Thus, a deficiency of vitamin K can cause coagulation problems, which in turn can result in bleeding and hemorrhage, and may also be associated with skeletal problems such as osteoporosis.

ANTIBIOTICS TO TREAT TUBERCULOSIS: ISONIAZID, ETHAMBUTOL, AND RIFAMPIN

Isoniazid has been reported to deplete vitamin B_6, vitamin B_3, vitamin D, and calcium.

❑ **Isoniazid and vitamin B_6 depletion:** Vitamin B_6 (pyridoxine) depletion can cause depression, insomnia, and an increased risk for cardiovascular disease.

■ **Depression:** Vitamin B_6 is necessary to convert the amino acid *tryptophan* into the neurotransmitter *serotonin*. A deficiency of serotonin in the brain is strongly associated with depression. Therefore, people taking drugs that deplete vitamin B_6 are at greater risk for developing depression.

■ **Insomnia:** In the brain, serotonin is converted into *melatonin*, a hormone that controls sleep. Because a vitamin B_6 deficiency inhibits the synthesis of serotonin, it also will decrease the amount of melatonin that can be produced in the brain. People who become deficient in melatonin are likely to suffer from *insomnia* and related sleep problems.

- **Cardiovascular disease:** Vitamin B_6 is one of the B vitamins necessary to metabolize *homocysteine,* an amino acid produced from the metabolism of the essential amino acid methionine. Homocysteine is a toxic substance capable of directly injuring the lining of the arteries — the type of damage that causes *atherosclerosis.* Under normal conditions, it exists only briefly. A lack of vitamin B_6, however, causes elevated levels of homocysteine in the blood. Even slight elevations of homocysteine represent a seriously increased risk for developing atherosclerosis, the leading cause of heart disease.

❑ **Isoniazid and niacin depletion:** Vitamin B_3 (niacin) depletion can produce problems with the skin, intestinal, and nervous systems. These problems usually develop only with a critical deficiency of niacin.

❑ **Isoniazid and vitamin D depletion:** Vitamin D depletion can lead to *osteoporosis* and other skeletal problems. Because vitamin D is necessary for calcium absorption, a vitamin D deficiency could cause a calcium deficiency as well. Vitamin D depletion also can result in muscle weakness and hearing loss.

❑ **Isoniazid and calcium depletion:** Vitamin D is necessary for calcium absorption. Because isoniazid causes a depletion of vitamin D, calcium could be depleted, too. This can lead to *osteoporosis,* heart irregularities, elevated blood pressure, and tooth decay.

Ethambutol has been reported to deplete zinc and copper.

❑ **Ethambutol and zinc depletion:** Zinc is a mineral important to the *immune system*. Zinc deficiency can cause a weakened immune system and slow healing of wounds. A zinc deficiency also results in loss of the senses of taste and smell. Zinc deficiency can also cause infertility and sexual dysfunction in men and women.

❑ **Ethambutol and copper depletion:** Insufficient copper can result in anemia and fatigue, problems with maintenance and repair of connective tissues, and elevated *serum cholesterol*.

Rifampin has been reported to deplete vitamin D.

Vitamin D is necessary for calcium absorption, which means that a vitamin D deficiency could produce a calcium deficiency. Vitamin D depletion, therefore, can result in osteoporosis and other skeletal problems. Vitamin D depletion also can produce muscle weakness and hearing loss.

AMINOGYLCOSIDES

Aminogylcosides are broad spectrum antibiotics that are used both topically and internally. Drugs that belong to the aminoglycoside class of antibiotics include amikacin, gentamicin, kanamycin, neomycin, streptomycin, and tobramycin. Topical use for short periods of time is of minimal concern. However, when used internally, they can deplete many nutrients including calcium, magnesium, nitrogen, potassium, sodium, vitamin, A, beta-carotene, fat, and the full range of B-vitamins and vitamin K that the beneficial bacteria in the intestinal tract normally produce. Rather than discuss each of these potential nutrient depletions separately, individuals using any of these drugs are encouraged to review each of the nutritional monographs and the introduction to the antibiotic section that discusses the importance of replenishing the beneficial bacteria in the gastrointestinal tract on pages 16–19.

PENICILLIN ANTIBIOTICS

Penicillin antibiotics deplete potassium.

❑ **Penicillin and potassium depletion:** Many of the various types of penicillin antibiotics have been reported to deplete potassium. Potassium depletion can produce muscular weakness, *tetany* (muscle spasms), and *postural hypotension*, (a term that refers to low blood pressure when changing from a lying or sitting position to a standing position) which can cause dizziness and fainting spells. Other symptoms associated with potassium depletion are irregular heartbeat, poor reflexes, fatigue, continuous thirst, *edema*, constipation, mental confusion, and nervous disorders. In a hospital setting, symptoms usually are treated and managed by giving intravenous potassium chloride.

TETRACYCLINE ANTIBIOTICS

Tetracycline antibiotics deplete calcium, magnesium, iron, and zinc, as well as the full range of B-vitamins and vitamin K that the beneficial bacteria in the intestinal tract normally produce. (See the introduction to Antibiotics, pages 16–19.)

Short-term use of tetracycline antibiotics — 1 to 2 weeks to treat an infection — is not likely to cause a significant depletion of nutrients. However, if *probiotics* are not taken after the course of antibiotics to reestablish the population of beneficial bacteria in the intestinal tract, a number of health problems can develop (see pages 16–19).

One of the greatest problems associated with tetracyclines arises when doctors prescribe them for teenage acne. In these cases, children are directed to take doses of the antibiotic daily, often for years. This can seriously disrupt the intestinal microflora, causing dysbiosis, which can result in nutritional depletions and other health problems. Tetracycline antibiotics easily react with and prevent the absorption of minerals such as calcium, iron, and magnesium.

❏ **Tetracyclines and calcium depletion:** Calcium depletion can result in the development of skeletal problems such as *osteoporosis* and *osteomalacia*. Osteoporosis refers to porous, brittle bones that break easily. Osteomalacia is a disease characterized by a gradual softening and bending of the bones with varying severity of pain. Calcium deficiency also can cause high blood pressure, muscle cramps, heart palpitations, tooth decay, back and leg pains, insomnia, and nervous disorders.

❏ **Tetracyclines and iron depletion:** Iron depletion causes anemia, which results in weakness and fatigue. Iron depletion also causes slow healing of wounds, and a general weakening of the *immune system*. However, iron supplementation is not recommended unless a lab test determines that iron deficiency is present.

❏ **Tetracyclines and magnesium depletion:** Magnesium depletion can cause *cardiac arrhythmias*, high blood pressure, and various other cardiovascular-related problems. Additional conditions associated with low magnesium levels are *osteoporosis*, muscle cramps, PMS, and an increase in the frequency and severity of asthma attacks.

❑ **Tetracyclines and zinc depletion:** Zinc is an important mineral for a healthy *immune system*. A zinc deficiency can cause slow healing of wounds and a weakened immune system, as well as a loss of the senses of taste and smell. Zinc deficiency can also cause infertility and sexual dysfunction in men and women.

TRIMETHOPRIM

Trimethoprim causes the depletion of folic acid.

Antibiotics containing trimethoprim cause a minor depletion of *folic acid*. As with antibiotics in general, when beneficial bacteria in the intestines are killed off, the production of all the B-vitamins and vitamin K is reduced. Because these antibiotics usually are taken for only a short period, these depletions probably are insignificant. Nevertheless, if *probiotics* are not taken after the course of antibiotics to reestablish the population of beneficial bacteria in the intestinal tract, a number of health problems can develop (see pages 16–19).

ANTICONVULSANTS

In 1998, *anticonvulsants*, also referred to as anti-seizure medications, represented the 10th largest dollar-volume category of prescription drugs in the United States, accounting for more than $2.078 billion in sales. In terms of numbers of prescriptions, this class of drugs ranked 17th in 1998, with 43,918,000 prescriptions written. Each of the anticonvulsant drugs — barbiturates, phenytoin, carbamazepine, primidone, and valproic acid — will be discussed separately, along with the nutrients they deplete.

BARBITURATES

Barbiturates can cause the depletion of calcium, folic acid, vitamin D, vitamin K, and biotin.

❑ **Barbiturates and calcium depletion:** Barbiturates and most of the other anticonvulsant drugs cause a decrease in the intestinal absorption of calcium, which results in the increased fecal excretion of calcium. Thus, individuals taking these medications have an increased risk of developing a calcium deficiency. *Calcium supplementation will not solve this problem* because the calcium deficiency is the result of a vitamin D deficiency, and vitamin D is necessary for calcium absorption. Therefore, the explanation for this problem is that barbiturates inhibit vitamin D production in the body, and this in turn decreases calcium absorption. To solve the problem, individuals should be given vitamin D supplements, which facilitate normalization of calcium absorption.

Calcium depletion can result in the development of skeletal problems such as *rickets* in children and *osteoporosis* or *osteomalacia* in adults. Osteoporosis refers to porous, brittle bones that break easily. Rickets and osteomalacia are essentially the same condition, characterized by gradual softening and bending of the bones with varying severity of pain. Calcium deficiency also can cause high blood pressure, muscle cramps, heart palpitations, tooth decay, back and leg pains, insomnia, and nervous disorders.

❑ **Barbiturates and folic acid depletion:** All anticonvulsant drugs deplete folic acid. This depletion can lead to some serious health problems, especially in women. Folic acid deficiency disrupts DNA metabolism, which causes the production of abnormal cells. This problem is especially acute in cells with the most rapid rates of turnover — red blood cells, leukocytes, and *epithelial cells* of the stomach, intestine, vagina, and uterine cervix. The need for folic acid is greater during pregnancy.

Insufficient folic acid is one of the most common vitamin deficiencies. In addition to people not eating enough green leafy vegetables, folic acid is easily destroyed by heat, light, and oxygen, and substantial losses also occur during food processing, cooking, and storage.

Folic acid deficiency can cause anemia, birth defects, cervical dysplasia, elevated homocysteine, headache, fatigue, depression, hair loss, anorexia, insomnia, diarrhea, nausea, and increased infections. Recent research indicates that folic acid deficiency is also associated with an increased risk of developing breast cancer and colorectal cancer. The major health issues related to folic acid deficiency are reviewed below in the hope that more people (especially women) will understand the importance of taking additional folic acid supplementation.

- **Anemia:** Folic acid is required for the production of *erythrocytes* (red blood cells), which carry oxygen from the lungs to the tissues and carbon dioxide from tissues to the lungs. Folic acid deficiency results in anemia and reduced tissue oxygenation, which in turn leads to a condition known as *megaloblastic anemia*, with symptoms including tiredness, weakness, diarrhea, and weight loss.

- **Birth defects:** Folic acid helps regulate neural development and the transfer of genetic material to new cells. During pregnancy, the rapidly growing fetus substantially increases a woman's need for folic acid, and folic acid deficiency during pregnancy dramatically increases the risk for birth defects such as spina bifida and cleft palate. The link between folic acid deficiency and birth defects is so strong that all women of childbearing age are urged to have their folic acid status checked before trying to become pregnant. If this practice were followed, thousands of birth defects would probably be prevented each year. A laboratory test called the Neutrophilic Hypersegmentation Index (NHI) has been developed, which easily identifies folic acid insufficiency.

■ **Cervical dysplasia:** The development of abnormal cells in the uterus, *cervical dysplasia*, is regarded as a *precancerous* condition. It usually is discovered when a woman has her annual Pap exam. This condition may contribute to an increased number of hysterectomies. Approximately 800,000 women have hysterectomies every year in the United States. Some health care professionals believe that the folic acid depletion caused by oral contraceptives and other medications is linked to this high incidence of cervical dysplasia and hysterectomies.

■ **Elevated homocysteine:** Also known as *hyperhomocysteinemia*, a high level of homocysteines is now recognized as a serious independent risk factor for *cardiovascular disease*. Excess homocysteine can cause direct damage to vascular endothelial cells. This means it can cause the type of damage that initiates plaque build-up in the arteries. Even moderate elevations of homocysteine represent a substantially increased risk for plaque build-up and blood clots.

Note. Physicians are urged to use caution when administering megadose folic acid therapy to patients who are on anticonvulsant medications, as there is a report of intravenous folic acid administration inducing a seizure in one patient.

❑ **Barbiturates and vitamin D depletion:** Vitamin D depletion can cause *rickets* in children and *osteomalacia* and *osteoporosis* in adults. These skeletal problems develop because vitamin D is necessary for calcium absorption. Vitamin D deficiency conditions result from insufficient deposition of calcium phosphate into the bone matrix. In children, this creates bones that are not strong enough to withstand the ordinary stresses and strains of weight-bearing, which can result in muscle weakness, pain, knock-knees, bowed legs, spinal curvature, pigeon breast, disfiguring of the skull, and tooth decay and dental problems. A lack of vitamin D in adults leads to *osteoporosis*, which makes the bones thin, porous, and more likely to fracture. Vitamin D deficiency also can result in hearing loss.

❑ **Barbiturates and vitamin K depletion:** Vitamin K regulates blood-clotting mechanisms. A deficiency of vitamin K can cause coagulation problems, which can result in bleeding and hemorrhage. The trauma of birthing can cause life-threatening intracranial bleeding in infants born to mothers who have been taking phenobarbital during pregnancy. Vitamin K is also necessary for bone metabolism and recent research indicates that vitamin K deficiency may contribute to bone loss.

❑ **Barbiturates and biotin depletion:** Biotin deficiency can result in hair loss, depression, skin problems, and an elevation of blood glucose and cholesterol levels.

PHENYTOIN

Phenytoin can cause the depletion of a wide range of nutrients including biotin, calcium, folic acid, vitamin B_1, vitamin B_{12}, vitamin D, and vitamin K.

Patients who are prescribed phenytoin usually have to take the drug for the rest of their lives. This long-term use can cause many health problems directly related to the nutritional depletions that the drug causes.

The most serious of the problems caused by depletion of these nutrients are birth defects in women as a result of folic acid deficiency and skeletal problems in children and adults alike from vitamin D and calcium depletions. Vitamin B_1 deficiency resulting from phenytoin therapy also has been reported to *lower IQ scores*. Two other potential problems are increased rates of *depression* and *cardiovascular disease* as a result of folic acid and vitamin B_{12} depletion.

❑ **Phenytoin and biotin depletion:** Biotin deficiency can result in hair loss, depression, skin problems, and an elevation of blood glucose and cholesterol levels.

❑ **Phenytoin and calcium depletion:** Phenytoin and most of the other anticonvulsant drugs cause a decrease in the intestinal absorption of calcium, which results in increased fecal excretion of calcium. Therefore, individuals taking these medications are at increased risk for developing a calcium deficiency. *Calcium supplementation is not an appropriate way to solve this problem* because the calcium deficiency is the result of a vitamin D deficiency. Vitamin D is necessary for calcium absorption. Thus, the explanation for this problem is that barbiturates inhibit vitamin D production in the body, and this in turn decreases calcium absorption. To solve the problem, patients have to be given vitamin D supplements, which facilitate normalization of calcium absorption.

Calcium depletion can result in the development of skeletal problems such as *rickets* in children and *osteoporosis* or *osteomalacia* in adults. These diseases are characterized by gradual softening and bending of the bones with varying severity of pain. Calcium deficiency also can cause high blood pressure, muscle cramps, heart palpitations, tooth decay, back and leg pains, insomnia, and nervous disorders.

❑ **Phenytoin and folic acid depletion:** All anticonvulsant drugs deplete folic acid. This depletion can cause some serious health problems, especially in women. Folic acid deficiency disrupts DNA metabolism, which causes the production of abnormal cells. This problem is especially acute in cells with the most rapid rates of turnover, including red blood cells, leukocytes, and *epithelial cells* of the stomach, intestine, vagina, and uterine cervix.

Folic acid needs are greater during pregnancy. Folic acid deficiency also is one of the most common vitamin deficiencies. In addition to people not eating enough green leafy vegetables, folic acid is easily destroyed by heat, light, and oxygen, and substantial losses occur during food processing, cooking and storage.

Folic acid deficiency can cause anemia, birth defects, *cervical dysplasia*, elevated *homocysteine* levels, headache, fatigue, depression, hair loss, anorexia, insomnia, diarrhea, nausea, and increased infections. Research also indicates that folic acid deficiency is associated with increased risk of developing breast cancer and colorectal cancer. The following is a synopsis of the major health problems related to folic acid deficiency. These affect women more than men and point up the need for supplementation in many circumstances.

■ **Anemia:** Folic acid is required for the production of *erythrocytes* (red blood cells), which carry oxygen from the lungs to the tissues and carbon dioxide from tissues to the lungs. Folic acid deficiency results in reduced tissue oxygenation. This causes a condition known as *megaloblastic anemia*, with symptoms of tiredness, weakness, diarrhea, and weight loss.

■ **Birth defects:** Folic acid helps regulate neural development and the transfer of genetic material to new cells in the fetus. During pregnancy, the rapidly growing fetus substantially increases a woman's need for folic acid, and folic acid deficiency during pregnancy dramatically increases the risk for birth defects such as spina bifida and cleft palate. The link between folic acid deficiency and birth defects is so strong that all women of childbearing age are urged to have their folic acid status checked before trying to become pregnant. If this practice were followed, thousands of birth defects probably would be prevented each year. A laboratory test called the Neutrophilic Hypersegmentation Index (NHI) has been developed, which easily identifies folic acid insufficiency.

- **Cervical dysplasia:** The development of abnormal cells in the uterus, *cervical dysplasia*, is regarded as a *precancerous* condition that usually is discovered when a woman has her annual Pap exam. This condition could contribute to an increased number of hysterectomies. Approximately 800,000 women have hysterectomies every year in the United States. Some health care professionals believe that the folic acid depletion caused by oral contraceptives and other medications is linked to this high incidence of cervical dysplasia and hysterectomies.

- **Elevated homocysteine,** also known as *hyperhomocysteinemia,* now is recognized as a serious independent risk factor for *cardiovascular disease.* Excess homocysteine is capable of directly damaging the vascular *endothelial cells,* causing the type of damage that initiates plaque build-up in the arteries. Even moderate elevations of homocysteine represent substantially increased risk for plaque build-up and blood clots.

Note. Physicians are urged to use caution when administering megadoses of folic acid therapy to patients who are on anticonvulsant medications. One case has been reported of intravenous folic acid administration inducing a seizure.

❑ **Phenytoin and vitamin B_1 depletion:** A deficiency of vitamin B_1 can cause depression, irritability, memory loss, muscle weakness, and *edema.* One study noted that administration of vitamin B_1 to individuals with a B_1 deficiency resulted in improvement in both verbal and nonverbal IQ scores.

❑ **Phenytoin and vitamin B$_{12}$ depletion:** A vitamin B$_{12}$ deficiency can cause *anemia*, which results in fatigue, tiredness, and weakness. A B$_{12}$ deficiency also is a common cause of depression, especially in the elderly population. Inadequate levels of B$_{12}$ result in elevated *homocysteine*, which poses a greatly increased risk for *cardiovascular disease*. If serious B$_{12}$ deficiencies are not corrected, they can lead to long-term irreversible neurological damage.

❑ **Phenytoin and vitamin D depletion:** Vitamin D depletion can cause *rickets* in children and *osteomalacia* and *osteoporosis* in adults. These skeletal problems develop because vitamin D is necessary for calcium absorption. In children, vitamin D deficiency conditions cause insufficient deposition of calcium phosphate into the bone matrix. This creates bones that are not strong enough to withstand the ordinary stresses and strains of weight bearing, and can result in muscle weakness, pain, knock-knees, bowed legs, spinal curvature, pigeon breast, disfiguring of the skull, and tooth decay and dental problems. When insufficient vitamin D causes a calcium deficiency in adults, osteoporosis develops, which makes the bones thin, porous, and more likely to fracture. Vitamin D deficiency also can result in hearing loss.

❑ **Phenytoin and vitamin K depletion:** Because vitamin K regulates blood-clotting mechanisms, a deficiency of vitamin K can cause coagulation problems. This, in turn, can result in bleeding and hemorrhage. Newborn babies have a greater risk of hemorrhaging problems if the mother has been taking vitamin K-depleting anticonvulsant drugs such as phenytoin. Vitamin K is also necessary for bone metabolism and recent research indicates that vitamin K deficiency may contribute to bone loss.

CARBAMAZEPINE

Carbamazepine can deplete biotin, folic acid, and vitamin D.

❑ **Carbamazepine and biotin depletion:** Biotin deficiency can result in hair loss, depression, skin problems, and an elevation of blood glucose and cholesterol levels.

❑ **Carbamazepine and folic acid depletion:** All anticonvulsant drugs deplete folic acid. This depletion can result in some serious health problems, especially in women. Folic acid deficiency disrupts DNA metabolism, which causes abnormal cells to be produced. This problem is especially acute in cells with the most rapid rates of turnover, including red blood cells, leukocytes, and *epithelial cells* of the stomach, intestine, vagina, and uterine cervix. Folic acid needs are greater during pregnancy. Insufficient folic acid also is one of the most common vitamin deficiencies. In addition to people not eating enough green leafy vegetables, folic acid is easily destroyed by heat, light, and oxygen, and substantial losses occur during food processing, cooking, and storage.

Folic acid deficiency can cause anemia, birth defects, cervical dysplasia, elevated homocysteine, headache, fatigue, depression, hair loss, anorexia, insomnia, diarrhea, nausea, and increased infections. Folic acid deficiency also has been associated with increased risk of developing breast cancer and colorectal cancer. The following discussion goes into more detail about the major folic acid deficiency-related health problems in the hope that more people (especially women) will understand the importance of taking additional folic acid supplementation.

- **Anemia:** Folic acid is required for the production of *erythrocytes* (red blood cells,(which carry oxygen from the lungs to the tissues and carbon dioxide from tissues to the lungs. Folic acid deficiency causes anemia and reduced tissue oxygenation. This results in a condition known as *megaloblastic anemia,* which produces symptoms of tiredness, weakness, diarrhea, and weight loss.

- **Birth defects:** Folic acid helps to regulate neural development in the fetus, as well as the transfer of genetic material to new cells. During pregnancy, the rapidly growing fetus substantially increases a woman's need for folic acid, and folic acid deficiency during pregnancy dramatically increases the risk of birth defects such as spina bifida and cleft palate. The link between folic acid deficiency and birth defects is so strong that all women of childbearing age are urged to have their folic acid status checked before trying to become pregnant. If this practice were followed, thousands of birth defects probably would be prevented each year. A laboratory test called the Neutrophilic Hypersegmentation Index (NHI) has been developed, which easily identifies folic acid insufficiency.

- **Cervical dysplasia:** The development of abnormal cells in the uterus, *cervical dysplasia,* is regarded as a *precancerous* condition that usually is discovered when a woman has her annual Pap exam. This condition might contribute to an increased number of hysterectomies. More than 800,000 women have hysterectomies every year in the United States. Some health care professionals believe that the folic acid depletion caused by oral contraceptives and other medications is linked to this high incidence of cervical dysplasia and hysterectomies.

■ **Elevated homocysteine:** Also known as *hyperhomocysteinemia,* elevated homocysteine now is recognized as a serious independent risk factor for *cardiovascular disease.* Excess homocysteine is capable of causing direct damage to vascular *endothelial cells,* which means that it can cause the type of damage that initiates plaque build-up in the arteries. Even moderate elevations of homocysteine represent a substantially increased risk for the development of plaque build-up and blood clots.

Note. Physicians are urged to use caution when administering megadoses of folic acid to patients who are on anticonvulsant medications, as intravenous folic acid administration induced a seizure in one reported patient.

❑ **Carbamazepine and vitamin D depletion:** Vitamin D depletion can cause *rickets* in children and *osteomalacia* and *osteoporosis* in adults. These skeletal problems develop because vitamin D is necessary for the absorption of calcium. In children, the vitamin D deficiency causes insufficient deposition of calcium phosphate into the bone matrix. This creates bones that are not strong enough to withstand the ordinary stresses and strains of weight bearing, which can result in muscle weakness, pain, knock-knees, bowed legs, spinal curvature, pigeon breast, a disfiguring of the skull, and tooth decay and dental problems. In adults, a lack of vitamin D causes a calcium deficiency, which leads to osteoporosis, in which the bones are thin, porous, and more likely to fracture. A vitamin D deficiency also can result in hearing loss.

PRIMIDONE

Primidone can cause the depletion of folic acid, and biotin.

As with other anticonvulsant drugs, the most significant problems arising from these depletions are skeletal problems arising from vitamin D and calcium depletion and potential birth defects resulting from folic acid depletion in pregnant women.

❑ **Primidone and biotin depletion:** Biotin deficiency can result in hair loss, depression, skin problems, and an elevation of blood glucose and cholesterol levels.

❑ **Primidone and folic acid depletion:** All anticonvulsant drugs deplete folic acid. This depletion can incite some serious health problems, especially in women. Folic acid deficiency disrupts DNA metabolism, which leads to the production of abnormal cells. This problem is especially acute in cells with the most rapid rates of turnover, including red blood cells, leukocytes, and *epithelial cells* of the stomach, intestine, vagina, and uterine cervix. Folic acid needs are greater during pregnancy. Folic acid deficiency also is one of the most common vitamin deficiencies in the United States. In addition to insufficient intake of green leafy vegetables, folic acid is easily destroyed by heat, light, and oxygen. Food processing, cooking, and storage also destroy folic acid.

Folic acid deficiency can cause anemia, birth defects, cervical dysplasia, elevated homocysteine, headache, fatigue, depression, hair loss, anorexia, insomnia, diarrhea, nausea, and increased infections. Folic acid deficiency also has been associated with an increased risk of developing breast cancer and colorectal cancer. The major folic acid deficiency-related health problems are explored in greater detail below in the hope that more people (especially women) will understand the importance of taking additional folic acid supplementation.

- **Anemia:** Folic acid is required for the production of *erythrocytes* (red blood cells), which carry oxygen from the lungs to the tissues and carbon dioxide from the tissues to the lungs. Folic acid deficiency results in anemia and reduced tissue oxygenation, causing a condition known as *megaloblastic anemia*, which produces symptoms of tiredness, weakness, diarrhea, and weight loss.

- **Birth defects:** Folic acid helps to regulate neural development and the transfer of genetic material to new cells. During pregnancy, the rapidly growing fetus substantially increases a woman's need for folic acid, and a folic acid deficiency during pregnancy dramatically increases the risk of birth defects such as spina bifida and cleft palate. The link between folic acid deficiency and birth defects is so strong that all women of childbearing age are urged to have their folic acid status checked before trying to become pregnant. If this practice were followed, thousands of birth defects probably would be prevented each year. A laboratory test called the Neutrophilic Hypersegmentation Index (NHI) has been developed, which easily identifies folic acid insufficiency.

- **Cervical dysplasia:** The development of abnormal cells in the uterus, *cervical dysplasia*, is regarded as a *precancerous* condition. It usually is discovered when a woman has her annual Pap exam. This condition may contribute to an increased number of hysterectomies. Approximately 800,000 women have hysterectomies every year in the United States. Some health care professionals believe that the folic acid depletion caused by oral contraceptives and other medications is linked to this high incidence of cervical dysplasia and hysterectomies.

■ **Elevated homocysteine:** Also known as *hyperhomocysteinemia*, elevated homocysteine now is recognized as an independent risk factor for *cardiovascular disease.* Because excessive homocysteine is capable of causing direct damage to vascular *endothelial cells*, it can produce the type of damage that initiates plaque build-up in the arteries. Even moderate elevations of homocysteine represent substantially increased risk for plaque build-up and blood clots.

Note. Physicians are urged to use caution when administering megadoses of folic acid to patients who are on anticonvulsant medications, as a report of intravenous folic acid administration induced a seizure in one patient.

VALPROIC ACID

Valproic acid can cause the depletion of folic acid, carnitine, copper, selenium, and zinc.

❑ **Valproic acid and folic acid depletion:** A deficiency of folic acid can cause a wide range of health problems including anemia, depression, *cervical dysplasia*, birth defects, and increased risks for developing *cardiovascular disease*, breast cancer, and colorectal cancer. For a detailed discussion of the problems associated with folic acid deficiency see pages 25–28, under the discussion of barbiturates and folic acid depletion.

❑ **Valproic acid and carnitine depletion:** Carnitine is an *amino acid* that facilitates the transport of fats across cellular membranes for metabolism and the production of energy. Although the body normally makes adequate levels of carnitine, administration of valproic acid can create a carnitine deficiency, which can cause fatigue, muscle weakness, and cramps.

❑ **Valproic acid and copper depletion:** Copper depletion can result in anemia and fatigue, problems with the maintenance and repair of connective tissues, and elevated levels of *serum cholesterol*.

❑ **Valproic acid and selenium depletion:** Selenium is an important *antioxidant* nutrient. A deficiency of selenium increases the risk for diseases such as *cancer* and *cardiovascular disease*. People who are selenium-deficient are subjected to increased *free radical* damage, which accelerates the aging process.

❑ **Valproic acid and zinc depletion:** Zinc is an important mineral for a healthy *immune system*. A zinc deficiency can cause slow healing of wounds and a weakened immune system, as well as a loss of the senses of taste and smell. Zinc deficiency can also cause infertility and sexual dysfunction in men and women.

ANTI-DIABETIC DRUGS

In 1998, antidiabetic medications, also called *oral hypo-glycemics*, represented the 11th largest category of pre-scription drugs in the United States, in terms of dollar volume, accounting for more than \$2.068 billion in sales. In terms of numbers of prescriptions written, this class of drugs ranked 10th in 1998, with 64,238,000 prescriptions written. The two classes of antidiabetic drugs, sulfonyl-ureas and biguanides, are discussed next, along with the nutrients they deplete.

SULFONYLUREAS

Sulfonylureas deplete coenzyme Q_{10}.

❑ **Sulfonylureas and Q_{10} depletion:** Coenzyme Q_{10} is an extremely important *antioxidant* and also per-forms vital roles in *generating energy* in the mito-chondria of all cells. Because the heart is the most active muscle in the human body, a decline in en-ergy resulting from a deficiency of CoQ_{10} first affects the heart, and now it is thought that a CoQ_{10} deficiency may be one of the primary causes of congestive heart failure.

In addition to providing antioxidant protection within the mitochondria, coenzyme Q_{10} protects *LDL-cholesterol* from *free radical* oxidation. Indi-viduals who are deficient in coenzyme Q_{10} have an increased risk for *cardiovascular disease* and also have more free radical damage, which accelerates the aging process.

BIGUANIDES

Biguanides deplete vitamin B_{12}, coenzyme Q_{10}, and folic acid.

❑ **Biguanides and vitamin B_{12} depletion:** One study reported that 30% of individuals taking biguanides developed an inability to absorb vitamin B_{12}. In this study, 50% of individuals who developed biguanide-related vitamin B_{12} deficiency actually developed a permanent inability to produce *intrinsic factor*. Because intrinsic factor is necessary for B_{12} absorption, these people may require vitamin B_{12} therapy indefinitely. Vitamin B_{12} depletion also can result in elevated levels of *homocysteine*, which poses a serious risk for *cardiovascular disease*. A long-term vitamin B_{12} deficiency can also result in irreversible nerve damage.

❑ **Biguanides and coenzyme Q_{10} depletion:** Coenzyme Q_{10} is an extremely important *antioxidant* and also performs critical roles in *generating energy* in the mitochondria of all cells. Because the heart is the most active muscle in the human body, a decline in energy from a deficiency of CoQ_{10} first affects the heart, and now it is thought that a CoQ_{10} deficiency may be one of the primary causes of congestive heart failure. In addition to providing *antioxidant* protection within the *mitochondria*, coenzyme Q_{10} protects *LDL-cholesterol* from *free radical* oxidation. Individuals who have a deficiency of coenzyme Q_{10} have an increased risk for *cardiovascular disease* and also have more *free radical* damage, which accelerates the aging process.

❑ **Biguanides and folic acid depletion:** Folic acid depletion can cause some serious health problems, especially in women. Folic acid deficiency disrupts

DNA metabolism, which causes abnormal cells to be produced. This problem is especially acute in cells with the most rapid rates of turnover, including red blood cells, leukocytes, and *epithelial cells* of the stomach, intestine, vagina, and uterine cervix. Folic acid needs are greater during pregnancy. Insufficient folic acid also is one of the most common vitamin deficiencies. In addition to people not eating enough green leafy vegetables, folic acid is easily destroyed by heat, light, and oxygen, as well as food processing, cooking, and storage.

Folic acid deficiency can cause anemia, birth defects, cervical dysplasia, elevated homocysteine, headache, fatigue, depression, hair loss, anorexia, insomnia, diarrhea, nausea, and increased infections. Folic acid deficiency also is associated with increased risk of developing breast cancer and colorectal cancer. The following sections review the major folic acid deficiency-related health problems.

- **Anemia:** Folic acid is required for the production of *erythrocytes* (red blood cells), which carry oxygen from the lungs to the tissues and carbon dioxide from the tissues to the lungs. Folic acid deficiency results in anemia and reduced tissue oxygenation. This causes a condition called *megaloblastic anemia*, which produces symptoms of tiredness, weakness, diarrhea, and weight loss.

- **Birth defects:** Folic acid helps to regulate neural development and the transfer of genetic material to new cells in the fetus. During pregnancy, the rapidly growing fetus substantially increases a woman's need for folic acid, and folic acid deficiency during pregnancy dramatically increases the risk for birth defects such as spina bifida and cleft palate. The link between folic acid deficiency and birth defects is so strong that all women of childbearing age are urged to have their folic acid status checked before trying to become pregnant. If this practice were followed, thousands of birth defects probably would be prevented each year. A laboratory test called the Neutrophilic Hypersegmentation Index (NHI) has been developed that easily identifies folic acid insufficiency.

- **Cervical dysplasia:** The development of abnormal cells in the uterus, *cervical dysplasia*, is regarded as a *precancerous* condition that usually is discovered when a woman has her annual Pap exam. This condition might contribute to an increased number of hysterectomies. Approximately 800,000 women have hysterectomies every year in the United States. Some health care professionals believe that the folic acid depletion caused by oral contraceptives and other medications is linked to this high incidence of cervical dysplasia and hysterectomies.

- **Elevated homocysteine,** also known as *hyperhomocysteinemia*, now is recognized as an independent risk factor for *cardiovascular disease*. Excess *homocysteine* is capable of directly damaging vascular *endothelial cells*, causing the type of damage that initiates plaque build-up in the arteries. Even moderate elevation of homocysteine represents substantial increased risk for the development of plaque build-up and blood clots.

ANTI-FUNGALS: AMPHOTERICIN B

Amphotericin B depletes calcium, magnesium, potassium, and sodium.

Amphotericin B remains the antifungal drug of choice for most *systemic* infections. A limiting factor for its use is the development of kidney toxicity. Amphotericin B-induced kidney toxicity causes a build-up of nitrogen compounds in the blood, renal tubular acidosis, impaired renal concentrating ability, and electrolyte abnormalities including depletion of potassium, sodium, and magnesium. All of these abnormalities occur to varying degrees in almost all patients who receive the drug. Upon withdrawal of therapy, renal function gradually returns to baseline, although in some instances permanent damage is sustained, especially when the cumulative dose exceeds 5g.

ANTIHISTAMINES: HYDROXYZINE

Hydroxyzine depletes melatonin. There are many other antihistamine medications, but studies on nutrient depletions have yet to be performed.

Melatonin is the brain hormone that triggers or induces sleep. A deficiency of melatonin results in insomnia and related sleep problems. Insomnia can lead to many other problems such as depression, poor performance at work, and an increase in accidents. Melatonin also is an important *antioxidant*, so a depletion of melatonin could result in more *free radical* damage and an acceleration of the aging process. Last, but not least, numerous studies have associated low levels of melatonin with an increased incidence of breast cancer.

ANTI-INFLAMMATORY DRUGS

In 1998, anti-inflammatory drugs, also called anti-arthritic medications, represented the 13th largest category of prescription drugs in the United States in terms of dollar volume, accounting for more than $1.875 billion in sales. In terms of numbers of prescriptions written, this class of drugs ranked sixth in 1998, with 76,925,000 prescriptions written. The categories of anti-inflammatory drugs, along with the nutrients they deplete are: corticosteroids, salicylates (aspirin), sulfasalazine, indomethacin, and nonsteroidal anti-inflammatory drugs (NSAIDs).

CORTICOSTEROIDS

Corticosteroid-induced nutrient depletions are of minimal importance when the drugs are taken for only a short period, as is the case with *dosepaks*, which provide 21 tablets to be taken within 6 days. People who are on long-term therapy with corticosteroid drugs, however, can develop significant nutrient depletion-related health problems. Each of the nutrient depletions mentioned above are discussed individually along with their associated health problems.

> *Corticosteroids (glucocorticoids) can cause depletion of calcium, vitamin D, potassium, zinc, magnesium, vitamin C, folic acid, vitamin B_{12}, selenium, chromium, and vitamin A.*

❑ **Corticosteroids and calcium depletion:** Corticosteroids cause increased urinary excretion of calcium. The resulting calcium depletion increases the probability of developing skeletal problems such as *rickets* in children and *osteoporosis* and *osteomalacia* in adults. These problems can cause soft, weak bones, resulting in skeletal deformities. In adults, calcium-depleted bones also increases the likelihood of fractures. Calcium deficiency also can cause high blood pressure, muscle cramps, heart palpitations, tooth decay, back and leg pains, insomnia, and nervous disorders.

❑ **Corticosteroids and vitamin D depletion:** Treatment with corticosteroids does not directly cause a depletion of vitamin D, but, by causing a depletion of calcium, creates a greater need for vitamin D to increase calcium absorption. Thus, by creating an indirect need for more vitamin D, corticosteroids can cause a vitamin D deficiency.

❑ **Corticosteroids and potassium depletion:** Corticosteroids cause increased urinary excretion of potassium, which can lead to *hypokalemia* (potassium depletion). This can produce muscular weakness, *tetany* (muscle spasms), and *postural hypotension* (low blood pressure when changing from a lying or sitting position to a standing position), which can cause dizziness and fainting spells. Other symptoms associated with potassium depletion are irregular heartbeat, poor reflexes, fatigue, continuous thirst, *edema*, constipation, mental confusion, and nervous disorders.

❑ **Corticosteroids and zinc depletion:** The use of corticosteroids can weaken the *immune system* and slow the healing of wounds. Zinc deficiency also can result in insulin resistance, a loss of the senses of taste and smell, and infertility and sexual dysfunction in both men and women.

❑ **Corticosteroids and magnesium depletion:** Corticosteroids cause increased urinary excretion of magnesium, which depletes magnesium levels in the body. Magnesium deficiency can cause *cardiac arrhythmias*, high blood pressure and various other cardiovascular-related problems, *osteoporosis*, muscle cramps, PMS, and an increase in the frequency and severity of asthma attacks.

❑ **Corticosteroids and vitamin C depletion:** The *immune system* can be weakened by the depletion of vitamin C resulting from use of corticosteroids. Low levels of vitamin C can accelerate aging damage via increased *free radical* damage. In one study, ophthalmologists expressed their concern that vitamin C depletion might increase the risk for glaucoma and cataracts.

❑ **Corticosteroids and folic acid depletion:** Folic acid depletion can cause some serious health problems, especially in women. Folic acid deficiency disrupts DNA metabolism, which results in the production of abnormal cells. This problem is especially acute in cells with the most rapid rates of turnover — red blood cells, leukocytes, and *epithelial cells* of the stomach, intestine, vagina, and uterine cervix. Folic acid needs are greater during pregnancy. Insufficient folic acid also is one of the most common vitamin deficiencies. In addition to people not eating enough green leafy vegetables, folic acid is easily destroyed by heat, light, and oxygen, as well as food processing, cooking, and storage.

Folic acid deficiency can cause anemia, birth defects, *cervical dysplasia*, elevated *homocysteine*, headacne, fatigue, depression, hair loss, anorexia, insomnia, diarrhea, nausea, and increased infections. Folic acid deficiency is associated with increased risk of developing breast cancer and colorectal cancer. The following paragraphs go into more detail about the major folic acid deficiency-related health problems in the hope that more people (especially women) will understand the importance of taking additional folic acid supplementation.

■ **Anemia:** Folic acid is required for the production of *erythrocytes*, red blood cells that carry oxygen from the lungs to the tissues and carbon dioxide from tissues to the lungs. Folic acid deficiency results in anemia and reduced tissue oxygenation. This leads to a condition known as *megaloblastic anemia*, accompanied by symptoms of tiredness, weakness, diarrhea, and weight loss.

■ **Birth defects:** Folic acid helps regulate neural development and the transfer of genetic material to new cells in the fetus. During pregnancy, the rapidly growing fetus substantially increases a woman's need for folic acid, and folic acid deficiency during pregnancy dramatically increases the risk of birth defects such as spina bifida and cleft palate. The link between folic acid deficiency and birth defects is so strong that all women of childbearing age are urged to have their folic acid status checked before trying to become pregnant. If this practice were followed, thousands of birth defects probably would be prevented each year. A laboratory test called the Neutrophilic Hypersegmentation Index (NHI) has been developed, which easily identifies folic acid insufficiency.

■ **Cervical dysplasia:** The development of abnormal cells in the uterus, *cervical dysplasia,* is regarded as a *precancerous* condition that usually is discovered when a woman has her annual Pap exam. This condition can contribute to an increased number of hysterectomies. Approximately 800,000 women have hysterectomies every year in the United States. Some health care professionals believe that the folic acid depletion caused by oral contraceptives and other medications is linked to the high incidence of cervical dysplasia and hysterectomies.

- **Elevated homocysteine:** Also known as *hyperhomocysteinemia,* elevated homocysteine now is recognized as a serious independent risk factor for *cardiovascular disease.* Excess *homocysteine* is capable of causing direct damage to vascular *endothelial cells.* Therefore, it can cause the type of damage that initiates plaque build-up in the arteries. Even moderate elevations of homocysteine represent a substantially increased risk for plaque build-up and blood clots.

❑ **Corticosteroids and vitamin B_{12} depletion:** A deficiency of vitamin B_{12} can cause anemia, characterized by tiredness, weakness, and fatigue. Inadequate vitamin B_{12} also can cause elevated levels of homocysteine, a risk factor for *cardiovascular disease.* Long-term B_{12} deficiency can result in permanent nerve damage. Depression is another common manifestation of vitamin B_{12} deficiency, especially in the elderly population.

❑ **Corticosteroids and selenium depletion:** Selenium is an important *antioxidant* nutrient. A deficiency of selenium increases the risk for diseases such as *cancer* and *cardiovascular disease.* People who are selenium-deficient are subjected to increased *free radical* damage, which accelerates the aging process.

❑ **Corticosteroids and chromium depletion:** Chromium deficiency can cause problems with blood sugar regulation, insulin resistance, and elevated cholesterol and *triglycerides.*

❑ **Corticosteroids and vitamin A depletion:** A deficiency of vitamin A weakens the immune system and increases the risks for infections. This is because vitamin A is necessary for healthy mucous membranes, which are an important part of the immune system that functions as a barrier against infections. Vitamin A deficiency can also cause dry skin and problems with vision.

SALICYLATES (ASPIRIN)

Salicylates cause the depletion of vitamin C, calcium, folic acid, iron, sodium, potassium, and pantothenic acid, which is also known as vitamin B₅.

☐ **Salicylates (aspirin) and vitamin C depletion:** Salicylates cause increased urinary excretion of vitamin C. In fact, the authors of one study stated that aspirin is the drug most likely to deplete vitamin C. A vitamin C deficiency can cause substantial weakening of the *immune system* and increased *free radical* damage, which accelerates the aging process.

☐ **Salicylates and calcium depletion:** aspirin and salicylates cause increased urinary excretion of calcium. Calcium depletion resulting from regular or long-term use increases the possibility of developing skeletal problems such as *rickets* in children and *osteoporosis* and *osteomalacia* in adults. These problems can cause soft, weak bones, resulting in skeletal deformities. In adults, calcium-depleted bones also increases the likelihood of fractures. Calcium deficiency also can cause high blood pressure, muscle cramps, heart palpitations, tooth decay, back and leg pains, insomnia, and nervous disorders.

☐ **Salicylates and folic acid depletion:** Folic acid depletion can cause a wide range of health problems including anemia, depression, and elevated *homocysteine*, which poses a seriously increased risk for *cardiovascular disease*. Folic acid deficiency also increases the risk of developing breast and colorectal cancers. The babies of women who become deficient in folic acid have a greater risk for birth defects, and their mothers for developing *cervical dysplasia*. (For a detailed discussion of folic acid deficiency problems, see pages 48–50.)

❑ **Salicylates and iron depletion:** Iron depletion can cause anemia, which produces weakness and fatigue. Other symptoms associated with iron deficiency include hair loss, brittle nails, and a weakened *immune system*. However, iron supplementation is not recommended unless a lab test determines that iron deficiency is present.

❑ **Salicylates and sodium and potassium depletion:** Depletion of sodium and potassium ions can result in muscle weakness, fatigue, dehydration, *tetany* (muscle spasms), and *postural hypotension*, which can cause dizziness and fainting spells. Other symptoms associated with potassium depletion include irregular heartbeat, poor reflexes, fatigue, continuous thirst, *edema*, constipation, mental confusion, and nervous disorders.

❑ **Salicylates and vitamin B$_5$ (pantothenic acid) depletion:** Although salicylates have been reported to deplete vitamin B$_5$, that vitamin is so widely available in foods that deficiency is rare. Experimentally induced deficiencies manifest as problems related to the skin, liver, thymus, and nerves. Fatigue and listlessness are also associated with vitamin B$_5$ deficiency.

SULFASALAZINE

Sulfasalazine has been reported to deplete folic acid.

Folic acid depletion can cause a wide range of health problems including anemia, depression, and elevated *homocysteine*, which is an increased risk factor for *cardiovascular disease*. Folic acid deficiency also increases the risk of developing breast and colorectal cancers. Women who become deficient in folic acid have greater risks for producing children with birth defects and of developing cervical dysplasia. (For a detailed discussion of folic acid deficiency problems, see pages 48–50.)

INDOMETHACIN

Indomethacin has been reported to cause a depletion of folic acid and iron.

❑ **Indomethacin and folic acid depletion:** Folic acid depletion can cause a wide range of health problems including anemia, depression, and elevated *homocysteine,* which is a serious risk factor for *cardiovascular disease.* Folic acid deficiency also increases the risk for developing breast and colorectal cancers. Women who become deficient in folic acid put the fetus at greater risk for birth defects, and the pregnant woman for developing *cervical dysplasia.* (For a detailed discussion of folic acid deficiency problems, see pages 48–50.)

❑ **Indomethacin and iron depletion:** Iron depletion can cause anemia, which produces weakness and fatigue. Other symptoms associated with iron deficiency include hair loss, brittle nails, and a weakened *immune system.* However, iron supplementation is not recommended unless a lab test determines that iron deficiency is present.

OTHER NON-STEROIDAL ANTI-INFLAMMATORY DRUGS (NSAIDs)

NSAIDs deplete folic acid.

This class of drugs was extremely successful when it was sold as a prescription drug. Now that NSAIDs are available without a prescription, there is greater concern because people can use the drugs without monitoring by physicians or pharmacists.

Folic acid deficiency poses greater risks for women because of the link to *cervical dysplasia,* as well as *birth defects* in their children. Other problems associated with folic acid depletion include anemia, depression, elevated *homocysteine* — a risk factor for *cardiovascular disease* — and increased risks for developing breast and colorectal cancers. (For more detailed description of folic acid deficiency problems, see pages 48–50.)

ANTI-PARKINSON'S DISEASE DRUGS

Levodopa depletes potassium, SAMe, and vitamin B$_6$.

❑ **Levodopa depletes potassium:** Potassium depletion can cause symptoms of muscular weakness, *tetany* (muscle spasms), and *postural hypotension* (low blood pressure when changing from a lying or sitting position to a standing position), which can cause dizziness and fainting spells. Other symptoms associated with potassium depletion include irregular heartbeat, poor reflexes, fatigue, continuous thirst, edema, constipation, mental confusion, and nervous disorders.

❑ **Levodopa depletes SAMe:** SAMe plays a key role in several important biochemical pathways involving the synthesis of DNA and RNA, phospholipids, proteins, and various neurotransmitters. SAMe deficiency increases the risk of cardiovascular disease, liver disease, depression, and insomnia.

❑ **Levodopa depletes vitamin B_6:** Depletion of vitamin B_6 can cause depression and insomnia, and an increased risk to *cardiovascular disease*. For a detailed discussion of vitamin B_6 depletion problems, see pages 58–59.

ANTI-PROTOZOALS: PENTAMIDINE

Pentamidine depletes magnesium.

Pentamidine, which is usually used with HIV and AIDS patients to prevent *opportunistic infections*, can cause a severe loss of magnesium. In turn, magnesium depletion can cause *cardiac arrhythmias*, high blood pressure, and various other cardiovascular-related problems. Additional conditions associated with low magnesium levels include *osteoporosis*, muscle cramps, PMS, and an increase in the frequency and severity of asthma attacks.

ANTIVIRALS

The antiviral drugs discussed in this section are the reverse transcriptase inhibitors and a single drug named foscarnet. Most of the research with reverse transcriptase inhibitors regarding nutrient depletions has been done with zidovudine (AZT). However, other related drugs that may cause similar nutrient depletions include didanosine, lamivudine, stavudine, zalcitabine, delavirdine, and nevirapine.

REVERSE TRANSCRIPTASE INHIBITORS:
ZIDOVUDINE (AZT) AND OTHER RELATED DRUGS

Zidovudine (AZT) depletes vitamin B_{12}, copper, zinc, and L-carnitine.

❑ **Zidovudine and vitamin B_{12} depletion:** A deficiency of vitamin B_{12} can cause anemia, which results in tiredness, weakness, and fatigue. Inadequate vitamin B_{12} also can cause elevated levels of *homocysteine*, which is a risk factor for cardiovascular disease. Long-term B_{12} deficiency can result in permanent nerve damage. Depression is another common manifestation of vitamin B_{12} deficiency, especially in elderly people.

❑ **Zidovudine and copper depletion:** Copper depletion can result in anemia and fatigue, problems with the maintenance and repair of connective tissues, and elevated levels of *serum cholesterol*.

❑ **Zidovudine and zinc depletion:** Zinc is an important mineral for a healthy *immune system*. A zinc deficiency can cause slow healing of wounds and a weakened immune system, as well as a loss of the senses of taste and smell. Zinc deficiency can also cause infertility and sexual dysfunction in men and women. It is somewhat of a paradox that a drug like this is given to AIDS patients, who have weakened immunity and need immune support, yet zidovudine depletes zinc, which weakens the immune system.

❑ **Zidovudine and carnitine depletion:** Carnitine is an *amino acid* that facilitates the transport of fats across cellular membranes for metabolism and the production of energy. Although the body normally produces adequate levels of carnitine, administration of zidovudine can create a carnitine deficiency, which can cause fatigue, muscle weakness and cramps.

FOSCARNET

Foscarnet is primarily used to prevent opportunistic infections in individuals with HIV.

Foscarnet depletes calcium, magnesium, and potassium.

❑ **Foscarnet and calcium depletion:** A low calcium level is one of the primary side effects with this drug. Calcium depletion can result in the development of skeletal problems such as *osteoporosis* and *osteomalacia*. Calcium deficiency also can also cause high blood pressure, muscle cramps, heart palpitations, tooth decay, back and leg pains, insomnia, and nervous disorders.

❑ **Foscarnet and magnesium depletion:** Magnesium depletion can cause *cardiac arrhythmias*, high blood pressure, and various other cardiovascular-related problems. Additional conditions associated with low magnesium levels include *osteoporosis*, muscle cramps, PMS, and an increase in the frequency and severity of asthma attacks.

❑ **Foscarnet and potassium depletion:** Potassium depletion can cause symptoms of muscular weakness, *tetany* (muscle spasms), and *postural hypotension* (low blood pressure when changing from a lying or sitting position to a standing position), which can cause dizziness and fainting spells. Other symptoms associated with potassium depletion include irregular heartbeat, poor reflexes, fatigue, continuous thirst, edema, constipation, mental confusion, and nervous disorders.

BRONCHODILATORS

THEOPHYLLINE AND THE BETA$_2$ ADRENERGIC AGONISTS (I.E., ALBUTEROL, TERBUTALINE, ETC.)

Theophylline depletes vitamin B$_6$ (pyridoxine).

❑ **Theophylline and Vitamin B$_6$ (pyridoxine) depletion:** Depletion of vitamin B$_6$ can cause depression and insomnia, and an increased risk to *cardiovascular disease*.

■ **Depression:** Pyridoxine is necessary for conversion of the amino acid *tryptophan* into the *neurotransmitter serotonin*. A deficiency of serotonin in the brain is strongly associated with depression. Therefore, people taking drugs that deplete vitamin B$_6$ are at greater risk for depression.

■ **Insomnia:** In the brain, serotonin is converted into *melatonin*, a hormone that controls sleep. Because a vitamin B$_6$ deficiency inhibits the synthesis of serotonin, it also decreases the amount of melatonin that can be produced in the brain. People who become deficient in melatonin will suffer from insomnia and related sleep problems.

■ **Cardiovascular disease:** Vitamin B$_6$ is one of the B vitamins necessary to metabolize *homocysteine*, an amino acid produced from metabolism of the essential amino acid methionine. Homocysteine is a toxic substance capable of directly injuring the lining of the arteries, which is the type of damage that causes *atherosclerosis.* Under normal conditions, it exists only a short time, but a lack of vitamin B_6 will cause elevated levels of homocysteine in the blood. Even slight elevations of homocysteine represent a seriously increased risk for developing atherosclerosis, which is the leading cause of heart disease.

❑ **The Beta$_2$ Adrenergic Agonists, which include albuterol and terbutaline, deplete potassium.** Potassium depletion can produce muscular weakness, *tetany* (muscle spasms), and *postural hypotension,* (a term that refers to low blood pressure when changing from a lying or sitting position to a standing position) which can cause dizziness and fainting spells. Other symptoms associated with potassium depletion are irregular heartbeat, poor reflexes, fatigue, continuous thirst, *edema,* constipation, mental confusion, and nervous disorders. In a hospital setting, symptoms usually are treated and managed by giving intravenous potassium chloride.

CARDIOVASCULAR DRUGS

The classes of cardiovascular drugs include ACE inhibitors, beta-blockers, calcium channel blockers, cardiac glycosides, clonidine and methyldopa, hydralazine-containing vasodilators, loop diuretics, potassium-sparing diuretics, and thiazide diuretics. Each of these will be discussed along with their nutrient depletions.

ACE INHIBITORS

In 1998, ACE inhibitors comprised the sixth largest dollar-volume category of prescription drugs in the United

States, accounting for more than $2.634 billion in sales. In terms of numbers of prescriptions written, this class of drugs ranked third in 1998, with 83,545,000 prescriptions written.

❑ **ACE inhibitors and zinc depletion.** The mineral zinc is important to the *immune system.* A zinc deficiency can cause slow healing of wounds and a weakened immune system. A zinc deficiency also can cause insulin resistance, a loss of the senses of taste and smell, and infertility and sexual dysfunction in both men and women.

BETA-BLOCKERS

In 1998, beta-blockers represented the seventh largest category of prescription drugs in the United States, with more than 71,868,000 prescriptions written. This class of drugs was not among the top 20 categories in terms of dollar sales.

> *Beta-blockers deplete coenzyme Q_{10} and melatonin.*

❑ **Beta-blockers and coenzyme Q_{10} depletion:** Beta-blockers comprise just one of numerous classes of drugs that deplete coenzyme Q_{10}, a nutrient that is an extremely important *antioxidant* and also performs vital roles in *generating energy* in the mitochondria of all cells. Because the heart is the most active muscle in the human body, a decline in energy resulting from a deficiency of CoQ_{10} first affects the heart, and now it is thought that a CoQ_{10} deficiency may be one of the primary causes of congestive heart failure. In addition to providing antioxidant protection within the mitochondria, coenzyme Q_{10} protects *LDL-cholesterol* from *free radical* oxidation. Individuals who are deficient in coenzyme Q_{10} are at increased risk for *cardiovascular disease* and also have more *free radical* damage, which accelerates the aging process.

❑ Beta-blockers and melatonin depletion: The beta-blockers propranolol, atenolol, and metaprolol have been found to inhibit the synthesis and release of *melatonin*, the brain hormone that triggers or induces sleep. A deficiency of melatonin results in insomnia and related sleep problems. Insomnia can lead to many other problems such as depression, poor performance at work, and an increase in accidents. Melatonin also is an important *antioxidant*, so a depletion of melatonin could result in more *free radical* damage and an acceleration of the aging process. Finally, many studies have associated low levels of melatonin with an increased incidence of breast cancer.

CALCIUM CHANNEL BLOCKERS: NIFEDIPINE AND VERAPAMIL

In 1998, calcium channel blockers comprised the fourth largest dollar-volume category of prescription drugs in the United States, accounting for more than $3.824 billion in sales. In terms of numbers of prescriptions written, this class of drugs ranked second in 1998, with 91,462,000 prescriptions written.

Nifedipine and Verapamil cause potassium depletion (also known as hypokalemia)

❑ Nifedipine and verapamil cause potassium depletion: Some of the cardiovascular side effects associated with nifedipine and verapamil stem from potassium depletion. This can cause symptoms of muscular weakness, *tetany* (muscle spasms) and *postural hypotension* (a term that refers to low blood pressure when changing from a lying or sitting position to a standing position), which can cause dizziness and fainting spells. Other symptoms associated with potassium depletion are irregular heartbeat, poor reflexes, fatigue, continuous thirst, *edema*, constipation, mental confusion, and nervous disorders.

CARDIAC GLYCOSIDES: DIGOXIN

Digoxin causes the depletion of calcium, magnesium, phosphorus, and vitamin B₁.

❑ **Cardiac glycosides and calcium depletion:** Digoxin causes an increase in urinary calcium excretion. To maintain adequate calcium in the blood, the body begins leaching calcium out of the bones, which can result in skeletal problems such as *osteoporosis* and *osteomalacia*. Calcium deficiency also can cause high blood pressure, muscle cramps, heart palpitations, tooth decay, back and leg pains, insomnia, and nervous disorders.

❑ **Cardiac glycosides and magnesium depletion:** Digoxin reduces the reabsorption of magnesium in the kidneys, which increases the urinary excretion of magnesium. Low magnesium levels are known to produce a wide variety of clinical symptoms, including irregular heartbeat, high blood pressure, and various other cardiovascular-related problems. Additional conditions associated with low magnesium levels include *osteoporosis,* muscle cramps, PMS, and an increase in the frequency and severity of asthma attacks.

❑ **Cardiac glycosides and phosphorus depletion:** Digoxin causes increased urinary excretion of phosphorus. A phosphorus deficiency can cause symptoms such as anxiety and nervousness, as well as skeletal problems.

❑ **Cardiac glycosides and vitamin B_1 depletion:** Digoxin causes a depletion of cellular thiamin and also hinders the cell's ability to incorporate thiamin. This vitamin B_1 deficiency can cause depression, irritability, memory loss, muscle weakness, and edema.

CENTRALLY ACTING ANTI-HYPERTENSIVE AGENTS: CLONIDINE AND METHYLDOPA

These are drugs that exert their effects by acting on centers within the brain that regulate blood pressure.

Clonidine and methyldopa deplete coenzyme Q_{10}.

❑ **Clonidine and methyldopa deplete coenzyme Q_{10}:** Coenzyme Q_{10} is an extremely important *antioxidant* and also performs critical roles in *generating energy* in the mitochondria of all cells. Because the heart is the most active muscle in the human body, a decline in energy resulting from a deficiency of CoQ_{10} first affects the heart, and now it is thought that a CoQ_{10} deficiency may be one of the primary causes of congestive heart failure. In addition to providing antioxidant protection within the mitochondria, coenzyme Q_{10} protects *LDL-cholesterol* from *free radical* oxidation. Individuals who are deficient in coenzyme Q_{10} have an increased risk for *cardiovascular disease* and also have more free radical damage, which accelerates the aging process.

HYDRALAZINE-CONTAINING VASODILATORS

Hydralazine-containing vasodilators deplete vitamin B$_6$ and coenzyme Q$_{10}$.

❑ **Hydralazine-containing vasodilators and vitamin B$_6$ depletion:** A depletion of vitamin B$_6$ (pyridoxine) can cause depression and insomnia and puts the person at increased risk for *cardiovascular disease.*

- **Depression:** Vitamin B$_6$ is necessary for converting the amino acid *tryptophan* into the *neurotransmitter serotonin.* A deficiency of serotonin in the brain is strongly associated with depression. Therefore, people taking drugs that deplete vitamin B$_6$ are at greater risk for developing depression.

- **Insomnia:** In the brain, serotonin is converted into *melatonin,* a hormone that controls sleep. Because a vitamin B$_6$ deficiency inhibits the synthesis of serotonin, it also decreases the amount of melatonin that can be produced in the brain. People who become deficient in melatonin will suffer from insomnia and related sleep problems.

- **Cardiovascular disease:** Vitamin B$_6$ is one of the B vitamins necessary to metabolize *homocysteine,* an *amino acid* produced from the metabolism of the essential amino acid *methionine.* Homocysteine is a toxic substance capable of directly injuring the lining of the arteries, which is the type of damage that causes *atherosclerosis.* Under normal conditions, it exists only briefly. A lack of vitamin B$_6$, however, will cause elevated levels of homocysteine in the blood. Even slight elevations of homocysteine represent a seriously increased risk for developing *atherosclerosis,* which is the leading cause of heart disease.

❏ **Hydralazine and coenzyme Q_{10} depletion:** Coenzyme Q_{10} is a nutrient that is an extremely important *antioxidant* and also performs critical roles in the *generation of energy* in the mitochondria of all cells. Because the heart is the most active muscle in the human body, a decline in energy resulting from a deficiency of CoQ_{10} first affects the heart, and it is now thought that a CoQ_{10} deficiency may be one of the primary causes of congestive heart failure. In addition to providing antioxidant protection within the mitochondria, coenzyme Q_{10} protects *LDL-cholesterol* from *free radical* oxidation. Individuals who are deficient in coenzyme Q_{10} are at increased risk for cardiovascular disease and also have more free radical damage, which accelerates the aging process.

LOOP DIURETICS

Loop diuretics cause a depletion of calcium, magnesium, potassium, vitamin B_1, vitamin B_6, vitamin C, sodium, and zinc.

❏ **Loop diuretics and calcium depletion:** Loop diuretics cause excessive urinary excretion of calcium. To maintain adequate calcium in the blood, the body begins leaching calcium out of the bones, which can result in the development of skeletal problems such as *osteoporosis* and *osteomalacia.* Calcium deficiency also can also cause high blood pressure, muscle cramps, heart palpitations, tooth decay, back and leg pains, insomnia, and nervous disorders.

❏ **Loop diuretics and magnesium depletion:** Loop diuretics cause an excess excretion of magnesium in the urine. Magnesium depletion can cause *cardiac arrhythmias*, high blood pressure and various other cardiovascular-related problems. Additional conditions associated with low magnesium levels include osteoporosis, muscle cramps, PMS, and an increase in the frequency and severity of asthma attacks.

❑ **Loop diuretics and potassium depletion:** Loop diuretics cause increased urinary excretion of potassium, which may lead to *hypokalemia* (potassium depletion). This can produce symptoms of muscular weakness, *tetany* (muscle spasms), and *postural hypotension* (a term that refers to low blood pressure when changing from a lying or sitting position to a standing position), which can cause dizziness and fainting spells. Other symptoms associated with potassium depletion are irregular heartbeat, poor reflexes, fatigue, continuous thirst, *edema*, constipation, mental confusion, and nervous disorders.

❑ **Loop diuretics and vitamin B_1 (thiamin) depletion:** Vitamin B_1 deficiency is a relatively common consequence of taking loop diuretics. Vitamin B_1 deficiency can cause depression, irritability, memory loss, muscle weakness, and edema. In one study, the authors noted that administration of vitamin B_1 resulted in improvement in both verbal and nonverbal IQ scores.

❑ **Loop diuretics and vitamin B_6 (pyridoxine) depletion:** Loop diuretics can cause a substantial urinary loss of pyridoxine. A depletion of pyridoxine (vitamin B_6) can cause depression, insomnia, and an increased risk for cardiovascular disease.

■ **Depression,** Vitamin B_6 is necessary for conversion of the amino acid *tryptophan* into the *neurotransmitter serotonin*. A deficiency of serotonin in the brain is strongly associated with depression. Therefore, people taking drugs that deplete vitamin B_6 are at greater risk for depression.

- **Insomnia:** In the brain, serotonin is converted into *melatonin*, a hormone that controls sleep. Because a vitamin B_6 deficiency inhibits the synthesis of serotonin, it also will decrease the amount of melatonin that can be produced in the brain. People who become deficient in melatonin will suffer from insomnia and related sleep problems.

- **Cardiovascular disease:** Vitamin B_6 is one of the B vitamins necessary to metabolize *homocysteine,* an *amino acid* produced from metabolism of the essential amino acid methionine. Homocysteine is a toxic substance capable of directly injuring the lining of the arteries — the type of damage that causes *atherosclerosis.* Under normal conditions, it exists only briefly. A lack of vitamin B_6, will cause an elevated level of homocysteine in the blood. Even a slight elevation of homocysteine is a serious risk factor for developing *atherosclerosis,* the leading cause of heart disease.

❑ **Loop diuretics and vitamin C depletion:** Increased urinary excretion of vitamin C begins within 3 hours after taking a dose of a loop diuretic. A vitamin C deficiency can result in a substantially weakened *immune system* and increased *free radical* damage, which accelerates the aging process.

❑ **Loop diuretics and sodium depletion:** Sodium depletion is the mechanism of action of loop diuretics, therefore, sodium replacement is **NOT** appropriate. However, too high a dose could cause excessive sodium depletion, which could produce symptoms that include muscle weakness, dehydration, loss of appetite, and poor concentration.

❑ **Loop diuretics and zinc depletion:** Zinc is important to a healthy *immune system*. A zinc deficiency can cause slow healing of wounds, a weakened immune system, decreased sperm motility and infertility and sexual dysfunction in both men and women. Zinc deficiency also can cause a loss of the senses of taste and smell.

POTASSIUM-SPARING DIURETICS

Potassium-sparing diuretics deplete calcium, folic acid, and zinc.

❑ **Potassium-sparing diuretics and calcium depletion:** Potassium-sparing diuretics cause a significant increase in urinary calcium excretion. To maintain adequate calcium in the blood, the body begins leaching calcium out of the bones, which can result in the skeletal problems such as *osteoporosis* and *osteomalacia*. Calcium deficiency also can cause high blood pressure, muscle cramps, heart palpitations, tooth decay, back and leg pains, insomnia, and nervous disorders.

❑ **Potassium-sparing diuretics and folic acid depletion:** The active ingredient in potassium-sparing diuretics is triamterene. Triamterene is classified as a folic acid *antagonist*, which means that it inhibits the conversion of folic acid to its active form in the body. A folic acid deficiency can result in numerous health problems, especially in women. Folic acid deficiency disrupts DNA metabolism, which causes the production of abnormal cells. This problem is especially acute in cells with the most rapid rates of turnover — red blood cells, leukocytes, and *epithelial cells* of the stomach, intestine, vagina, and uterine cervix. Folic acid needs are greater during pregnancy. Insufficient folic acid also is one of the most common vitamin deficiencies. In addition to people not eating enough green leafy vegetables, folic acid is easily destroyed by heat, light, and oxygen, and substantial losses also occur during food processing, cooking, and storage.

Folic acid deficiency can cause anemia, birth defects, cervical dysplasia, elevated homocysteine, headache, fatigue, depression, hair loss, anorexia, insomnia, diarrhea, nausea, and increased infections. Folic acid deficiency also is associated with increased risk for breast cancer and colorectal cancer. The major folic acid deficiency-related health problems are described briefly below.

- **Anemia:** Folic acid is required for the production of *erythrocytes* (red blood cells), which carry oxygen from the lungs to the tissues and carbon dioxide from the tissues to the lungs. Folic acid deficiency causes anemia and reduced tissue oxygenation. This results in a condition known as *megaloblastic anemia*, which produces symptoms of tiredness, weakness, diarrhea, and weight loss.

- **Birth defects:** Folic acid helps regulate neural development and the transfer of genetic material to new cells in the fetus. During pregnancy, the rapidly growing fetus substantially increases a woman's need for folic acid, and folic acid deficiency during pregnancy dramatically increases the risk of birth defects such as spina bifida and cleft palate. The link between folic acid deficiency and birth defects is so strong that all women of childbearing age are urged to have their folic acid status checked before trying to become pregnant. If this practice were followed, thousands of birth defects probably would be prevented each year. A laboratory test called the Neutrophilic Hypersegmentation Index (NHI) has been developed, which easily identifies folic acid insufficiency.

- **Cervical dysplasia:** The development of abnormal cells in the uterus, *cervical dysplasia*, is regarded as a *precancerous* condition that usually is discovered when a woman has her annual Pap exam. This condition may contribute to an increased number of hysterectomies. Approximately 800,000 women have hysterectomies every year in the United States. Some health care professionals believe that the folic acid depletion caused by oral contraceptives and other medications is linked to this high incidence of cervical dysplasia and hysterectomies.

- **Elevated homocysteine,** also known as *hyperhomocysteinemia*, now is recognized as a serious independent risk factor for *cardiovascular disease.* Excess homocysteine is capable of causing direct damage to vascular *endothelial cells*, which means that it can cause the type of damage that initiates plaque build-up in the arteries. Even moderate elevations of homocysteine represent a substantially increased risk for the development of plaque build-up and blood clots.

❑ **Potassium-sparing diuretics deplete zinc:** Triamterene, which is the primary ingredient in potassium-sparing diuretics, causes an increased urinary excretion of zinc. Zinc is a nutrient that is extremely important to the immune system. Thus, a zinc deficiency can cause slow wound healing and a weakened immune system. Other zinc deficiency problems include a loss of the senses of taste and smell, decreased sperm motility and infertility and sexual dysfunction in both men and women.

THIAZIDE DIURETICS

Thiazide diuretics deplete coenzyme Q_{10}, magnesium, potassium, sodium, and zinc.

❑ **Thiazide diuretics and coenzyme Q_{10} depletion:** Coenzyme Q_{10} is an extremely important *antioxidant* and also performs vital roles in the *generation of energy* in the mitochondria of all cells. Because the heart is the most active muscle in the human body, a decline in energy arising from a deficiency of CoQ_{10} first affects the heart, and now it is thought that a CoQ_{10} deficiency might be one of the primary causes of congestive heart failure. In addition to providing antioxidant protection within the mitochondria, coenzyme Q_{10} protects LDL-cholesterol from *free radical* oxidation. Individuals who are deficient in coenzyme Q_{10} have an increased risk for *cardiovascular disease* and also will incur more free radical damage, which accelerates the aging process.

❑ **Thiazide diuretics and magnesium depletion:** Thiazide diuretics cause excess magnesium to be lost in the urine. Low magnesium levels are known to produce a wide variety of clinical symptoms, including irregular heartbeat, high blood pressure, and various other cardiovascular-related problems. Additional conditions associated with low magnesium levels include *osteoporosis*, muscle cramps, PMS, and an increase in the frequency and severity of asthma attacks.

❑ **Thiazide diuretics and potassium depletion:** Thiazide diuretics cause increased urinary excretion of potassium, which may lead to *hypokalemia* (potassium depletion). This can cause symptoms of muscular weakness, *tetany* (muscle spasms), and *postural hypotension* (a term that refers to low blood pressure when changing from a lying or sitting position to a standing position), which can cause fainting spells. Other symptoms associated with potassium depletion are irregular heartbeat, poor reflexes, fatigue, continuous thirst, edema, constipation, mental confusion, and nervous disorders.

❑ **Thiazide diuretics and sodium depletion:** Sodium depletion is the mechanism of action of thiazide diuretics, therefore, sodium replacement is **NOT** appropriate. However, too high a dose could cause excessive sodium depletion. Symptoms associated with sodium depletion include muscle weakness, dehydration, loss of appetite, and poor concentration.

❑ **Thiazide diuretics and zinc depletion:** Thiazide diuretics cause a substantial increase in urinary zinc output. Zinc is extremely important to the immune system. A zinc deficiency can cause slow healing of wounds and a weakened immune system. Zinc deficiency also can result in a loss of the senses of taste and smell, decreased sperm motility and infertility and sexual dysfunction in both men and women.

CHEMOTHERAPY DRUGS

Many of the drugs used to treat cancer are capable of causing multiple nutrient depletions by several different mechanisms. Some of these drugs damage the cells lining the intestinal tract, which inhibits the absorption of nutrients. The damage to these cells also creates inflammation and pain, which becomes more intense when food and digestives juices come into contact with the damaged cells. Ulceration in the mouth and throat may also develop. Frequently cancer patients lose their appetite because it is too painful to eat, which also contributes to nutrient depletions. Many chemotherapy medications also cause nausea, diarrhea and vomiting, which can further exacerbate nutrient depletions. Administration of intravenous vitamins and minerals can be very helpful to cancer patients who are too sick to eat properly and absorb nutrients.

CHOLESTEROL-LOWERING DRUGS

There are four classes of cholesterol-lowering drugs, which are the HMG-CoA reductase inhibitors (the statins), the bile acid sequesterants, the "fibrates" which include clofibrate and fenofibrate, and gemfibrozil, an individual cholesterol-lowering drug that does not fit into either of the other categories.

HMG-CoA REDUCTASE INHIBITORS (THE STATINS)

In 1998, the "statin" cholesterol-lowering drugs comprised the third largest category of prescription drugs in the United States, accounting for more than $4.596 billion in sales. The statins were the ninth largest category of drugs in terms of numbers of prescriptions, with an estimated 67,889,000 prescriptions written during that same year.

In 1998, Lipitor, the largest selling statin drug, was the third leading drug in the United States, accounting for over $1.544 billion in sales. During the same year, Lipitor was the seventh largest selling drug in 1998 in terms of prescriptions, with an estimated 24,897,000 prescriptions filled.

Statin drugs deplete coenzyme Q_{10}.

The "statin" drugs, also known as HMG-CoA Reductase Inhibitors, represent one of numerous classes of drugs that deplete coenzyme Q_{10}, an extremely important *antioxidant* that also performs vital roles in *generating energy* in the mitochondria of all cells. Because the heart is the most active muscle in the human body, a decline in energy resulting from a deficiency of CoQ_{10} first affects the heart, and now it is thought that a CoQ_{10} deficiency might be one of the main causes of congestive heart failure. In addition to providing antioxidant protection within the mitochondria, coenzyme Q_{10} protects *LDL-cholesterol* from *free radical* oxidation. Individuals who are deficient in coenzyme Q_{10} are at increased risk for *cardiovascular disease* and also incur more free radical damage, which accelerates the aging process.

BILE ACID SEQUESTRANTS

The two drugs in this class of cholesterol-lowering medication are cholestyramine and colestipol. Because these drugs are seldom used these days, the nutrient depletions associated with them are summarized instead of discussing each nutrient depletion separately. These drugs function by inhibiting the absorption of cholesterol in the intestines. In doing so, however, they inhibit the absorption of many other nutrients. Individuals who are taking one of these drugs are urged to take nutritional supplements several hours before taking a dose of the medication, which will give the nutrients a better chance of being absorbed before the medication arrives in the intestines.

❑ Cholestyramine depletes all of the fat-soluble vitamins, which include vitamins A, D, E, and K.

Other nutrients that are depleted are vitamin B_{12}, folic acid, beta-carotene, and the minerals calcium, iron, magnesium, phosphorus, and zinc.

❑ Colestipol depletes the fat-soluble vitamins, including vitamins A, D, E, and K. Other nutrients that are depleted include beta-carotene, folic acid, vitamin B_{12}, and iron.

THE "FIBRATES," WHICH INCLUDE CLOFIBRATE AND FENOFIBRATE, DEPLETE VITAMIN E, VITAMIN B_{12}, COPPER, AND ZINC.

❑ **Clofibrate and fenofibrate deplete vitamin E:** Vitamin E is one of the body's most important *antioxidant* nutrients. A deficiency of vitamin E results in more free radical damage, which accelerates the aging process. One of the most immediate consequences of vitamin E depletion is increased oxidation of *LDL-cholesterol*, which speeds up the process of *atherosclerosis*.

❑ **Clofibrate and fenofibrate deplete vitamin B_{12}:** Vitamin B_{12} deficiency can cause anemia, which results in fatigue, tiredness, and weakness, and B_{12} deficiency is a common cause of depression, especially in elderly people. Inadequate B_{12} also causes elevated *homocysteine*, which poses a seriously increased risk for *cardiovascular disease*. If serious B_{12} deficiencies are not corrected, long-term irreversible neurological damage can occur.

❑ **Clofibrate and fenofibrate deplete copper:** Copper depletion can result in anemia and fatigue, problems with the maintenance and repair of connective tissues, and elevated levels of *serum cholesterol*.

❑ **Clofibrate and fenofibrate deplete zinc:** Zinc is important to a healthy *immune system.* Indications of a zinc deficiency are slow healing of wounds and a weakened immune system. Other zinc deficiency problems include insulin resistance, a loss of the senses of taste and smell, and infertility and sexual dysfunction in both men and women.

GEMFIBROZIL

> *Gemfibrozil depletes coenzyme Q_{10} and vitamin E and gamma tocopherol.*

Although it effectively improves blood cholesterol, gemfibrozil reportedly causes a 41.5% decline in coenzyme Q_{10}, a 39.7% decline in vitamin E (alpha tocopherol), and a 50% decline in gamma tocopherol (another form of vitamin E, with anti-cancer properties).

❑ **Gemfibrozil and coenzyme Q_{10} depletion:** Coenzyme Q_{10} is an extremely important *antioxidant* and also performs critical roles in the *generation of energy* in the mitochondria of all cells. Because the heart is the most active muscle in the human body, a decline in energy resulting from a deficiency of CoQ_{10} first affects the heart, and now it is thought that a CoQ_{10} deficiency may be one of the primary causes of congestive heart failure. In addition to providing antioxidant protection within the mitochondria, coenzyme Q_{10} protects *LDL-cholesterol* from *free radical* oxidation. Individuals who are deficient in coenzyme Q_{10} are at increased risk for *cardiovascular disease* and also have more free radical damage, which accelerates the aging process.

❑ **Gemfibrozil and vitamin E depletion:** Vitamin E is one of the body's most important *antioxidant* nutrients. A deficiency of vitamin E results in more free radical damage, which accelerates the aging process. One of the most immediate consequences of vitamin E depletion is increased oxidation of *LDL-cholesterol*, which speeds up the process of *atherosclerosis*.

❏ **Gemfibrozil and gamma tocopherol depletion:** Gamma tocopherol is a form of vitamin E that also has fat-soluble *antioxidant* properties. Gamma tocopherol actually may provide stronger anticancer activity than the alpha tocopherol form of vitamin E. Thus, the depletion of gamma tocopherol might weaken a portion of an individual's *immune system* that protects against cancer.

ELECTROLYTE REPLACEMENT:
TIMED RELEASE POTASSIUM CHLORIDE

Timed release potassium chloride medications cause a depletion of Vitamin B_{12}.

Timed release potassium chloride medications make the ileal section of the intestinal tract more acidic, which inhibits the absorption of vitamin B_{12}. A vitamin B_{12} deficiency can cause anemia, which results in fatigue, tiredness, and weakness, and B_{12} deficiency is a common cause of depression, especially in elderly people. Inadequate B_{12} also causes elevated *homocysteine*, which poses a seriously increased risk for *cardiovascular disease*. If serious B_{12} deficiencies are not corrected, long-term irreversible neurological damage can occur.

FEMALE HORMONES

The two main categories of female hormones are oral contraceptives, used for birth control, and estrogen replacement therapy (ERT), prescribed for the symptoms of menopause as well as the prevention of *osteoporosis* and *cardiovascular disease.*

ORAL CONTRACEPTIVES

In 1998, oral contraceptives constituted the 14th largest category of prescription drugs in the United States, accounting for more than $1.653 billion in sales. In terms of numbers of prescriptions, oral contraceptives ranked eighth that year, with an estimated 68,671,000 prescriptions filled.

Oral contraceptives deplete folic acid, vitamin B_6, vitamin B_{12}, vitamin B_1. vitamin B_2, vitamin B_3, vitamin C, and the minerals magnesium, selenium, and zinc.

❑ **Oral contraceptives and folic acid depletion:** Folic acid depletion can cause some serious health problems, especially in women. Folic acid deficiency disrupts DNA metabolism, which causes the disruption of abnormal cells. This problem is especially acute in cells with the most rapid rates of turnover, which includes red blood cells, leukocytes, and *epithelial cells* of the stomach, intestine, vagina, and uterine cervix. Folic acid needs are greater during pregnancy. Insufficient folic acid also is one of the most common vitamin deficiencies. In addition to people not eating enough green leafy vegetables, folic acid is easily destroyed by heat, light, and oxygen, and substantial losses occur during food processing, cooking, and storage.

Folic acid deficiency can cause anemia, birth defects, *cervical dysplasia,* elevated *homocysteine,* headache, fatigue, depression, hair loss, anorexia, insomnia, diarrhea, nausea, and increased infections. Folic acid deficiency also is associated with an increased risk for developing breast cancer and colorectal cancer. The major health problems related to folic acid insufficiency are outlined below in the hope that more people (especially women) will understand the importance of taking additional folic acid supplementation.

■ **Anemia:** Folic acid is required for the production of *erythrocytes* (red blood cells), which carry oxygen from the lungs to the tissues and carbon dioxide from the tissues to the lungs. Folic acid deficiency causes anemia and reduced tissue oxygenation. This results in a condition known as *megaloblastic anemia,* which produces of tiredness, weakness, diarrhea, and weight loss.

■ **Birth defects:** Folic acid helps regulate neural development and the transfer of genetic material to new cells in the fetus. During pregnancy, the rapidly growing fetus substantially increases the woman's need for folic acid and folic acid deficiency during pregnancy dramatically increases the risk of birth defects such as spina bifida and cleft palate. The link between folic acid deficiency and birth defects is so strong that all women of childbearing age are urged to have their folic acid status checked before trying to become pregnant. If this practice were followed, thousands of birth defects probably would be prevented each year. A laboratory test called the Neutrophilic Hypersegmentation Index (NHI) has been developed, which easily identifies folic acid insufficiency.

- **Cervical dysplasia:** The development of abnormal cells in the uterus *cervical dysplasia,* is a *precancerous* condition that usually is discovered when a woman has her annual Pap exam. This condition may contribute to an increased number of hysterectomies. Approximately 800,000 women have hysterectomies every year in the United States. Some health care professionals believe that the folic acid depletion caused by oral contraceptives and other medications is linked to this high incidence of cervical dysplasia and hysterectomies.

- **Elevated homocysteine:** Also known as *hyperhomocysteinemia,* elevated homocystein now is recognized as a independent risk factor for *cardiovascular disease.* Excess *homocysteine* is capable of causing direct damage to vascular *endothelial cells,* which means that it can cause the type of damage that initiates plaque build-up in the arteries. Even moderate elevations of homocysteine represent substantially increased risk for plaque build-up and blood clots.

❑ **Oral contraceptives and vitamin B_6 depletion:** Depletion of vitamin B_6 (pyridoxine) can cause depression and insomnia, and it poses an increased risk for *cardiovascular disease.*

- **Depression:** Vitamin B_6 is necessary to convert the *amino acid* tryptophan into the *neurotransmitter serotonin.* A deficiency of serotonin in the brain is strongly associated with depression. Therefore, people taking drugs that deplete vitamin B_6 are at greater risk for depression.

- **Insomnia:** In the brain, serotonin is converted into *melatonin,* a hormone that controls sleep.

Because a vitamin B_6 deficiency inhibits the synthesis of serotonin, it also decreases the amount of melatonin that can be produced in the brain. People who become deficient in melatonin will incur insomnia and related sleep problems.

- **Cardiovascular disease:** Vitamin B_6 is one of the B vitamins that are necessary to metabolize *homocysteine*, an *amino acid* produced from the metabolism of the essential amino acid methionine. Homocysteine is a toxic substance capable of directly injuring the lining of the arteries, the type of damage that causes *atherosclerosis*. Under normal conditions, it exists only briefly. A lack of vitamin B_6, however, causes elevated homocysteine in the blood. Even slight elevations of homocysteine represent a seriously increased risk for developing *atherosclerosis*, which is the leading cause of heart disease.

❑ **Oral contraceptives and vitamin B_{12} depletion:** Vitamin B_{12} deficiency can cause anemia, which results in fatigue, tiredness, and weakness, and B_{12} deficiency is a common cause of depression, especially in elderly people. Inadequate B_{12} also causes elevated *homocysteine*, which poses a seriously increased risk for *cardiovascular disease*. If serious B_{12} deficiencies are not corrected, long-term irreversible neurological damage can occur.

Note: I want to draw special attention to the fact that oral contraceptives deplete all three of the B-vitamins necessary for the metabolism of homocysteine, which are folic acid, vitamin B_6, and vitamin B_{12}. A deficiency of any one of these increases homocysteine, which damages the arteries and initiates plaque build-up. The sad part about this scenario is that it is a silent killer. Frequently there are no symptoms until arteries are more than 90% blocked. This greatly increases the risks for a stroke or a heart attack. Women who are taking oral contraceptives are urged to carefully consider these nutrient depletions and begin taking nutritional supplements now to help prevent serious health problems that may take decades to develop.

❑ **Oral contraceptives deplete vitamin B_1:** A deficiency of vitamin B_1 can cause depression, irritability, memory loss, muscle weakness, and *edema*. One study noted that administration of vitamin B_1 to individuals with a B_1 deficiency resulted in improvement in both verbal and nonverbal IQ scores.

❑ **Oral contraceptives and vitamin B_2 depletion:** Symptoms associated with vitamin B_2 (riboflavin) deficiency include problems with the skin, eyes, mucous membranes, and nerves.

❑ **Oral contraceptives and vitamin B_3 depletion:** Women have disturbances in the metabolism of tryptophan and outbreaks of *pellagra* at twice the rate of men. This is presumably because estrogen medications inhibit the conversion of tryptophan to niacin. Niacin deficiency, or pellagra-like symptoms, include problems with the skin and gastrointestinal and nervous systems.

❑ **Oral contraceptives and vitamin C depletion:** Vitamin C depletion can result in a weakened *immune system*. Low levels of vitamin C can accelerate aging damage because of increased *free radical* damage. In one study, ophthalmologists expressed their concern that vitamin C depletion might increase the risk of developing glaucoma and cataracts.

❑ **Oral contraceptives and magnesium depletion:** In general, magnesium depletion can cause *cardiac arrhythmias*, high blood pressure and various other cardiovascular-related problems, *osteoporosis*, muscle cramps, PMS, and an increase in the frequency and severity of asthma attacks.

For women who are taking estrogen-containing medications, the issue of magnesium depletion deserves a more detailed explanation. Frequently, the following two factors interact at the same time to increase health problems:

a) Oral contraceptives deplete magnesium.

b) Many women take calcium to prevent osteoporosis.

Taking calcium without extra magnesium magnifies the problem of magnesium depletion, because calcium and magnesium function as a mineral pair and the relative ratio or balance between these minerals is important. For example, they control the blood-clotting mechanism: Excess calcium increases clotting, whereas magnesium thins the blood to prevent clotting. They also regulate muscle contraction, with calcium causing contractions while magnesium is working to relax muscles. Thus, the two minerals are counter-regulatory.

Therefore, you can see that two factors contribute to, and magnify, the resulting imbalance when women who take oral contraceptives (which deplete magnesium) also take calcium (without magnesium). One of the most frequent side effects associated with oral contraceptives is *thrombus* formation, or blood clots. Now it is clear why this happens, a depletion of magnesium and an excess of calcium increases the likelihood of clot formation. This also helps to explain why so many women have painful muscle cramps around the time of menstruation every month because excess calcium increases muscle contraction.

❑ **Oral contraceptives and selenium depletion:** Selenium is an important *antioxidant* nutrient. A deficiency of selenium increases the risk for diseases such as *cancer* and *cardiovascular disease*. People who are selenium-deficient are subjected to increased *free radical* damage, which accelerates the aging process.

❑ **Oral contraceptives and zinc depletion:** Zinc is a mineral that is important to the *immune system*. A zinc deficiency can cause slow healing of wounds and a weakened immune system. A zinc deficiency also results in insulin resistance, a loss of the senses of taste and smell, and infertility and sexual dysfunction in both men and women.

ESTROGEN REPLACEMENT THERAPY

In 1998, *estrogen replacement therapy (ERT)* as a category of prescription drugs ranked 13th in terms of number of prescriptions, with an estimated 59,187,000 prescriptions filled. This class did not rank in the top 20 categories of drugs in terms of dollar volume of sales. It is worth emphasizing, however, that in 1998, Premarin was the number-one prescribed drug in the United States, with an estimated 46,759,000 prescriptions filled. Premarin ranked 15th in dollar volume, accounting for more than $853 million in sales.

A substantial body of research has been published on the nutritional depletions caused by orally ingested estrogen in the form of oral contraceptives. Little research has been done, however, on the estrogen-containing medications used for ERT, also referred to as *hormone replacement therapy (HRT)*. To date, studies have reported that orally ingested estrogen medications taken for hormone replacement therapy deplete vitamin B_6 and magnesium. However, women should be aware that the estrogens in oral contraceptives also deplete folic acid, vitamin B_1, vitamin B_2, vitamin B_3, vitamin B_{12}, vitamin C, and zinc. Women are urged to read about the health problems associated with depletion of these nutrients, presented previously in the discussion on oral contraceptives.

❑ **Estrogen replacement therapy and vitamin B_6 depletion:** Vitamin B_6 (pyridoxine) depletion can lead to depression, insomnia, and an increased risk for *cardiovascular disease.*

■ **Depression:** Vitamin B_6 is necessary to convert the amino acid *tryptophan* into the *neurotransmitter serotonin.* A deficiency of serotonin in the brain is strongly associated with depression. Therefore, people taking drugs that deplete vitamin B_6 are at greater risk for depression.

■ **Insomnia:** In the brain, serotonin is converted into *melatonin,* a hormone that controls sleep. Because a vitamin B_6 deficiency inhibits the synthesis of serotonin, it also decreases the amount of melatonin that can be produced in the brain. People who are deficient in melatonin have insomnia and related sleep problems.

■ **Cardiovascular disease:** Vitamin B_6 is one of the B-vitamins necessary to metabolize *homocysteine,* an *amino acid* produced from metabolism of the essential amino acid methionine. Homocysteine is a toxic substance capable of directly injuring the lining of the arteries. This is the type of damage that causes *atherosclerosis*. Under normal conditions, homocysteine exists only briefly. A lack of vitamin B_6, however, causes elevated homocysteine in the blood, and even slight elevations of homocysteine pose a seriously increased risk for atherosclerosis, the leading cause of heart disease.

❑ **Estrogen replacement therapy and magnesium depletion:** In general, magnesium depletion can cause *cardiac arrhythmias*, high blood pressure, and various other cardiovascular-related problems, *osteoporosis*, muscle cramps, PMS, and an increase in the frequency and severity of asthma attacks.

For women taking estrogen-containing medications, however, the issue of magnesium depletion deserves a more detailed explanation, because frequently two factors happening at the same time interact to increase health problems. First, estrogen replacement therapy medications deplete magnesium. Second, many women take calcium to prevent *osteoporosis*. Taking calcium without extra magnesium magnifies the problem of magnesium depletions because calcium and magnesium function as a mineral pair and the relative ratio or balance between these minerals is important. For example, they control the blood-clotting mechanism; excess calcium increases clotting, whereas magnesium thins the blood to prevent clotting. The two also regulate muscle contraction, with calcium causing contractions while magnesium is working to relax muscles. Thus, they are counter-regulatory.

You can see, then, that two factors contribute to and magnify the imbalance that women who take estrogen medications (which deplete magnesium) who also take calcium (without magnesium) incur. One of the most frequent side effects associated with estrogen-containing medication is *thrombus,* or blood clot, formation. Now it is clear why this happens, a depletion of magnesium and an excess of calcium increases the likelihood of clot formation. This also helps to explain why so many women have painful muscle cramps around the time of menstruation, because excess calcium increases muscle contraction.

GOUT MEDICATIONS: COLCHICINE

Colchicine depletes vitamin B_{12}, sodium, potassium, beta-carotene, calcium, and phosphorus.

❑ **Colchicine and vitamin B_{12} depletion:** A deficiency of vitamin B_{12} can cause anemia, characterized by fatigue, tiredness, and weakness. A B_{12} deficiency also is a common cause of depression, especially in elderly people. Inadequate levels of B_{12} increase *homocysteine* levels, increasing the risk for *cardiovascular disease.* If serious B_{12} deficiencies are not corrected, they can lead to long-term irreversible neurological damage.

❑ **Colchicine and sodium depletion:** Colchicine can cause widespread alteration of intestinal mucus, which hinders intestinal absorption of nutrients and causes increased fecal excretion. Sodium is one of several nutrients reported to be depleted in this manner. Symptoms associated with sodium depletion include muscle weakness, dehydration, loss of appetite, and poor concentration.

❑ **Colchicine and potassium depletion:** Colchicine can cause widespread alteration of the intestinal mucus, which hinders intestinal absorption of nutrients, causing increased fecal excretion. Potassium is one of several nutrients reported to be depleted in this manner. Loss of potassium can lead to *hypokalemia* (potassium depletion). This can be accompanied by muscular weakness, *tetany* (muscle spasms), and *postural hypotension* (a term that refers to low blood pressure when changing from a lying or sitting position to a standing position), which can cause fainting spells. Other symptoms associated with potassium depletion include irregular heartbeat, poor reflexes, fatigue, continuous thirst, *edema*, constipation, mental confusion, and nervous disorders.

❑ **Colchicine and beta-carotene depletion:** Colchicine can cause widespread alteration of the intestinal mucus, which hinders intestinal absorption of nutrients and causes increased fecal excretion. Beta-carotene is one of several nutrients reported to be depleted in this manner.

❑ **Colchicine and calcium depletion:** Calcium depletion can result in skeletal problems such as *osteoporosis* and *osteomalacia*. Calcium deficiency also can cause high blood pressure, muscle cramps, heart palpitations, tooth decay, back and leg pains, insomnia, and nervous disorders.

❑ **Colchicine and phosphorus depletion.** A phosphorus deficiency can cause symptoms such as anxiety and nervousness, as well as skeletal problems.

LAXATIVES

The three classes of laxatives are those containing mineral oil, bisacodyl, and the phosphate enemas.

LAXATIVES CONTAINING MINERAL OIL

Mineral-oil laxatives deplete fat-soluble nutrients, which include vitamins A, D, E, K, and beta-carotene, as well as the minerals calcium and phosphorus.

The following points summarize the various ways in which regular use of mineral oil-containing laxatives can cause the depletion of nutrients.

❑ Mineral oil is capable of absorbing the fat-soluble vitamins A, D, E, K, and beta-carotene, which prevents them from being absorbed.

❑ Mineral oil hastens movement of the bowel content, which may prevent complete digestion and absorption of nutrients.

❑ Mineral oil may interfere with the process of absorption throughout the lower intestines. By partially covering the surface area of the intestines, it establishes a mechanical barrier to absorption and digestion with consequent symptoms of "indigestion."

❑ Mineral oil interferes with the utilization and retention of calcium and phosphorus. This interference is possibly of a dual nature: (a) Mineral oil interferes with the absorption of these minerals by forming a mechanical barrier along the intestinal tract, and (b) it alters the metabolic processes of calcium and phosphorus by interfering with the absorption of vitamin D.

❑ Mineral oil mechanically coats food particles and, consequently, prevents their complete absorption through the intestinal walls. This statement is borne out by the fact that the continuous use of mineral oil frequently causes a severe loss in weight.

BISACODYL

Bisacodyl causes potassium depletion.

Loss of potassium can lead to *hypokalemia* (potassium depletion). This can produce symptoms of muscular weakness, *tetany* (muscle spasms), and *postural hypotension* (a term that refers to low blood pressure when changing from a lying or sitting position to a standing position), which can cause fainting spells. Other symptoms associated with potassium depletion include irregular heartbeat, poor reflexes, fatigue, continuous thirst, *edema*, constipation, mental confusion, and nervous disorders.

PHOSPHATE ENEMAS

Phosphate enemas deplete calcium and magnesium.

❏ **Phosphate enemas and calcium depletion:** Calcium depletion can result in skeletal problems such as *osteoporosis* and *osteomalacia*. Calcium deficiency also can cause high blood pressure, muscle cramps, heart palpitations, tooth decay, back and leg pains, insomnia, and nervous disorders.

❏ **Phosphate enemas and magnesium depletion:** Depletion of magnesium can cause *cardiac arrhythmias*, high blood pressure, and various other cardiovascular-related problems. Additional conditions associated with low magnesium levels include *osteoporosis*, muscle cramps, PMS, and an increase in the frequency and severity of asthma attacks.

PSYCHOTHERAPEUTIC DRUGS

The following classes of psychotherapeutic drugs are capable of depleting nutrients in the body: the tricyclic antidepressants, phenothiazines, monoamine oxidase inhibitors (phenelzine), butyrophenones (haloperidol), and lithium.

TRICYCLIC ANTIDEPRESSANTS

Tricyclic antidepressants deplete vitamin B_2 and coenzyme Q_{10}.

❑ **Tricyclic antidepressants and vitamin B_2 depletion:** Symptoms associated with vitamin B_2 (riboflavin) deficiency include problems with the skin, eyes, mucous membranes, and nerves.

❑ **Tricyclic antidepressants and coenzyme Q_{10} depletion:** Coenzyme Q_{10} is an extremely important *antioxidant* and also performs critical roles in the *generation of energy* in the mitochondria of all cells. The heart is the most active muscle in the human body, and a decline in energy resulting from a deficiency of CoQ_{10} first affects the heart. Now it is thought that a CoQ_{10} deficiency may be one of the primary causes of congestive heart failure. In addition to providing antioxidant protection within the mitochondria, coenzyme Q_{10} protects *LDL-cholesterol* from *free radical* oxidation. Individuals who are deficient in coenzyme Q_{10} have an increased risk for cardiovascular disease and also have higher levels of *free radical* damage, which accelerates the aging process.

PHENOTHIAZINES

Phenothiazines deplete vitamin B_2, coenzyme Q_{10}, and melatonin.

❑ **Phenothiazines and vitamin B_2 depletion:** Symptoms associated with vitamin B_2 (riboflavin) deficiency include problems with the skin, eyes, mucous membranes, and nerves.

❏ **Phenothiazines and coenzyme Q$_{10}$ depletion:** Coenzyme Q$_{10}$ is an extremely important *antioxidant* and also performs critical roles in the *generation of energy* in the mitochondria of all cells. Because the heart is the most active muscle in the human body, a decline in energy resulting from a deficiency of CoQ$_{10}$ first affects the heart, and now it is thought that a CoQ$_{10}$ deficiency might be one of the main causes of congestive heart failure. In addition to providing antioxidant protection within the mitochondria, coenzyme Q$_{10}$ protects *LDL-cholesterol* from *free radical* oxidation. Individuals who are deficient in coenzyme Q$_{10}$ have an increased risk for *cardiovascular disease* and also have more *free radical* damage, which accelerates the aging process.

❏ **Phenothiazines and melatonin depletion:** Chlorpromazine depletes *melatonin*, the brain hormone that triggers or induces sleep. A deficiency of melatonin results in insomnia and related sleep problems. Insomnia can lead to many other problems such as depression, poor performance at work, and an increase in accidents. Melatonin is also an important antioxidant, so a depletion of melatonin could result in more *free radical* damage and an acceleration of the aging process. Finally, many studies have associated low levels of melatonin with a higher incidence of breast cancer.

MONOAMINE OXIDASE INHIBITORS (MAOIS) (PHENELZINE)

❏ **Phenelzine depletes vitamin B$_6$:** Vitamin B$_6$ (pyridoxine) depletion can cause depression and insomnia, and it increases the risk for *cardiovascular* *disease.* For a more detailed explanation of these vitamin B$_6$-deficiency problems, see pages 58–59.

BUTYROPHENONES (HALOPERIDOL)

Haloperidol depletes melatonin and vitamin E.

❑ **Haloperidol and melatonin depletion.** *Melatonin* is the brain hormone that triggers or induces sleep. A deficiency results in insomnia and related sleep problems. Insomnia also can lead to depression, poor performance at work, and an increase in accidents, among other problems. Melatonin is an important antioxidant, so a depletion of melatonin could result in more free radical damage and an acceleration of the aging process. Finally, low levels of melatonin have been associated with an increased incidence of breast cancer.

❑ **Haloperidol depletes vitamin E:** Vitamin E is one of the body's most important *antioxidant* nutrients. A deficiency of vitamin E results in more free radical damage, which accelerates the aging process. One of the most immediate consequences of vitamin E depletion is increased oxidation of *LDL-cholesterol,* which speeds up the process of *atherosclerosis.*

LITHIUM

Lithium depletes inositol.

❑ Lithium reduces brain inositol levels by inhibiting the enzyme inositol monophosphatase. In one study, 80% of patients with bipolar depression who were being treated with lithium were found to have reduced levels of inositol in the brain. Excessive urination and excessive thirst are side effects related to inositol deficiency.

STEROID, ANABOLIC

❏ **Stanozolol depletes iron:** Iron depletion can cause anemia, which produces weakness and fatigue. Other symptoms associated with iron deficiency include hair loss, brittle nails, and a weakened *immune system*. However, iron supplementation is not recommended unless a lab test determines that iron deficiency is present.

THYROID MEDICATIONS

❏ **Levothyroxine depletes iron:** Iron depletion can cause anemia, which produces weakness and fatigue. Other symptoms associated with iron deficiency include hair loss, brittle nails, and a weakened *immune system*. However, iron supplementation is not recommended unless a lab test determines that iron deficiency is present.

ULCER MEDICATIONS

In 1998, anti-ulcer medications comprised the number-one category of prescription drugs in the United States, accounting for more than $6.215 billion in sales. During the same year, this class of drugs ranked fourth in terms of numbers of prescriptions, with an estimated 81,434,000 prescriptions filled.

The two classes of anti-ulcer medications are the H-2 receptor antagonists and the proton pump inhibitors. The purpose of these drugs is to decrease the acidity in the stomach and intestinal tract. Less acid frequently improves the symptoms of acid indigestion and decreases the pain when an ulcer is present. However, the absorption of numerous vitamins and minerals requires a slightly acidic pH in the intestinal tract. When these drugs make the intestinal tract less acidic, they inhibit the absorption of many nutrients.

Gastritis (inflammation of the cells lining the stomach and/or intestinal tract) and ulcers often are caused by a bacteria known as *Helicobacter pylori*, or *H. pylori*. Actually, *H. pylori* is the most common gastric infection worldwide, and some experts estimate that 90% of ulcers are caused by this bacterium. *H. pylori* causes gastritis and ulcers by burrowing through the protective mucus layer that lines the stomach and intestinal tract.

Taking one of these anti-ulcer drugs decreases the amount of acid, which reduces the pain in the inflamed or ulcerated tissue. *H. pylori*, however, thrive in an alkaline environment. Therefore, taking anti-ulcer drugs treats the symptoms but does not eradicate the cause of the problem. Creating a more alkaline environment actually increases the likelihood that the *H. pylori* bacteria will grow and multiply.

Currently, several protocols are used to treat ulcers and destroy *H. pylori*. These involve taking one or two different antibiotics along with a proton pump inhibitor for 1 to 2 weeks. A different protocol reported a 30% cure rate in people who took 5 grams of vitamin C daily. This included curing the ulcers and completely eradicating the *H. pylori* bacteria. One wonders what the level of success would be if people were to take 10 or 15 grams of vitamin C daily in divided doses. Because ulcers and infection with *H. pylori* are associated with higher rates of gastric cancer, this issue should be taken very seriously.

The fact that the H-2 blocker drugs have been made available without a prescription creates another level of concern. This allows people to use these drugs indiscriminately without any checks and balances from a health care professional. Most people are not aware of the fact that (a) these drugs treat only the symptoms, and (b) altering the acid/base balance actually creates an environment that is more favorable for *H. pylori.*

H_2 Blockers

H_2 blockers deplete vitamin B_{12}, vitamin D, calcium, iron, zinc, and folic acid.

❏ **H_2 blockers and vitamin B_{12} depletion:** Stomach acid and pepsin are required to cleave or separate vitamin B_{12} from food, and then a protein known as *intrinsic factor* is necessary for vitamin B_{12} absorption. All of these processes require a slightly acidic environment. Taking anti-ulcer drugs, which decreases acidity, inhibits vitamin B_{12} digestion and absorption processes.

Vitamin B_{12} deficiency can cause anemia, which results in fatigue, tiredness, and weakness, and B_{12} deficiency is also a common cause of depression, especially in elderly people. Inadequate levels of B_{12} increases *homocysteine*, which is a risk factor for *cardiovascular disease*. If serious B_{12} deficiencies are not corrected, long-term irreversible neurological damage can occur.

❏ **H_2 blockers and vitamin D depletion:** These drugs seem to inhibit the metabolism of vitamin D, which can lead to *osteoporosis* and other skeletal problems. Vitamin D is necessary for calcium absorption, which means that a vitamin D deficiency could cause a calcium deficiency. Vitamin D depletion also can result in muscle weakness and hearing loss.

❑ **H₂ blockers and calcium depletion:** Studies have been contradictory, so at this time it is not clear if calcium supplements are necessary. The alterations in calcium may be secondary to the effects on vitamin D metabolism. If calcium is truly depleted, it can lead to skeletal problems such as *osteoporosis* and *osteomalacia*. Calcium deficiency also can cause high blood pressure, muscle cramps, heart palpitations, tooth decay, back and leg pains, insomnia, and nervous disorders.

❑ **H₂ blockers and iron depletion:** Iron depletion can cause anemia, which produces weakness and fatigue. Other symptoms associated with iron deficiency include hair loss, brittle nails, and a weakened *immune system*. However, iron supplementation is not recommended unless a lab test determines that iron deficiency is present.

❑ **H₂ blockers and zinc depletion:** Zinc is important to a healthy *immune system*. Indications of a zinc deficiency are slow healing of wounds and a weakened immune system. A zinc deficiency also can cause insulin resistance, a loss of the senses of taste and smell, and infertility and sexual dysfunction in both men and women.

❑ **H₂ blockers and folic acid depletion:** Therapy with H₂ blocker drugs causes a slight but noticeable reduction in folic acid levels. Folic acid depletions could become significant during long-term or intensive use of these medications, especially in individuals who are on diets that supply only small amounts of folic acid to begin with. A deficiency of folic acid can cause a wide range of health problems including anemia, depression, cervical dysplasia, birth defects, and increased risks for cardiovascular disease, breast cancer, and colorectal cancer. For a detailed discussion of the problems associated with folic acid deficiency, see pages 48–50.

PROTON PUMP INHIBITORS

Proton pump inhibitors deplete vitamin B_{12}.
(please read the introductory section to Anti-Ulcer Drugs, pages 94–96.)

In 1998, Prilosec was the number-one selling drug in the United States, accounting for nearly $3 billion in sales. In terms of numbers of prescriptions, Prilosec ranked fifth, with an estimated 26,662,000 prescriptions filled that year.

Like the H-2 receptor antagonists, the proton pump inhibitors function by decreasing the amount of acidity in the intestinal tract. The difference is that these two classes of anti-ulcer drugs decrease acidity by two different mechanisms, yet the net result is the same — a change in the acid/base levels in the intestinal tract.

To date, studies have only reported that the proton pump inhibitors deplete vitamin B_{12}, whereas the H-2 receptor antagonists deplete vitamin B_{12}, folic acid, vitamin D, calcium, iron, and zinc. One possible explanation for these differences is that the proton pump inhibitors are a much newer class of drugs, so studies researching other nutrient depletions have yet to be conducted. There is certainly the likelihood that altered acid/base levels will inhibit the absorption of many nutrients in addition to vitamin B_{12}.

❑ **Proton pump inhibitors and vitamin B_{12} depletion:** Stomach acid and pepsin are required to cleave or separate vitamin B_{12} from food, and then a protein known as *intrinsic factor* is necessary for vitamin

B_{12} absorption. To proceed, all of these processes require a slightly acidic environment. Taking anti-ulcer drugs, which decreases acidity, inhibits vitamin B_{12} digestion and absorption processes.

A deficiency in Vitamin B_{12} can cause anemia, which results in fatigue, tiredness, and weakness, and a B_{12} deficiency is also a common cause of depression, especially in elderly people. Inadequate levels of B_{12} cause elevated *homocysteine*, which poses increased risk for *cardiovascular disease*. If serious B_{12} deficiencies are not corrected, long-term irreversible neurological damage can occur.

MISCELLANEOUS DRUGS

The miscellaneous drugs discussed here are methotrexate, penicillamine, EDTA, and ritodrine.

METHOTREXATE

❑ **Methotrexate and folic acid depletion:** Initially, methotrexate was used as a form of cancer chemotherapy. When it is used in cancer therapy, the drug interferes with cancer metabolism by inhibiting the metabolism of folic acid, so folic acid supplementation is not appropriate. Methotrexate, however, is now being used for other conditions such as rheumatoid arthritis. Studies have reported that folic acid supplementation does not reduce the therapeutic effectiveness of methotrexate when it is used for arthritis but it may have a positive effect in lowering the toxic side effects associated with the drug.

A deficiency of folic acid can cause a wide range of health problems including anemia, depression, *cervical dysplasia*, and birth defects, as well as increased risks for developing *cardiovascular disease*, breast cancer, and colorectal cancer. For a detailed discussion of the problems associated with folic acid deficiency, see pages 48–50.

PENICILLAMINE

Penicillamine is used to treat copper, mercury, zinc, and lead poisoning by promoting the urinary excretion of those metals. Penicillamine also depletes vitamin B_6, magnesium, and zinc.

❑ **Penicillamine and copper depletion:** Penicillamine therapy causes a substantial increase in urinary copper excretion. Copper depletion can result in anemia and fatigue, problems with the maintenance and repair of connective tissues, and elevated levels of *serum cholesterol*.

❑ **Penicillamine and vitamin B_6 depletion:** Vitamin B_6 (pyridoxine) depletion can cause depression and insomnia, and it increases the risk for *cardiovascular disease*.

■ **Depression:** Vitamin B_6 is necessary for converting the amino acid *tryptophan* into the *neurotransmitter serotonin*. A deficiency of serotonin in the brain is strongly associated with depression. Therefore, people taking drugs that deplete vitamin B_6 are at greater risk for depression.

■ **Insomnia:** In the brain, serotonin is converted into *melatonin*, a hormone that controls sleep. Because a vitamin B_6 deficiency inhibits the synthesis of serotonin, it also will decrease the amount of melatonin that can be produced in the brain. People who become deficient in melatonin will suffer from insomnia and related sleep problems.

■ **Cardiovascular disease:** Vitamin B$_6$ is one of the B-vitamins that are necessary to metabolize *homocysteine*, an *amino acid* produced from the metabolism of the essential amino acid methionine. Homocysteine is a toxic substance capable of directly injuring the lining of the arteries, which is the type of damage that causes *atherosclerosis*. Under normal conditions, it exists only briefly. A lack of vitamin B$_6$, however, will produce elevated homocysteine in the blood, and even slight elevations of homocysteine represent a seriously increased risk for developing *atherosclerosis*, the leading cause of heart disease.

❑ **Penicillamine and magnesium depletion:** This combination can cause *cardiac arrhythmias*, high blood pressure, and various other cardiovascular-related problems. Additional conditions associated with low magnesium levels include *osteoporosis*, muscle cramps, PMS, and an increase in the frequency and severity of asthma attacks.

❑ **Penicillamine and zinc depletion:** The mineral zinc is important to a healthy *immune system*. A zinc deficiency can cause slow healing of wounds and a weakened immune system. Insufficient zinc also results in insulin resistance, loss of the senses of taste and smell, and infertility and sexual dysfunction in both men and women.

EDTA

EDTA (ethylene-diamine tetraacetic acid) is often given intravenously as *chelation* therapy. EDTA interacts with calcium, causing excess urinary calcium loss.

❑ **EDTA and calcium depletion:** Depletion of this mineral can result in skeletal problems such as *osteoporosis* and *osteomalacia.* Calcium deficiency also can also cause high blood pressure, muscle cramps, heart palpitations, tooth decay, back and leg pains, insomnia, and nervous disorders.

RITODRINE

Ritodrine inhibits uterine contractions. It is used to delay or prevent contractions in women who are going into pre-term labor.

Ritodrine depletes calcium and potassium.

❑ **Ritodrine and calcium depletion:** Calcium depletion under these conditions will most likely cause symptoms of high blood pressure, muscle cramps, heart palpitations, back and leg pains, insomnia, and nervousness.

❑ **Ritodrine and potassium depletion:** Potassium depletion can produce symptoms of muscular weakness, *tetany* (muscle spasms), and *postural hypotension* (a term that refers to low blood pressure when changing from a lying or sitting position to a standing position), which can cause dizziness and fainting spells. Other symptoms associated with potassium depletion are irregular heartbeat, poor reflexes, fatigue, continuous thirst, *edema,* constipation, mental confusion, and nervousness.

BETA-CAROTENE

OVERVIEW

Drugs that deplete Beta-Carotene
✔ Cholestyramine
✔ Colchicine
✔ Colchicine and probenicid
✔ Colestipol
✔ Mineral oil
✔ Neomycin

Beta-carotene belongs to a group of plant compounds called *carotenoids*. To date, more than 500 carotenoids have been found in nature. *Beta-carotene* is the most abundant carotenoid in foods that people eat and is thought to be the most important carotenoid for humans.

Beta-carotene which is also known as provitamin A, consists of 2 molecules of vitamin A linked together. *Enzymes* in the lining of the intestinal tract split beta-carotene into two separate molecules of vitamin A whenever the body needs it. This makes beta-carotene the most abundant precursor of vitamin A in fruits and vegetables.

SYMPTOMS AND CAUSES OF DEFICIENCY

❑ Because beta-carotene is the dietary precursor of vitamin A, deficiencies of this nutrient are the same as deficiencies in vitamin A.

❑ Low dietary intake of beta-carotene is associated with a weakened *immune system*, probably a result of increased damage from *free radicals*.

❑ Many types of cancer are associated with low dietary intake of beta-carotene.

❑ Although several drugs are capable of reducing blood levels of beta-carotene, the main cause of a deficiency is not eating enough of the colored fruits and vegetables which are known to contain ample beta-carotene.

BIOLOGICAL FUNCTIONS AND EFFECTS

❑ Beta-carotene functions as a chain-breaking *antioxidant*. This means it traps free radicals, which stops the chain reaction of free radical destruction.

❑ Beta-carotene is the natural agent that is most capable of quenching singlet oxygen free radicals in humans.

SIDE EFFECTS AND TOXICITY

No known toxicities are associated with beta-carotene. Ingesting large doses of beta-carotene, however, can result in a harmless side effect called *carotenosis* which denotes an orange coloration that is most noticeable on the palms of the hands and the soles of the feet. The discoloration subsides when the dosage is lowered or stopped.

RDA AND DOSAGE

❑ No *RDA* has been established for beta-carotene.

❑ The most common supplemental dose of beta-carotene is 25,000 *I.U.* daily.

DIETARY SOURCES

Beta-carotene occurs exclusively in plant (fruit and vegetable) foods. Foods containing high amounts of beta-carotene include:

❑ green leafy vegetables

❑ sweet potatoes

❑ spinach

❑ peaches

❑ green, yellow, and red peppers

❑ carrots

❑ squash

❑ apricots

❑ cantaloupe

BIFIDOBACTERIA BIFIDUM (BIFIDUS)

OVERVIEW

Drugs that deplete Bificobacteria bifidum
✔ Aminoglycosides
✔ Cephalosporins
✔ Co-trimoxazole
✔ Fluoroquinolones
✔ Macrolides
✔ Penicillins
✔ Sulfonamides
✔ Tetracyclines

Bifidobacteria bifidum, also known as bifidus, is the main strain of beneficial bacteria that inhabit the large intestine. If the balance between the beneficial and the pathological bacteria gets upset, a condition known as *dysbiosis* develops. A frequent cause of dysbiosis is the use of antibiotics. When a person takes antibiotics, most of the bifidobacteria are killed along with the pathological bacteria.

SYMPTOMS AND CAUSES OF DEFICIENCY

❑ Symptoms of a deficiency of bifidobacteria bifidum include gas, bloating, diarrhea or constipation, and bad breath.

❑ The primary cause of a deficiency is the use of antibiotic drugs. Other causes are prolonged high stress levels, exposure to or ingestion of toxic metals or pesticides, and a poor diet containing large quantities of sugar, fat, and refined and processed foods lacking in fiber content.

BIOLOGICAL FUNCTIONS AND EFFECTS

❑ Bifidobacteria produce fatty acids in the colon, which slightly increase the acidic environment, making it unfavorable for the growth of pathological bacteria, yeasts, and molds.

❑ The fatty acids that the bifidobacteria produce are the main source of energy for the *colonocytes* which are the cells that form the inner surface of the colon.

SIDE EFFECTS AND TOXICITY

No toxicity is associated with *probiotics*, and they do not interfere with other medications.

RDA AND DOSAGE

❑ No RDA has been set.

❑ Dosages for probiotics are measured in *cfu's* (colony forming units), which refers to the number of viable (live) organisms.

❑ To prevent problems, healthy people can take a probiotic containing 1–2 billion cfu per day.

❑ Many probiotic products contain a combination of acidophilus and bifidobacteria.

❑ Individuals with dysbiosis and those who are taking antibiotics should take 10–15 billion cfu (a combination of acidophilus and bifidobacteria) twice daily for 2 weeks.

DIETARY SOURCES

Because foods do not contain substantial amounts of bifidobacteria, they are best obtained by purchasing commercial probiotic products containing bifidobacteria.

BIOTIN

OVERVIEW

Drugs that deplete Biotin
✔ Amionglycosides
✔ Barbiturates
✔ Carbamazepine
✔ Cephalosporins
✔ Fluoroquinolones
✔ Macrolides
✔ Penicillins
✔ Phenobarbital
✔ Phenytoin
✔ Primidone
✔ Sulfonamides
✔ Tetracyclines
✔ Trimethoprim

Biotin is one of the more recently discovered water-soluble B vitamins. It was first isolated in 1936 and was synthesized in 1943. Biotin is essential to many *enzyme* systems. Biotin consumed from plant and animal sources is bound to proteins and the biotin is not released until it comes into contact with the enzymes in the upper part of the small intestine. It is also absorbed from the lower part of the small intestine where it is synthesized by the "friendly" intestinal bacteria.

SYMPTOMS AND CAUSES OF DEFICIENCY

❑ Biotin deficiency in humans is rare. Some diabetic individuals have an abnormality in a biotin-dependent enzyme, which can lead to dysfunctions of the nervous system.

❑ Deficiency symptoms include progressive hair loss, loss of hair color, depression, scaly dermatitis, sores on the nose and in the mouth, anorexia, nausea, numbness and tingling of the extremities, muscle pain, and heart irregularities.

BIOLOGICAL FUNCTIONS AND EFFECTS

❑ Biotin-containing enzymes play a vital role in the production of energy from the metabolism of carbohydrates and fats.

❑ Biotin-containing enzymes also are involved in the manufacture of fats and the excretion of byproducts from the metabolism of protein.

❑ Biotin-containing enzymes participate in carboxylation reactions (adding carbon dioxide to acceptor molecules) decarboxylation reactions (which remove carbon dioxide) and deamination reactions (removing NH_2 groups from certain amino acids).

❑ Biotin is the vitamin that produces healthy hair and helps prevent graying and baldness. Supplementation in cases of severe deficiency will help, but because biotin deficiency is rare, these claims are suspect.

❑ Biotin helps with "uncombable hair syndrome," a condition in which children have multiple cowlicks (the hair sticks up in all directions and won't lie down).

❑ In many cases, biotin helps people with dry, splitting fingernails.

SIDE EFFECTS AND TOXICITY

Biotin has no known toxic effects. Excessive levels are easily eliminated through urination.

RDA AND DOSAGE

❑ The RDA for biotin is 0.3 milligrams (mg) per day.

❑ *Pharmacologic* doses in the scientific literature range from 0.3 mg up to 3 mg.

❑ Because biotin is seldom deficient in humans, taking large doses is seldom necessary.

DIETARY SOURCES

Biotin is found abundantly in many plant and animal foods. A considerable amount of biotin also is synthesized by the "friendly" intestinal bacteria. The best food sources are:

❑ liver
❑ brewer's yeast
❑ grapefruit
❑ strawberries

❑ milk
❑ bananas
❑ watermelon
❑ peanuts

BORON

OVERVIEW

Boron is a *trace mineral* that is most prevalent in nature as borax, a mixture of boron, sodium, and oxygen. Although boron has been recognized as an essential nutrient for plants for almost 100 years, not until the mid-1980s was it discovered to be essential to humans. Therefore, some of the information about its metabolic activity and function is still speculative. Research in the past decade is strongly implicating that boron plays vital roles in metabolism and in the health of bones.

SYMPTOMS AND CAUSES OF DEFICIENCY

❑ A deficiency of boron results in increased loss of calcium and magnesium through the urine.

❑ A boron deficiency causes a more rapid rate of bone demineralization, which probably hastens the development of *osteoporosis* in postmenopausal women.

BIOLOGICAL FUNCTIONS AND EFFECTS

❑ Boron has a powerful effect on the metabolism of calcium. In one study, when boron was given to women deficient in boron, it produced a 44 percent reduction in the urinary excretion of calcium.

❑ Boron plays an important role in the metabolism of magnesium.

❑ Boron has a regulatory effect on the production of estrogens and testosterone.

❑ Biochemically, boron facilitates *hydroxylation* reactions. Because the synthesis of estrogens and testosterone both require hydroxylation, there is strong indication that boron influences production of these hormones.

❑ Boron may play a role in preventing osteoporosis in postmenopausal women, as boron has been shown to substantially reduce calcium loss through the urine.

❑ Boron may influence the synthesis of vitamin D, which plays a role in the prevention of bone loss.

❑ People living in geographical areas with low levels of boron in the soil have a higher than usual incidence of *osteoarthritis*.

SIDE EFFECTS AND TOXICITY

❑ An excessive intake of boron can cause nausea, vomiting, diarrhea, skin rashes, and fatigue.

❑ No health or medical problems have been reported in areas of the world where the daily diet supplies up to 41 mg per day of boron.

RDA AND DOSAGE

❑ No RDA has been set for boron.

❑ Based on animal studies, the human requirement for boron is estimated to be from 1 to 2 mg/day.

❑ *Pharmacological* doses in the scientific literature range from 3 mg to 6gm daily.

❑ Available forms of boron are sodium borate and boron chelates, the latter of which include boron citrate, aspartate, and glycinate.

DIETARY SOURCES

Boron is readily available from fruits and vegetables, and it is easily absorbed from the intestinal tract.

CALCIUM

OVERVIEW

Drugs that deplete Calcium
✔ Aluminum hydroxide-containing products
✔ Amionglycosides
✔ Amphotericin B
✔ Aspirin
✔ Barbiturates
✔ Bumetanide
✔ Cholestyramine
✔ Cimetidine
✔ Colchicine
✔ Corticosteroids
✔ Digoxin
✔ EDTA
✔ Ethacrynic acid
✔ Famotidine
✔ Fosphenytoin
✔ Furosemide
✔ Hydrocholorthiazide and Triamterene
✔ Magnesium-containing products
✔ Mineral oil
✔ Nizatidine
✔ Phenobartibal
✔ Phenytoin
✔ Ranitidine
✔ Tetracyclines
✔ Torsemide
✔ Triamterene

Calcium is the most abundant mineral in the human body, and the fifth most common substance behind carbon, hydrogen, oxygen, and nitrogen. Average healthy male bodies contain about 2.5 to 3 pounds of calcium, and female bodies contain about 2 pounds. Approximately 99 percent of our calcium is present in the bones and teeth, which leaves only about 1 percent in cells and body fluids. Even though only a small amount of calcium is in the blood, the body goes to great lengths to maintain blood-calcium levels within a relatively narrow range.

Three regulatory mechanisms control blood-calcium. If levels drop too low:

1. The intestines absorb calcium at a faster rate.

2. The bones release more calcium.

3. The kidneys excrete less calcium.

In addition:

❑ Phosphorus displaces calcium. Eating a lot of foods that contain phosphorus prompts increased urinary excretion of calcium, which in turn can prompt the body to leach calcium from the bones and thereby contribute to osteoporosis. The main sources of dietary phosphorus are soft drinks and animal protein.

❑ In bones and teeth, calcium exists primarily as hydroxyapatite, which is a calcium carbonate/calcium phosphate compound that gives these tissues rigidity and strength.

❑ The appropriateness of cow's milk as a source of calcium has been questioned for the following three reasons: First, milk is a frequent cause of food allergies. Second, many people have digestive problems as a result of lactose intolerance. Third, an enzyme from cow's milk, called xanthine oxidase, can damage the arterial membranes, and antibodies to bovine (cow) xanthine oxidase have been found in the blood of individuals who have *atherosclerosis*.

SYMPTOMS AND CAUSES OF DEFICIENCY

❑ *Rickets* is the classic calcium-deficiency disease. It occurs most frequently in children and results in a variety of bone deformities. A lack of vitamin D and a lack of sunshine (which promotes the formation of Vitamin D in the body) can produce the calcium deficiency that leads to rickets.

❑ Symptoms of calcium deficiency include muscle cramps, heart palpitations, high blood pressure, brittle or soft bones, tooth decay, back and leg pains, insomnia, nervous disorders, rickets, osteoporosis and osteomalacia.

❑ The two main adult conditions caused by calcium deficiency are *osteoporosis* and *osteomalacia*, characterized by bone deformities and propensity for fractures.

❑ Magnesium deficiency causes various abnormalities in the metabolism of calcium.

❑ Eating foods that are high in phosphorus (soft drinks and animal protein) promote the urinary loss of calcium.

❑ Inflammatory conditions in the intestinal tract will decrease the body's absorption of calcium.

❑ Other significant factors that can lower calcium levels include caffeine intake, excess dietary fat and fiber, lack of exercise, and the numerous drugs that can cause calcium depletion.

BIOLOGICAL FUNCTIONS AND EFFECTS

❑ The most important documented function of calcium is its role in the development and maintenance of healthy bones and teeth. The need for calcium is greatest in childhood and adolescence and during pregnancy and lactation.

❑ Calcium supplements are only minimally effective when they are taken alone. In one osteoporosis study, a nutritional supplement containing a broad range of *micronutrients* increased bone density 2 to 3 times more effectively than calcium alone.

❑ Low levels of calcium are associated with *hypertension,* and many studies have shown that the blood pressure of hypertensive patients who take calcium supplements is slightly lowered. The gains are so small, though, that calcium cannot be suggested as a treatment.

❑ Several studies report that men with low levels of calcium intake have higher rates of colorectal cancer. Calcium supplementation in high-risk individuals also decreases the rate of abnormal cell division in the colon.

❑ Calcium helps to initiate muscle contractions. As such, it plays a vital role in the contraction-relaxation cycle that regulates a normal heartbeat.

❑ Calcium is involved in several steps of the blood-clotting mechanism.

❑ Ionized calcium regulates the passage of fluids across cellular membranes by affecting the *permeability* of cell walls.

❑ Calcium activates various *enzyme* systems responsible for muscle contraction, fat digestion, and protein metabolism.

SIDE EFFECTS AND TOXICITY

❑ Large doses of calcium are excreted efficiently by the body and usually do not produce toxic effects.

❑ Regularly taking large doses of calcium may interfere with the absorption of zinc, iron, and magnesium.

RDA AND DOSAGE

❑ The RDA for calcium is 1,000 mg/day.

❑ Pharmacologic doses in the scientific literature range from 1,000 mg to 2,000 mg/day.

❑ Available forms are calcium citrate, aspartate, ascorbate, lactate, phosphate, carbonate, glycinate, malate, amino acid chelates, and microcrystalline hydroxyapatite compound (MCHC).

DIETARY SOURCES

❑ Milk and dairy products are the major source of dietary calcium for most people.

❑ Other good sources are dark green leafy vegetables, broccoli, legumes, nuts, and whole grains.

CARNITINE

OVERVIEW

Drugs that deplete Carnitine
✔ Nevirapine
✔ Valproic acid
✔ Zidovudine

Although carnitine is a nonessential *amino acid*, it has vitamin-like properties. It can be synthesized from the essential amino acids lysine and methionine. The highest concentrations of carnitine are found in the heart, muscles, liver, and kidney.

SYMPTOMS AND CAUSES OF DEFICIENCY

❑ Carnitine deficiencies are rare because the body produces carnitine relatively easily.

❑ Symptoms of deficiency include elevated levels of *blood lipids*, abnormal liver function, muscle weakness, less energy, and impaired glucose control.

BIOLOGICAL FUNCTIONS AND EFFECTS

❑ The primary function of carnitine seems to be the regulation of heart function by controlling the production of energy in muscle tissue.

❑ Carnitine regulates fat metabolism by facilitating the transport of fats across cell membranes into the *mitochondria* for energy production.

❑ Carnitine helps the body oxidize amino acids to produce energy when necessary.

❑ Carnitine helps to metabolize *ketones*.

❑ Although this area has not been well researched, many athletes take carnitine supplements to increase their energy and endurance.

❑ The ability of carnitine to increase the oxidation of fats suggests that it might be useful in weight-loss diets.

SIDE EFFECTS AND TOXICITY

Carnitine seems to be safe, with no significant side effects reported, even at high doses.

RDA AND DOSAGE

❑ No RDA has been established for carnitine.

❑ The dosage range for carnitine is 1,500–4,000 mg/day in divided doses.

CHLORIDE

OVERVIEW

Drugs that deplete Chloride
No studies reporting drug-induced depletion of chloride have been found.

Chloride is one of the body's three major *electrolytes* (the other two are sodium and potassium). They are the *dissociated ions*, responsible for *osmotic pressure* in body fluids. Osmotic pressure is rigidly controlled, primarily by regulatory mechanisms that determine the rate of *resorption* of ions and water through the kidneys. The ionic strength of electrolytes enables them to influence the *solubility* of proteins and other substances throughout the body.

SYMPTOMS AND CAUSES OF DEFICIENCY

❑ Chloride deficiency is rare as a result of the widespread availability and use of salt (sodium chloride).

❑ Chloride deficiency creates a condition called *metabolic alkalosis*, which can cause diarrhea, vomiting and sweating.

❑ Chloride deficiency can be caused by extensive diarrhea, frequent vomiting, adrenal insufficiency, long-term use of diuretics, and systemic acidosis.

❑ Other symptoms of chloride deficiency include weakness, poor digestion and loss of appetite, and hair loss.

❑ Increased sweating can cause chloride depletion.

❑ Control of chloride, sodium, and potassium is mediated by the hormones of the adrenal cortex and the anterior pituitary gland.

❑ Chloride and the other electrolytes are readily absorbed through the intestinal tract and are excreted primarily in the urine and sweat.

❑ Under normal conditions, chloride represents about 3 percent of the total mineral content of the body.

BIOLOGICAL FUNCTIONS AND EFFECTS

❑ Chloride is the primary *anion* functioning in the *extracellular* fluids throughout the body, which include the blood, lymph, and the fluid in the spaces between cells. Approximately 85 percent of the chloride ions reside in extracellular fluids and 15 percent in the *intracellular* fluids.

❑ Chloride, along with sodium and potassium, helps to maintain normal osmotic equilibrium by controlling the distribution and balance of water throughout the body.

❑ Chloride, along with phosphate and sulfate ions, helps to maintain the acid/alkaline pH balance throughout the body.

❑ As part of the hydrochloric acid in the stomach, chloride is necessary to maintain the normal acidity of the stomach for the processes of digestion.

❑ Chloride helps regulate removal of CO_2 from cells and its transport to the lungs for excretion.

❑ The electrolytes, in conjunction with calcium and magnesium, maintain nerve transmission and normal muscle activity (contraction and relaxation).

SIDE EFFECTS AND TOXICITY

❑ Excess chloride is efficiently excreted through the kidneys and, therefore, chloride toxicity is virtually impossible in humans.

❑ Because of the efficient excretion of excess chloride, side effects are a nonissue.

RDA AND DOSAGE

❑ No RDA has been set for chloride because it is so readily available in foods.

❑ Estimated safe and adequate intake of chloride for adults is from 1.5 to 5grams/day.

DIETARY SOURCES

❑ The primary dietary source of chloride is table salt (sodium chloride).

❑ Chloride also occurs abundantly in vegetables and animal foods.

CHOLINE

OVERVIEW

Drugs that deplete Choline
No studies that report choline depletion have been found.

Choline is a member of the water-soluble B vitamin group. Classifying choline as a vitamin is questionable because the human body synthesizes it naturally. Because the rate of synthesis is not normally sufficient to meet human metabolic needs, however, choline has been included as an essential vitamin nutrient.

SYMPTOMS AND CAUSES OF DEFICIENCY

❑ Choline deficiency in humans is virtually non-existent.

BIOLOGICAL FUNCTIONS AND EFFECTS

❑ Choline is the precursor to, and a component of, the *neurotransmitter* acetylcholine. As such, choline is intimately involved in a wide range of neurological activities, including the functions of movement, coordination, and the stimulation of muscle contraction. It also plays a critical role in the brain functions of thought, memory, and intellect.

❑ Choline is a *lipotropic* (fat-emulsifying) agent.

❑ Structurally, choline contains three methyl groups that enable it to serve as a methyl donor in many important biochemical pathways.

❑ Choline is also a part of phosphatidyl choline, a *phospholipid* that is a major structural component of cell walls and cellular membranes throughout the body.

❑ As part of phosphatidyl choline, choline functions in the metabolism of fat and in the transport of fat from the liver.

❑ After being converted to betaine, choline functions in the synthesis of *amino acids* and proteins.

❑ One of the main characteristics of Alzheimer's disease is a deficiency of acetylcholine. With high doses of phosphatidyl choline, some individuals with mild to moderate Alzheimer's disease show improved memory and cognitive function.

❑ Choline is useful in reducing the tremors associated with *tardive dyskinesia* and other diseases of the nervous system.

SIDE EFFECTS AND TOXICITY

❑ The toxicity of choline is very low.

❑ Orally taking high doses of choline salts such as choline chloride can readily produce nausea, diarrhea, and dizziness.

❑ Orally taking choline produces an unpleasant "fishy" odor as a result of intestinal bacteria metabolizing the choline and releasing the odorous substance trimethylamine.

RDA AND DOSAGE

❑ No RDA has been set for choline.

❑ Pharmacologic doses in the scientific literature range from 2 grams up to 10 grams in divided doses. Larger doses are not practical because they cause diarrhea and the unpleasant "fishy" odor.

❑ Available forms are choline bitartrate, choline citrate, choline chloride, CDP-choline, and in phosphatidyl choline, also known as lecithin.

DIETARY SOURCES

❑ The richest source of dietary choline is egg yolk.

❑ Other good sources include organ meats, brewer's yeast, wheat germ, soy beans, peanuts and other legumes.

CHROMIUM

OVERVIEW

Drugs that deplete Chromium
✔ Corticosteriods
✔ Sugar
Although sugar is not a drug, it should be mentioned because the overconsumption of sugar throughout much of the United States causes increased urinary excretion of chromium.

Chromium is an essential *trace mineral* that is commonly deficient in American diets. One survey reported that the diets of 90 percent of Americans contained less than the Recommended Dietary Allowance (RDA) for chromium. The body of an average healthy individual contains only a few milligrams. This small amount, however, plays important roles in enhancing the effectiveness of *insulin*, regulating blood sugar levels, and activating various enzymes for energy production.

Chromium is biologically active only when it forms complexes with organic compounds. One such complex is the *glucose tolerance factor (GTF)*. In addition to potentiating the effect of insulin, GTF seems to help lower elevated blood cholesterol and triglyceride levels.

SYMPTOMS AND CAUSES OF DEFICIENCY

❑ Chromium deficiency is claimed to be one of the major nutritional deficiencies in the United States. The main cause of chromium deficiency is low dietary intake.

❑ High sugar consumption is a major contributing cause of chromium deficiency because sugar raises blood chromium levels, increasing urinary excretion and accelerating chromium deficiency.

❑ *Adult-onset (Type II) diabetes* is one of the main indications or results of chromium deficiency. The deficiency impairs GTF activity, which increases insulin levels. Elevated insulin causes increased urinary excretion of chromium, which makes the deficiency worse, contributing to the development of diabetes.

❑ Insufficient dietary intake of chromium contributes to impaired glucose tolerance.

❑ A low level of chromium is associated with *cardiovascular disease.*

❑ Chromium deficiency symptoms parallel those of diabetes and include elevated blood sugar, numbness and tingling in the extremities, nerve disorders in the limbs, and glucose intolerance.

❑ Disturbances in protein and lipid metabolism have been reported in conjunction with chromium deficiency.

BIOLOGICAL FUNCTIONS AND EFFECTS

❑ Some studies suggest that chromium is helpful in preventing *adult-onset (Type II) diabetes.* This seems to be a significant finding for a large percentage of the elderly population.

❑ Chromium, as a component of glucose tolerance, enhances the blood-sugar lowering effects of insulin by facilitating the uptake of glucose into cells. Chromium actually increases the activity of insulin, thereby reducing the amount of insulin required to control blood sugar.

❑ Many studies indicate that chromium decreases total cholesterol, *LDL cholesterol* (the "bad" cholesterol), and *triglycerides* while increasing levels of *HDL cholesterol* (the "good" cholesterol). Other studies, however, have not shown these benefits.

❑ Chromium in combination with niacin has been shown to effectively lower elevated blood cholesterol levels. This enables the dose of niacin to be low enough so that niacin flush is no longer a problem.

❑ Chromium may be helpful in the treatment of *hypoglycemia.*

❏ Some studies have shown that supplemental chromium increases *lean body mass,* which enhances *body composition.* However, other studies have shown no improvement in lean body mass.

SIDE EFFECTS AND TOXICITY

Side effects and toxicity from taking supplemental chromium are virtually nonexistent in humans.

RDA AND DOSAGE

❏ There is no RDA for chromium. In 1989, however, the National Research Council recommended the Safe and Adequate Range for adults to be from 50 to 200 mcg/day.

❏ Pharmacologic doses in the scientific literature range are frequently in the 200 to 400 mcg/day range.

❏ Available forms are chromium picolinate, chromium polynicotinate, chromium chloride, and chromium-enriched yeast (yeast grown in a growth medium enriched with chromium)

DIETARY SOURCES

Good chromium food sources are:

❏ whole-grain breads and cereals ❏ lean meats
❏ cheeses   ❏ black pepper
❏ thyme

COENZYME Q_{10}

OVERVIEW

Drugs that deplete Coenzyme Q10	
✔ Acetohexamide	✔ Imipramine
✔ Amitriptyline	✔ Indapamide
✔ Amoxapine	✔ Lovastatin
✔ Atorvastatin	✔ Mesoridazine
✔ Benzthiazide	✔ Metformin
✔ Beta-blockers	✔ Methyclothiazide
✔ Cerivastatin	✔ Methyldopa
✔ Chlorothiazide	✔ Metolazone
✔ Chlorpromazine	✔ Nortriptyline
✔ Clomipramine	✔ Perphenazine
✔ Clonidine	✔ Polythiazide
✔ Desipramine	✔ Pravastatin
✔ Doxepin	✔ Prochlorperazine
✔ Fluphenazine	✔ Promazine
✔ Fluvastatin	✔ Promethazine
✔ Gemfibrozil	✔ Protriptyline
✔ Glimepiride	✔ Quinethazone
✔ Glyburide	✔ Simvastatin
✔ Haloperidol	✔ Thiethylperazine
✔ Hydralazine	✔ Thioridazine
✔ Hydralazine and hydrochlorothiazide	✔ Tolazamide
✔ Hydralazine, hydrochlorothiazide, and reserpine	✔ Tolbutamide
✔ Hydrochlorothiazide	✔ Trichlomethiazide
✔ Hydroflumethiazide	✔ Trifluoperazine
	✔ Trimipramine

Coenzyme Q_{10} (CoQ_{10}) is one of the most important nutrients in the human body. It is a fat-soluble vitamin-like compound also known as ubiquinone, from the word ubiquitous, which means "everywhere." Coenzyme Q or ubiquinone compounds are synthesized in the cells of all living organisms — plants, animals, and humans. Of the ten coenzyme Q compounds that occur throughout nature, only coenzyme Q_{10} is synthesized in humans.

In 1958, Professor Karl Folkers elucidated the chemical structure of coenzyme Q_{10} while employed at Merck. Working with tiny quantities, Folkers was able to determine that CoQ_{10} had great promise in treating *cardiovascular disease*. However, he was not able to convince his superiors to pursue the development of CoQ_{10}, because Merck had recently launched its new blockbuster drug in the cardiovascular arena, called Diuril. Consequently, the formula and patent rights for coenzyme Q_{10} were sold to a Japanese company.

The Japanese quickly developed new methods of synthesizing large quantities of coenzyme Q_{10}, and it has become one of the best-selling and most effective treatments for cardiovascular disease in Japan. The benefits of this miracle nutrient, coenzyme Q_{10}, are just beginning to be recognized in the United States.

SYMPTOMS AND CAUSES OF DEFICIENCY

Dietary sources contain only a limited amount of coenzyme Q_{10}. Most of the CoQ_{10} in humans is manufactured by the body's cells. The biosynthesis of coenzyme Q_{10} is a 17-step process that requires the following nutrients: riboflavin (B_2), niacinamide (B_3), pantothenic acid (B_5), pyridoxine (B_6), cobalamin (B_{12}), folic acid, vitamin C, and many other trace elements. Consequently, the complex synthesis of coenzyme Q_{10} can be interrupted in many ways. Many people with health problems probably have a deficiency of coenzyme Q_{10} as a result of inadequate dietary intake of the necessary nutrients or ingestion of one or more drugs that interrupt the synthesis of coenzyme Q_{10}.

❑ Coenzyme Q_{10} deficiency can cause congestive heart failure, high blood pressure, angina, mitral valve prolapse, stroke, cardiac arrhythmias, cardiomyopathies, lack of energy, gingivitis, and generalized weakening of the immune system.

❑ Coenzyme Q$_{10}$ is intimately involved in the production of energy. Therefore, a deficiency of CoQ$_{10}$ first affects the heart and cardiovascular system because the heart is the most energy-demanding muscle in the human body. The results of some studies suggest that congestive heart failure is primarily a coenzyme Q$_{10}$ deficiency disease.

BIOLOGICAL FUNCTIONS AND EFFECTS

❑ Coenzyme Q$_{10}$ plays essential roles in the production of energy within the *mitochondria*. It is a coenzyme for numerous enzymes that are involved in the production of *adenosine triphosphate (ATP)*, the high-energy fuel for all living cells.

❑ Coenzyme Q$_{10}$ is an important *antioxidant*. Because it is fat-soluble, it is able to reside in the cell membranes, where it provides protection against damage from *free radicals*.

❑ Coenzyme Q$_{10}$ is transported in the blood stream on molecules of LDL-cholesterol. As such, it plays a major role in preventing the oxidation of LDL and reducing the risk of atherosclerosis.

❑ CoQ$_{10}$ is reportedly useful in treating all kinds of cardiovascular diseases.

❑ CoQ$_{10}$ has been found to be effective in treating *periodontal* (gum) *disease.*

❑ Coenzyme Q$_{10}$ helps to protect against the toxic side effects of widely used drugs such as adriamycin, beta-blockers, and drugs used for psychiatric disorders.

SYMPTOMS OF TOXICITY

Coenzyme Q$_{10}$ seems to be safe. No studies have reported toxicity or adverse side effects.

RDA AND DOSAGE

- ❑ No RDA has been set for coenzyme Q_{10}.
- ❑ Normal supplement dosages range from 30 mg to 100 mg per day.
- ❑ Some reports have indicated treating health conditions such as severe cardiovascular disease and advanced breast cancer with dosages from 300 mg to 360 mg per day. Utilizing high dosages to treat severe health problems should be done only under the supervision of a physician.

DIETARY SOURCES

Coenzyme Q compounds exist in the cells of all plants and animals. The level of coenzyme Q_{10} that we obtain from the diet, however, is believed to be inadequate to meet our needs for optimal health and wellness. Therefore, supplementation is advisable.

COPPER

OVERVIEW

Drugs that deplete Copper
✔ Clofibrate
✔ Ethambutol
✔ Fenofibrate
✔ Nevirapine
✔ Penicillamine
✔ Valproic acid
✔ Zidovudine

Copper is an essential *trace mineral* that is a *co-factor* in many copper-dependent enzyme systems throughout the body. Copper is absorbed in the small intestine and carried to the liver, where it is incorporated into liver enzymes and secreted into the blood on *ceruloplasmin*. The results of some dietary surveys suggest that the diet of most Americans provides only half of the Recommended Dietary Allowance for copper.

SYMPTOMS AND CAUSES OF DEFICIENCY

Although severe copper deficiency is rare, marginal copper deficiency is common, as the diet of many Americans supplies only about 50 percent of the RDA. Symptoms of copper deficiency include loss of color in the hair and skin (because of decreased synthesis of melanin), *anemia*, fatigue, kinky hair, low body temperature, breakdown of connective tissue, various cardiovascular problems, nervous system disorders, and reduced resistance to infection.

❑ Zinc interferes with copper absorption, so a high intake of zinc supplements can lead to copper deficiency.

❑ Menkes' disease, also called kinky or steely hair syndrome, is a genetic defect in copper absorption characterized by stunted growth, abnormalities in cardiovascular and skeletal development, progressive *cognitive decline*, and premature death.

❑ Some researchers have shown that copper deficiency is associated with elevated blood cholesterol and *triglyceride levels*, as well as the development of atherosclerosis. Thus, copper deficiency may play a role in the risk of cardiovascular disease.

BIOLOGICAL FUNCTIONS AND EFFECTS

❑ Copper is required for the synthesis and function of *hemoglobin* and, as such, it plays a central role in the transport of oxygen throughout the body. Copper also stimulates the absorption of iron.

❑ The synthesis of *collagen*, which determines the integrity of bone, cartilage, skin, and tendons, requires copper.

❑ Copper is involved in the production of *elastin*.

❑ The production of *melanin*, which imparts color to the skin and hair, requires copper.

❑ Copper is a component of many important *enzymes*.

❑ Because copper *chelates* are anti-inflammatory agents, they are effective in combatting some forms of arthritis. A double-blind study has shown that wearing copper bracelets helps some arthritic individuals.

❑ The role of copper in cardiovascular disease remains controversial. Various studies have shown that both high and low copper levels can increase cardiovascular abnormalities.

❑ Some studies have indicated that copper may play a role in *osteoporosis* and *diabetes*.

SIDE EFFECTS AND TOXICITY

❑ Copper toxicity is rare, occurring only when intakes are about 200 to 500 times above normal. Symptoms include intestinal disturbances, excess production of saliva, a metallic taste in the mouth, headache, dizziness, and weakness. Severe cases cause hypertension, liver damage, kidney failure, and possibly even death.

❑ In cases of elevated copper, the problems that develop may not be a result of copper toxicity but, rather, its interference with the absorption and distribution of other metal ions such as iron and zinc.

❑ Wilson's disease is a genetic disorder that causes a toxic accumulation of copper in the liver, kidney, cornea of the eye, and central nervous system. Treatment involves a low-copper diet and use of penicillamine, which facilitates the excretion of copper.

❑ Occasional copper toxicity has been reported in individuals who live in houses with copper water pipes, which leaches copper into the drinking water.

RDA AND DOSAGE

❑ The RDA for copper is 2 mg per day.

❑ Pharmacologic doses of copper in scientific studies usually range from 2 mg to 4 mg/day.

❑ Available forms are copper gluconate, amino acid chelates, glycinate, lysinate, citrate, sulfate, and sebacate.

DIETARY SOURCES

Copper-containing foods include:

❑ oysters
❑ whole-grain breads and cereals
❑ dark green leafy vegetables
❑ nuts

❑ organ meats
❑ shellfish
❑ dried legumes
❑ chocolate

FLUORIDE

OVERVIEW

Drugs that deplete Flouride
No studies reporting drug-induced fluoride depletions have been found.

Fluoride is a controversial nutrient. Fluoridation of community water supplies is the main issue. Proponents claim that fluoridation reduces the incidence of dental caries (cavities) and strengthens bone. Opponents claim it does more harm than good. This issue is far from being resolved. Hotly contested, emotionally charged debates still take place in scientific journals and in communities considering fluoridation.

It is generally accepted that Fluoride prevents cavities and has an effect on bone metabolism. It hardens tooth enamel and increases the stability of the bone mineral matrix. Health benefits include teeth that are less prone to developing cavities and possibly creating bones that are less susceptible to osteoporosis.

Critics of fluoridation, on the other hand, cite studies indicating that children in fluoridated cities have about the same incidence of dental caries as those in nonfluoridated communities. They also cite studies reporting higher rates of bone fractures in fluoridated communities.

Cancer is another concern. In 1977, results of a study presented at a Congressional hearing revealed that people living in the 10 largest fluoridated U.S. cities had a 15 percent higher incidence of cancer than those living in the 10 largest nonfluoridated cities. In 1989 the American Dental Association reduced its longstanding official estimate of 60 percent benefit and now states that fluoride provides a 25 percent reduction in tooth decay.

Whether municipal water supplies should or should not be fluoridated is a medical, social, and political issue, and is far from being resolved. Two points in the fluoride debate are beyond argument.

1. Ingesting too much fluoride can produce a number of undesirable side effects.

2. There is a relatively narrow dosage range between benefits and side effects, and there are big differences in an individual's sensitivity to fluoride.

SYMPTOMS AND CAUSES OF DEFICIENCY

The major symptom of fluoride deficiency is an increase in the incidence of dental caries in areas of the country where natural levels of fluoride are low and municipal water supplies are not fluoridated.

BIOLOGICAL FUNCTIONS AND EFFECTS

❑ The primary function of fluoride is the prevention of dental caries. In children, fluoride creates stronger teeth because it gets incorporated into dental structure during tooth formation. Its effects are greatest when given during early childhood when teeth are still forming. After teeth have erupted, topical fluoride gets deposited into the enamel, creating a stronger protective surface.

❑ Fluoride replaces the hydroxy portion of hydroxyapatite in bones, producing a less water-soluble, more stable substance called fluorapatite.

❑ Some reports suggest that fluoride protects against *osteoporosis* and also is useful in the treatment of osteoporosis. Fluoride works in conjunction with calcium to stimulate new bone growth, and it also is incorporated into the bone, making it stronger. However, some studies report that fluoride produces bones that are more brittle and prone to fracture.

SIDE EFFECTS AND TOXICITY

❑ Fluorosis is the main side effect from excess fluoride. This is a mottling discoloration of the teeth that occurs in children if they ingest too much fluoride during tooth development.

❑ Some studies report that in sensitive individuals fluoride damages the *nervous* and *immune systems*, possibly setting the stage for multiple chemical sensitivities. Fluoride also may interfere with various *enzyme* systems, harm a developing fetus, and play a role in arthritis, gastric ulcers, *atherosclerosis*, kidney disorders, and migraine headaches.

❑ It is relatively easy to get too much fluoride, as it is found in soils, plants, animal tissues, water supplies, dental products, and fluoride vitamin supplements, as well as foods and beverages processed with fluoridated water.

❑ Moderate fluorosis occurs in 1 to 2 percent of children exposed to 1ppm (parts per million) fluoride and in approximately 10 percent of children exposed to 2ppm. Moderate to severe fluorosis occurs in varying percentages up to as high as 33 percent of children exposed to 2.4 to 4.1ppm.

❑ The groups at potentially higher risk for fluoride-associated problems consist of formula-fed infants, heavy exercisers, individuals with high consumption of water-based beverages, people with malfunctioning kidneys, and the elderly.

RDA AND DOSAGE RANGES

❑ No RDA has been established for fluoride.

❑ The U. S. Environmental Protection Agency's limits for fluoride in municipal water supplies are 0.7 to 1.2 ppm. The maximal acceptable limit is 4 ppm.

DIETARY SOURCES

Fluoride content varies widely in soils, water, plants, and animals in different areas of the United States. Many cities have fluoridated water supplies. However, more and more people believe that municipal water supplies contain unacceptably high levels of toxins and opt for bottled or filtered water. Fluoride also is available in toothpastes, mouth-washes, topical dental applications, fluoride vitamin sup-plements, and in foods processed with fluoridated water.

FOLIC ACID (FOLACIN)

OVERVIEW

Drugs that deplete Folic Acid (Folacin)
✔ Aluminum-containing antacids
✔ Aspirin
✔ Barbiturates
✔ Carbamazepine
✔ Cholestyramine
✔ Choline magnesium trisalicylate
✔ Choline salicylate
✔ Cimetidine
✔ Co-Trimoxazole
✔ Colestipol
✔ Corticosteroids
✔ Famotidine
✔ Fosphenytoin
✔ Hydrochlorthiazide and triamterene
✔ Indomethacin
✔ Magnesium-containing antacids
✔ Metformin
✔ Methotrexate
✔ Nizatidine
✔ Nonsteroidal anti-inflammatory drugs
✔ Oral contraceptives
✔ Phenobartibal
✔ Phenytoin
✔ Primidone
✔ Ranitidine
✔ Salsalate
✔ Sulfasalazine
✔ Triamterene
✔ Trimethoprim
✔ Valproic acid and derivatives

Folic acid is a member of the B vitamin group. Isolated in 1946 from spinach leaves, its name comes from "folium," the Latin word for leaf. In the body, folic acid is converted to its biologically active form, tetrahydrofolic acid (THFA). Niacin and vitamin C are necessary for this conversion. Structurally, folic acid consists of a pteridine (containing two rings) nucleus, conjugated with para-aminobenzoic acid, and glutamic acid. Hence, its chemical name is pteroylmonoglutamate.

SYMPTOMS AND CAUSES OF DEFICIENCY

Folic acid deficiency disrupts DNA metabolism, which causes abnormal cellular development, especially in red blood cells, leukocytes, and cells of the stomach, intestine, vagina, and cervix. Folic acid needs are greater during pregnancy. Folic acid is one of the most commonly deficient vitamins. Heat, light, and oxygen easily destroy it, so destruction of folic acid occurs during food processing, cooking, and storage. One study reported that cooking can destroy up to 98% of the free folic acid in foods while another study reported that 88% of Americans consume less than 400 mcg of folic acid daily.

Effects of folic acid deficiency include *megaloblastic anemia*, birth defects, cervical dysplasia, elevated homocysteine, headache, fatigue, hair loss, anorexia, insomnia, diarrhea, nausea, infections, and increased rates of breast and colorectal cancer. More recently, folic acid deficiency has also been reported to cause an increased risk of breast cancer and colorectal cancer.

❑ **Anemia.** Folic acid is required for the production of red blood cells (erythrocytes), which carry oxygen from the lungs to the tissues and carbon dioxide from tissues to the lungs. A deficiency in folic acid causes anemia and reduced oxygenation of tissues. This results in a condition known as *megaloblastic anemia*, characterized by enlarged, abnormal red blood cells. This condition can produce tiredness, weakness, diarrhea, and weight loss.

❑ **Birth defects.** Folic acid helps regulate the development of nerves and the transfer of genetic material to new cells. Many drugs have been shown to deplete folic acid. During pregnancy, the rapidly growing fetus increases a woman's need for folic acid substantially, and a folic acid deficiency during pregnancy dramatically increases the risk for birth defects such as spina bifida and cleft palate. The link between folic acid deficiency and birth defects is so strong that all women of childbearing age should have their folic acid status checked before trying to become pregnant. Following this practice probably would prevent thousands of birth defects each year. A laboratory test called the Neutrophilic Hypersegmentation Index (NHI) can easily identify the earliest stages of folate insufficiency.

❑ **Cervical dysplasia.** The development of abnormal cells in the uterus, *cervical dysplasia*, is regarded as a precancerous condition that usually is discovered when a woman has her annual Pap exam. This condition may contribute to an increased number of hysterectomies. More than 800,000 women have hysterectomies every year in the United States. Some health care professionals believe that the folic acid depletion caused by oral contraceptives and other medications is linked to this high incidence of cervical dysplasia and hysterectomies.

❑ **Elevated homocysteine,** also known as hyperhomocysteinemia, is now recognized as a serious risk factor for *cardiovascular disease.* Excessive *homocysteine* is capable of directly damaging the cells in the lining of arteries, which causes plaque build-up and atherosclerosis. Even moderate elevations of homocysteine represent a substantially increased risk for the development of plaque build-up and blood clots.

BIOLOGICAL FUNCTIONS AND EFFECTS

❑ Like vitamin B_{12}, folic acid is intimately involved in the synthesis of both DNA and RNA. Hence, it is essential for proper cell division and the transmission of one's genetic code to all newly formed cells.

❑ Folic acid may protect against certain types of cancers including: a) precancerous cervical dysplasia in women (especially those taking oral contraceptives), b) bronchial squamous metaplasia in long-time heavy cigarette smokers, c) dysplasia associated with ulcerative colitis and colon cancer, and d) breast cancer.

❑ Folic acid prevents birth abnormalities such as neural tube defects, cleft palate, and cleft lip.

❑ Folic acid is essential for the healthy maturation of both red and white blood cells.

❑ Folic acid supplementation has been shown to prevent cervical dysplasia, which is recognized as a precancerous condition.

❑ Folic acid is required for the conversion of homocysteine to methionine. High blood levels of homocysteine are associated with the development of *atherosclerosis.*

SYMPTOMS OF TOXICITY

❑ Folic acid is essentially nontoxic, even at high doses.

❑ Large doses of folic acid can mask an underlying vitamin B_{12} deficiency, which, if undetected, could result in irreversible nerve damage. Consequently, folic acid is limited to 800 mcg in over-the-counter nutritional supplements.

RDA AND DOSAGE

❑ The RDA for folic acid is 200 mcg/day.

❑ Pregnant and lactating women require dosages higher than the RDA.

❑ Pharmacologic dosages in the scientific literature range from 400 mcg up to 4,000 mcg.

DIETARY SOURCES

❑ Folic acid is found in a wide variety of foods. Best sources include dark green leafy vegetables, brewer's yeast, liver, and eggs.

❑ Other good sources are beets, broccoli, Brussels sprouts, orange juice, cabbage, cauliflower, cantaloupe, kidney and lima beans, wheat germ, and whole-grain cereals and breads.

❑ Folic acid also is synthesized by the "friendly" intestinal bacteria.

INOSITOL

OVERVIEW

Drugs that deplete Inositol
✔ Aminoglycosides
✔ Cephalosporins
✔ Fluoroquinolones
✔ Macrolides
✔ Penicillins
✔ Sulfonamides
✔ Tetracyclines
✔ Trimethoprim

Although inositol has been known for a long time, scientists first realized it was a vitamin in 1940. Inositol is a sugar-like, water-soluble substance that is a member of the B vitamin complex. It is found in the liver, kidney, skeletal, and heart muscle, and in the leaves and seeds of most plants. In animal tissues, inositol is a component of *phospholipids,* and in plants it usually occurs as *phytic acid.* In humans, inositol is synthesized in the intestinal tract by the normal or "friendly" bacteria.

SYMPTOMS AND CAUSES OF DEFICIENCY

No inositol deficiency has been identified in humans, and a deficiency is not likely because of its widespread occurrence in foods.

BIOLOGICAL FUNCTIONS AND EFFECTS

❑ Inositol is an essential component of phospholipids in cellular membranes of animals and humans.

❑ The metabolically active form of inositol is myoinositol, which occurs abundantly in muscle tissue.

❑ As part of phospholipids in cellular membranes, phosphatidylinositol helps to mediate cellular responses to external stimuli. Phosphatidylinositol also facilitates the production of arachidonic acid.

❑ Myoinositol may be helpful in the treatment of diabetic neuropathy.

❑ Several studies have shown that inositol can be effective in treating depression, panic and obsessive-compulsive disorders.

SIDE EFFECTS AND TOXICITY

No toxicity has been reported or observed.

RDA AND DOSAGE

❑ No RDA has been set for inositol.

❑ Pharmacologic doses in the scientific literature range from 100 mg to 1,000 mg.

DIETARY SOURCES

❑ Myoinositol occurs in foods in three different forms: free myoinositol, phytic acid, and inositol-containing phospholipids.

❑ The richest sources of myoinositol are the seeds of plants such as beans, grains, and nuts.

❑ The richest animal sources are organ meats. Free myoinositol predominates in brain and kidney, whereas phospholipid-inositol is concentrated in skeletal muscle, heart, liver, and pancreas.

IODINE

OVERVIEW

Drugs that deplete Iodine
No known studies have reported drug-induced iodine depletions.

The only known function of iodine is the role it plays in the thyroid hormones diiodotyrosine, triiodothryonine (T_3), and thyroxine (T_4). Dietary iodine is converted to iodide in the intestinal tract, where it is easily absorbed and transported to the thyroid gland. In the thyroid gland, iodine is stored in a protein complex called thryoglobulin.

Iodine metabolism and thyroid hormone production are regulated by a hormonal control system. A decline in blood thyroid hormones triggers the hypothalamus to release thyroid releasing hormone (TRH), which in turn signals the pituitary gland to release thyroid stimulating hormone (TSH). An increase in TSH stimulates the thyroid gland to increase the uptake of iodine and synthesize more thyroid hormones. TSH also stimulates the thyroid gland to produce *enzymes* that release the thyroid hormones into circulation for delivery to cells throughout the body.

SYMPTOMS AND CAUSES OF DEFICIENCY

A deficiency of iodine can produce the following conditions:

❑ **Hypothyroidism.** A lack of iodine decreases thyroid hormone synthesis. The lower thyroid activity reduces the rate of energy production and can cause fatigue and weight gain.

❑ **Goiter.** A deficiency of iodine can result in enlargement of the thyroid gland. When this becomes visible, it is called a simple goiter. This condition can be prevented and frequently cured by administering iodine.

❑ **Cretinism.** Iodine deficiency during pregnancy can cause cretinism in the developing fetus, a severe condition characterized by both mental and physical retardation.

❑ **Myxedema.** Iodine deficiency is one of the causes of myxedema, and the resulting hypofunction (lower function) of the thyroid gland causes a slower metabolic rate, anemia, enlarged tongue, slow speech, puffiness of the hands and face, problems with the skin and hair, drowsiness, and mental apathy.

Goitrogens are naturally occurring substances in some foods that can inhibit the synthesis and secretion of thyroid hormones. Some common foods containing goitrogens are raw cabbage, turnips, cauliflower, soy beans, and peanuts. Problems are unlikely unless an iodine-deficient individual consumes large amounts of these foods over a period of time. Cooking deactivates the goitrogen compounds in these foods.

BIOLOGICAL FUNCTIONS AND EFFECTS

❑ The effects of iodine are all related to the activity and function of the hormones of the thyroid gland.

❑ The iodine-dependent thyroid hormones regulate cellular oxygen consumption, *basal metabolism*, and energy production throughout the body. As a result, the thyroid hormones control a variety of biological and physiological activities, including body temperature, physical growth, reproduction, neuromuscular function, the synthesis of proteins, and the growth of skin and hair.

❑ Iodine deficiency may be a contributing factor to fibrocystic breasts. Iodine supplementation has caused complete relief of symptoms in some women.

- Iodine-containing products such as SSKI (saturated solution of potassium iodide) and Organidin are frequently effective for loosening up irritating mucus secretions. These *mucolytic agents* require a doctor's prescription.
- If the thyroid gland is damaged or absent, the basal metabolic rate can decline to as low as 55 percent of normal, resulting in impaired growth and development.
- When the thyroid gland is hyperactive, the basal metabolic rate can go up as high as 160 percent of normal, causing *tachycardia*, nervousness, and excitability.

SIDE EFFECTS AND TOXICITY

- Iodine is a relatively benign *trace element* that generally causes no harm at dosages 10 to 20 times above normal daily needs. The thyroid gland absorbs more iodine, but thyroid synthesis remains normal.
- Chronic excessive intake of iodine can cause enlargement of the thyroid gland resembling goiter. The condition is called "iodine goiter."

RDA AND DOSAGE

- The RDA for iodine is 150 mcg/day.
- Pharmacologic doses for iodine in scientific studies are generally in the range of 3 mg to 6 mg/day.

DIETARY SOURCES

- The most common source of iodine in the United States is iodized salt.
- Iodine-rich foods include seafood, sea vegetables (seaweed), and vegetables grown in iodine-rich soils.

IRON

OVERVIEW

Drugs that deplete Iron
✔ Aspirin
✔ Cholestyramine
✔ Choline magnesium trisalicylate
✔ Choline salicylate
✔ Cimetidine
✔ Choestipol
✔ Famotidine
✔ Indomethacin
✔ Levothyroxine
✔ Neomycin
✔ Nizatidine
✔ Penicillamine
✔ Ranitidine
✔ Salicylates
✔ Stanozolol
✔ Tetracyclines

Iron plays a vital role in many biochemical pathways. It is involved in oxygen transport within blood and muscle, electron transfer in the cellular uptake of oxygen, and conversion of blood sugar to energy. Iron also is part of many *enzymes* involved with making new cells, *amino acids*, hormones, and *neurotransmitters*. In the body, iron exists in various functional forms (in hemoglobin and in enzymes) and in transport and storage forms (ferritin, transferrin, and hemosiderin).

SYMPTOMS AND CAUSES OF DEFICIENCY

The iron lost in menstrual bleeding is the most common cause of iron deficiency. About 80 percent of the iron in the body is in the blood, so iron loss is greatest whenever blood is lost. To replace their monthly losses, menstruating women require approximately twice as much iron intake as men.

Individuals at risk for iron deficiency include infants, adolescent girls, pregnant women, menstruating women, and people with bleeding ulcers. Vegetarians are at risk for anemia because the main dietary source of iron is from meat/animal protein foods.

Iron-deficiency anemia is the classic condition in which red blood cells contain less than optimum *hemoglobin* and consequently carry less oxygen. Symptoms of iron-deficiency anemia are weakness, fatigue, skin pallor, headache, hair loss, labored breathing after exertion, spooning of fingernails, brittle nails, and greater susceptibility to infections. Additional considerations include the following.

❑ Deliberately consuming large quantities of ice, called pagophagia, is related to iron deficiency and is completely resolved with low-level iron supplementation.

❑ Hypochlorhydria, which refers to a low production of hydrochloric acid in the stomach, causes decreased iron absorption. Low production of hydrochloric acid occurs often in the elderly and can lead to iron deficiency anemia.

❑ Antacids and drugs that alter gastric acidity inhibit iron absorption.

❑ Complexing agents, such as phytates, oxalates, and phosphates, form insoluble iron complexes, which reduce absorption. Vitamin E also inhibits the absorption of iron. Although taking vitamin E generally is not a cause of iron deficiency, it is not advisable to take supplemental doses of iron and vitamin E at the same time.

❑ Diarrhea, intestinal inflammation, and other conditions that increase intestinal motility also reduce absorption.

❑ Iron deficiency can cause hair loss.

❑ Athletes may be more susceptible to iron loss.

BIOLOGICAL FUNCTIONS AND EFFECTS

The functions of iron in the body are summarized in the following.

❑ The major function of iron is for oxygen transport by hemoglobin. Hemoglobin is the oxygen-carrying protein in red blood cells. The heme portion of hemoglobin contains 4 atoms of iron. Iron picks up the oxygen in the lungs where the concentration is high. Iron binds the oxygen and then transports it to the tissues and releases it wherever it is needed.

❑ *Myoglobin* is an iron-containing protein in muscles that accepts oxygen and serves as an oxygen storage reservoir in muscle.

❑ Iron is one of the substances necessary for optimal immune response.

❑ Iron is necessary for the synthesis of the *amino acid* carnitine, which plays an essential role in the metabolism of fatty acids.

❑ Much of iron's functional activity in electron transport and energy production has to do with its ability to convert back and forth between its reduced or ferrous state (Fe^{++}) and its oxidized ferric state (Fe^{+++}).

❑ Iron plays an important role in liver detoxification *enzymes*, which remove toxins from the body.

❑ Iron is part of the enzymes that initiate the synthesis of the *neurotransmitters serotonin* and *dopamine*.

❑ The synthesis of collagen and elastin require iron.

SIDE EFFECTS AND TOXICITY

When the body's iron stores are full, the body absorbs less iron. Therefore, iron toxicity is rare, but it can occur. The primary causes of iron toxicity are:

❑ Ingesting too much iron.

❑ A genetic defect, called hemochromatosis, usually occurring in men, which causes excessive iron absorption, resulting in damage to the heart, liver, spleen and pancreas.

❑ Alcoholism, which can cause intestinal and liver damage leading to increased iron absorption.

RDA AND DOSAGE RANGES

- ❑ The RDA for iron is 15 mg/day for women and 10 mg/day for men.
- ❑ Pharmacologic doses in the scientific literature range from 10 mg/day to 50 mg/day.
- ❑ Available forms are ferrous sulfate, ferrous gluconate, ferrous fumerate, ferrous glycinate, and ferric ammonium citrate.

DIETARY SOURCES

- ❑ Liver is by far the richest iron-containing food. Other good sources of iron-rich foods are organ meats, fish, and poultry.
- ❑ Dried beans and vegetables are the best plant sources, followed by dried fruits, nuts, and whole-grain breads and cereals.
- ❑ Fortified cereals, flours, and breads with iron have contributed significantly to daily consumption of dietary iron.

LACTOBACILLUS ACIDOPHILUS

OVERVIEW

Drugs that deplete Lactobacillus Acidophilus
✔ Aminoglycosides
✔ Cephalosporins
✔ Co-trimoxazole
✔ Fluoroquinoones
✔ Macrolides
✔ Penicillins
✔ Sulfonamides
✔ Tetracyclines

Lactobacillus acidophilus is the primary strain of beneficial bacteria that inhabit the small intestine. If the balance between the beneficial and the *pathological* bacteria gets upset, a condition known as *dysbiosis* develops. The use of antibiotics is the most common cause of dysbiosis because antibiotics kill most of the acidophilus bacteria along with the pathological bacteria. Maintaining a healthy colonization of intestinal microflora with beneficial bacteria such as L. acidophilus is a key factor in maintaining a healthy *immune system*. Products containing beneficial bacteria are frequently referred to as probiotics.

SYMPTOMS AND CAUSES OF DEFICIENCY

❑ A deficiency of L. acidophilus bacteria can result in the growth and proliferation of pathological organisms in the intestinal tract. This can decrease digestion and absorption of nutrients, as well as increase production of gas, bloating, and toxins.

❑ The most common cause of a deficiency of L. acidophilus bacteria is the use of antibiotic drugs.

❑ Other factors that can cause a reduction of L. acidophilus include the use of drugs that increase intestinal pH, stress, diarrhea, intestinal infections, high sugar/low fiber diets, and toxins in the intestine.

BIOLOGICAL FUNCTIONS AND EFFECTS

- ❏ Lactobacillus acidophilus bacteria act as a barrier against infection by producing natural antibiotics in the intestinal tract that have been shown to inhibit the growth of more than 20 types of harmful bacteria.

- ❏ The metabolism of L. acidophilus bacteria produces lactic acid and hydrogen peroxide, which create an environment unfavorable for the growth of yeasts and other harmful bacteria.

- ❏ L. acidophilus bacteria promote healthy digestion by producing enzymes that help digest fats, proteins, and dairy products.

- ❏ L. acidophilus organisms produce a wide range of B vitamins and vitamin K in the intestinal tract.

- ❏ Oral ingestion of acidophilus has been shown to enhance the activity of the immune system throughout the whole body.

- ❏ L. acidophilus bacteria metabolize cholesterol, so they can help to lower elevated cholesterol levels and reduce the risk of *cardiovascular disease*.

SIDE EFFECTS AND TOXICITY

L. acidophilus has no known toxic effects, and these beneficial bacteria do not interfere with other medications.

RDA AND DOSAGE

- ❏ No RDA has been set for Lactobacillus acidophilus.

- ❏ Dosages for *probiotics* are measured in terms of *cfu* (colony forming units), which denotes the number of live organisms per dose.

- ❏ Dosage range for prevention: Healthy people can take from 1–2 billion cfu per day.

❑ Patients with dysbiosis or after taking antibiotics: 10–15 billion cfu twice daily (with food) for 2 weeks.

DIETARY SOURCES

Small amounts of L. acidophilus occur in cultured food products such as yogurt and acidophilus milk. To be effective therapeutically, however, larger quantities should be consumed in the form of probiotic supplements.

MAGNESIUM

OVERVIEW

Drugs that deplete Magnesium
✔ Aminoglycosides
✔ Amphotericin B
✔ Benzthiazide
✔ Bumetanide
✔ Chlorothiazide
✔ Chlorotrianisene
✔ Cholestyramine
✔ Corticosteroids
✔ Diethylstilbesterol
✔ Digoxin
✔ Estrogens, conjugated
✔ Estrogens, esterified
✔ Ethacrynic acid
✔ Foscarnet
✔ Furosemide
✔ Hydrochlorothiazide
✔ Hydroflumethiazide
✔ Indapamide
✔ Metolazone
✔ Oral contraceptives
✔ Penicillamine
✔ Pentamidine
✔ Polythiazide
✔ Quinestrol
✔ Quinethazone
✔ Tetracyclines
✔ Torsemide
✔ Trichlormethiazide

Magnesium is a co-factor in more than 300 enzymatic reactions in the body. It is necessary for the transmission of nerve impulses, muscular activity, temperature regulation, detoxification reactions, and for the formation of healthy bones and teeth. It also plays a crucial role in energy production and the synthesis of DNA and RNA.

A U. S. Department of Agriculture survey revealed that approximately 75 percent of Americans do not ingest the RDA of magnesium, making it one of the most commonly deficient nutrients in the United States. Less than optimal magnesium intake compromises all tissues, especially tissues of the heart, nerves, and kidneys.

Magnesium is an extremely important nutrient for the cardiovascular system. A deficiency is associated with an increased incidence of *atherosclerosis, hypertension,* strokes, and heart attacks. Low levels of magnesium can cause stiffness in the blood vessels, which elevates blood pressure, and a contraction or spasm in the heart muscle, which can result in sudden death. Many heart attacks occur in individuals with a relatively healthy heart; a magnesium deficiency is the instigator of the heart spasm that results in death.

Magnesium single-handedly influences many of the activities associated with a wide variety of cardiac medications. For example, magnesium inhibits platelet aggregation (like aspirin), thins the blood (like Coumadin), blocks calcium uptake (like calcium channel-blocking drugs such as Procardia), and relaxes blood vessels (like ACE inhibitors such as Vasotec). Magnesium also increases oxygenation of the heart muscle by improving the heart's ability to contract.

SYMPTOMS AND CAUSES OF DEFICIENCY

❑ Although a critical deficiency of magnesium is rare in the United States, a marginal deficiency seems to be widespread. Some studies report that approximately 75 percent of Americans ingest less than the RDA.

❑ Deficiency symptoms include muscle cramps, weakness, insomnia, loss of appetite, intestinal disorders, kidney stones, *osteoporosis*, nervousness, restlessness, irritability, fear, anxiety, confusion, depression, fatigue, and high blood pressure.

❑ Magnesium depletion creates an elevated calcium to magnesium ratio, which can cause a cardiac muscle spasm resulting in a heart attack and, frequently, death.

❑ Food processing is a major cause of magnesium depletion. For example, up to 85 percent of magnesium is lost when whole wheat is refined to produce white flour.

❑ Modern farming techniques contribute to the depletion of magnesium in the soil. Artificial fertilizers usually do not contain any magnesium.

❑ Poor food choices, excess calcium intake, intestinal malabsorption, alcohol abuse, liver and kidney disease, and diabetes also can cause deficiencies.

❑ Hypomagnesemia occurs in approximately 25 percent of patients with diabetes. Low levels of magnesium have been reported in childhood Type I diabetes and in adults with Type I or Type II *diabetes*.

BIOLOGICAL FUNCTIONS AND EFFECTS

❑ In general, magnesium is required for the metabolism of carbohydrates, proteins, and fats, as well as activity related to calcium, phosphorus, and vitamin C. It is vital for the health of nervous and muscular tissues throughout the body.

❑ Magnesium is a *co-factor* for oxidative phosphorylation in the production of *ATP*. As such, it is essential for the production and transfer of energy for synthesis of protein and lipids, contractibility of muscle, and nerve transmission.

❑ Adequate magnesium intake reduces the risk of cardiovascular disease and increases the rate of survival following a heart attack. Administering intravenous magnesium in early stages of a heart attack results in a 70 percent decrease in deaths within one month following the event.

❑ Magnesium influences many aspects of cardiovascular health. It acts to decrease platelet stickiness, helps to thin the blood, blocks calcium uptake, and relaxes blood vessels.

❑ More than 30 clinical trials have reported that magnesium can lower high blood pressure. The effect usually is only moderate, however. Therefore, magnesium should not be viewed as a primary treatment for hypertension.

❑ Many studies report that women with premenstrual syndrome (PMS) have low levels of magnesium, and some studies report that magnesium helps to relieve PMS symptoms.

❑ Various studies report low magnesium levels in asthma patients. Consuming adequate magnesium may reduce the risk of developing asthma and frequently is useful as part of an overall treatment program.

❑ Magnesium is extremely important for bone health. It is involved in calcium metabolism, the synthesis of vitamin D, and the integrity of skeletal bone-crystal formation.

❑ Magnesium helps to bind calcium to tooth enamel, thereby creating an effective barrier to tooth decay.

SIDE EFFECTS AND TOXICITY

❑ Kidney excretion of excess magnesium makes magnesium toxicity rare.

❑ Excess magnesium intake frequently causes diarrhea.

RDA AND DOSAGE

❑ The RDA for magnesium is 400 mg/day.

❑ Pharmacologic doses in the scientific literature range from 500 mg to 1,500 mg/day.

❑ Available forms include magnesium oxide, hydroxide, gluconate, glycinate, sulfate, chloride, aspartate, malate, succinate, fumarate, ascorbate, and citrate.

DIETARY SOURCES

Magnesium content in foods varies widely, as does its content in soil. Good food sources include:

❑ nuts   ❑ legumes
❑ cereal grains ❑ dark green leafy vegetables

MANGANESE

OVERVIEW

Drugs that deplete Manganese
No studies reporting drug-induced manganese depletion have been found.

Manganese is a *co-factor* that aids in the activation of a wide variety of *enzymes*. Manganese-containing enzymes influence many biological activities, including the synthesis of *collagen*, protein, *mucopolysaccharides*, *cholesterol*, and fatty acids. It also is necessary for the normal growth of bones and the metabolism of amino acids.

The average human body contains only about 20 mg of manganese, most of which is stored in the bones. Smaller amounts are concentrated in the pituitary, liver, pancreas, and intestinal mucus. Absorption takes place throughout the entire small intestine.

SYMPTOMS AND CAUSES OF DEFICIENCY

Manganese deficiency in humans is relatively uncommon because the mineral magnesium is capable of substituting for manganese in many of the enzyme-related functions of manganese.

❑ The most notable symptoms of manganese deficiency are skeletal abnormalities such as loss of muscle coordination, propensity for sprains and strains, and weak ligaments. These problems develop as a result of the reduced synthesis of collagen and mucopolysaccharides.

❑ Some indications are that manganese deficiency impairs glucose metabolism and produces abnormalities in the secretion of *insulin*.

❑ Low manganese levels often are found in people with epilepsy, *hypoglycemia*, *schizophrenia*, and *osteoporosis*.

❑ Women with osteoporosis have been shown to have low levels of manganese.

❑ Manganese is necessary for the biosynthesis of cholesterol and *hypocholesterolemia* may be associated with manganese deficiency. Intestinal absorption is hindered by ingesting calcium, phosphate, iron, and phytate.

BIOLOGICAL FUNCTIONS AND EFFECTS

❑ Manganese is necessary for the production of mucopolysaccharides, glycoproteins, and lipopolysaccharides, which are necessary for the growth and maintenance of connective tissue and cartilage.

❑ In conjunction with vitamin K, manganese plays a role in the synthesis of prothrombin and the regulation of blood clotting.

❑ Manganese influences the activity of osteoblasts and osteoclasts, which makes it essential for normal bone growth and development.

❑ Manganese is the central metal *co-factor* in mitochondrial superoxide dismutase, and as such, it is essential for optimal functioning of one of the body's most important *antioxidant* defense systems, protecting against the toxic effects of oxygen during energy production.

❑ Manganese is necessary in the synthesis of thyroxin, the principal hormone of the thyroid gland.

❑ Manganese is involved with the production of *dopamine* and *melanin* and in the synthesis of fatty acids.

SIDE EFFECTS AND TOXICITY

❑ Manganese is safe, and people can tolerate relatively large oral doses with no apparent adverse effects.

❑ Miners have developed toxicity to manganese after inhaling manganese dust.

❏ Toxicity can produce dementia, psychiatric disorders resembling schizophrenia, and neurologic disorders resembling Parkinson's disease.

RDA AND DOSAGE

❏ The safe and adequate range for manganese is from 2 to 5 mg/day.
❏ Pharmacologic doses, according to the scientific literature, range from 2 to 50 mg/day.

DIETARY SOURCES

Manganese is widely distributed in foods of plant and animal origin. Best food sources include:

❏ whole-grain breads and cereals
❏ dried beans and peas
❏ raisins
❏ nuts
❏ vegetables
❏ pineapple

MELATONIN

OVERVIEW

Drugs that deplete Melatonin
✔ Alprazolam
✔ Atenolol
✔ Chlorpromazine
✔ Diazepam
✔ Haloperidol
✔ Hydroxyzine
✔ Metoprolol
✔ Propranolol

Melatonin is a naturally occurring hormone that regulates sleep. It is secreted by the pineal gland in the brain. The body's levels of melatonin decline with aging. Adults experience about a 37 percent decline in daily melatonin output between 20 and 70 years of age, with most of the decline occurring after age 40. Melatonin output is regulated by the amount of light that enters our eyes.

Melatonin products are available as sublingual (fast-acting), regular tablets or capsules, and timed release (long-acting) products. The sublingual dosage form is best for people who have trouble falling asleep. The timed-release products work better for individuals who wake up during the night.

SYMPTOMS AND CAUSES OF DEFICIENCY

❑ Insomnia and other sleep disturbances are the primary symptoms of melatonin deficiency.

❑ A deficiency of vitamin B$_6$ can inhibit the synthesis of *serotonin*, and subsequently, the conversion of serotonin to melatonin. Therefore, all drugs that deplete vitamin B$_6$ (see page 201) can potentially inhibit the synthesis of melatonin and cause insomnia.

❑ Research in cell cultures and with animals indicates that melatonin may provide protection against certain types of cancer. Low levels of melatonin could constitute an increased risk for breast cancer. One possible explanation has to do with melatonin's *antioxidant* activity. Thus, a melatonin deficiency could result in increased levels of *free radical* damage, which could lead to cancer.

BIOLOGICAL FUNCTIONS AND EFFECTS

❑ Melatonin is a master control hormone that regulates our 24-hour *circadian rhythm*.

❑ The primary function of melatonin seems to be its role in regulating the sleep/wake cycle. When darkness falls, melatonin levels rise, which triggers the sleep cycle.

❑ Melatonin possesses important antioxidant activity.

❑ Melatonin also controls the output of growth hormone and the sex hormones.

❑ Melatonin has been used successfully to treat jet lag.

RDA AND DOSAGE

❑ No RDA has been set for melatonin.

❑ Common nighttime dosages range from 0.5 mg to 3.0 mg.

❑ The normal dosage ranges from 0.5 mg to 3 mg nightly. Dosages for specific therapeutic applications can be much higher.

❑ Melatonin is available in sublingual (fast-acting) tablets, regular, and timed-release forms.

SIDE EFFECTS AND TOXICITY

❑ Melatonin seems to be safe and nontoxic. To date, however, long-term studies have not been conducted with humans.

❑ Taking too much melatonin can cause morning grogginess and undesired drowsiness.

FOOD SOURCES

Melatonin does not occur in foods in any significant amount.

MOLYBDENUM

OVERVIEW

Drugs that deplete Molybdenum
No studies that report drug-induced molybdenum deficiency have been located.

Even though molybdenum is one of the rarest substances on earth, small amounts of this mineral are found in all tissues of the human body. Molybdenum is a component of several important *metalloenzymes* that participate in liver detoxification. Most biochemistry textbooks acknowledge that little is known about this *trace mineral* beyond its role as a *co-factor* for several *enzymes.*

SYMPTOMS AND CAUSES OF DEFICIENCY

Molybdenum deficiency in humans is rare because so little is needed. In a healthy state, body tissues contain less than 0.1 parts per million.

❑ Molybdenum co-factor deficiency syndrome has recently been identified as a rare genetic condition that has caused previously unexplained seizures and developmental delays in newborns.

❑ Molybdenum deficiency has developed occasionally in individuals who have been receiving prolonged *total parenteral nutrition (TPN).* Symptoms include *tachycardia,* headache, mental disturbances, and coma.

❑ Increased intake of sulfate or copper can cause excess excretion of molybdenum.

BIOLOGICAL FUNCTIONS AND EFFECTS

❑ Molybdenum is necessary for the function of three enzymes: xanthine oxidase, aldehyde oxidase, and sulfite oxidase.

❑ Xanthine oxidase metabolizes xanthine to uric acid for urinary excretion.

- Uric acid usually is considered to be a negative substance because of its association with gouty arthritis. At certain levels, however, uric acid is a powerful *antioxidant* that neutralizes *free radicals*. Thus, molybdenum may help regulate important antioxidant functions.

- Sulfite oxidase catalyzes the last step in the metabolism of sulfur-containing amino acids. It enables the conversion to sulfite, (that is toxic to the nervous system) to sulfate for excretion.

- Molybdenum affects the absorption of iron, copper, and sulfate.

- Aldehyde oxidase catalyzes the conversion of aldehydes to acids.

SIDE EFFECTS AND TOXICITY

- Molybdenum toxicity is rare.

- Excess intake (10 to 15 mg/day) can cause a gout-like syndrome due to excess production of uric acid.

RDA AND DOSAGE

- The National Academy of Sciences had determined that from 10 to 500 mcg/day is a reasonable dietary level of molybdenum.

- Pharmacologic doses in the scientific literature range from 100 to 1000 mcg/day.

DIETARY SOURCES

- Good food sources of molybdenum are whole grains, organ meats, leafy green vegetables, legumes, and beans.

- The availability of molybdenum varies widely according to the molybdenum content of the soil. Vegetables grown in molybdenum-rich soil can contain up to 500 times more molybdenum than those grown in molybdenum-deficient soils.

NICKEL

OVERVIEW

Drugs that deplete Nickel
No studies that report drug-induced depletion of nickel have been found.

In 1974, nickel was discovered to be an essential nutrient in baby chicks. Since then, it has been found to have an essential physiological role in the metabolism of other animals and in humans. Its functions, however, are still far from being understood at this time.

Nickel is present in the blood, various organs, teeth, bone, skin, and the brain of humans, with the largest concentrations found in skin and bone marrow. Nickel is so ubiquitous in nature (it occurs in air, plants and animals) that scientists have only recently been able to effectively prepare nickel-deficient diets so the biological effects of this mineral could begin to be tested. To date, more is known about the effects of nickel in various animals than in humans.

SYMPTOMS AND CAUSES OF DEFICIENCY

❑ Nickel is so common in the environment that deficiency is rare.

❑ Nickel deficiency depresses iron absorption.

❑ Low levels of nickel are associated with smaller litter sizes in animals.

❑ Nickel deficiency causes abnormal changes in the livers of laboratory animals.

❑ Rats raised on nickel-deficient diets develop anemia related to a reduction in iron absorption.

BIOLOGICAL FUNCTIONS AND EFFECTS

❑ Nickel has been found to be present normally in *ribonucleic acid (RNA)*.

❑ The biological activities of nickel are thought to involve hormone, *lipid* (fat), and cellular membrane metabolism.

❑ Studies with rabbits and dogs have shown that nickel increases the *hypoglycemic* effect of insulin.

❑ Nickel is part of a protein called nickeloplasmin that is synthesized in the liver.

❑ Serum concentrations of nickel increase in response to stressful situations, such as a heart attack, a stroke, and even in women during labor.

❑ Nickel concentrations have been shown to influence the levels of a number of mitochondrial and liver enzymes.

SIDE EFFECTS AND TOXICITY

❑ Under normal conditions, nickel is not a toxic element.

❑ Nickel sensitivity from jewelry is relatively common in people who get their ears pierced.

❑ Some individuals with the skin conditions of *psoriasis* and *eczema* have been found to have elevated levels of nickel in the blood and skin.

❑ Occasionally in industry, nickel combines with carbon monoxide to form a toxic compound called nickel carbonyl. Industrial exposure to this compound has caused hospitalizations and several deaths.

❑ Excess exposure to or ingestion of nickel and nickel carbonyl is suspected to cause cancer. These compounds are found in tobacco and cigarette smoke.

❑ Inhalation of large quantities of certain nickel compounds has been shown to cause lung cancer in laboratory animals.

❑ Long-term intake of excessive nickel causes degeneration of the heart, brain, lungs, liver, and kidney.

RDA AND DOSAGE

❑ There is no RDA for nickel.

❑ Nickel is so ubiquitous in the environment that studies on its supplementation have not been conducted.

DIETARY SOURCES

❑ Grains and vegetables are the best dietary sources of nickel.

❑ Animal foods are relatively poor sources of nickel.

PHOSPHORUS

OVERVIEW

Drugs that deplete Phosphorus
✔ Aluminum hydroxide-containing medications
✔ Cholestyramine
✔ Colchicine
✔ Digoxin
✔ Magnesium-containing compounds

Phosphorus is the second most abundant mineral in the human body, after calcium. Approximately 80 percent of phosphorus is present in the skeleton, and the other 20 percent is active metabolically and plays a role in the metabolism of every cell in the body. In fact, phosphorus participates in more biological processes than any other mineral. A complete discussion of its functions would require delving into virtually every metabolic process in the body.

SYMPTOMS AND CAUSES OF DEFICIENCY

❑ Phosphorus deficiency has been reported in animals, but it is rare in humans.

❑ Long-term use of aluminum-containing antacids could lead to phosphate depletion.

❑ Individuals who might be at risk for phosphorus depletion include alcoholics, people with kidney malfunction, individuals with intestinal malabsorption syndromes such as celiac disease or Crohn's disease, and individuals on starvation diets.

BIOLOGICAL FUNCTIONS AND EFFECTS

❑ Phosphorus, along with calcium, forms the insoluble calcium phosphate crystals that provide the strength and rigidity in bones and teeth.

❑ Unlike calcium, phosphorus is also an integral part of the structure of soft tissues. As part of *phospholipids*, such as phosphatidylcholine, it is a component of all cellular membranes.

❑ *ATP* contains three phosphate groups and, thus, phosphorus is an essential part of energy storage and production processes in every cell throughout the body.

❑ Phosphorus is a part of many *coenzymes* and takes part in a wide variety of enzymatic reactions.

❑ As phosphoric acid and its salts, phosphorus is part of one of the body's major buffer systems.

❑ Phosphorus is part of DNA and RNA and thus is necessary for all cellular reproduction and protein synthesis.

SIDE EFFECTS AND TOXICITY

❑ Excessive consumption of foods high in phosphorus, such as animal protein and cola soft drinks, may inhibit calcium absorption and contribute to skeletal problems such as *osteoporosis*.

❑ Excess phosphorus can increase hyperthyroidism, increase bone *resorption,* increase soft tissue calcium deposition, and decrease bone mass.

RDA AND DOSAGE

The RDA for phosphorus is 1000 mg/day. Most Americans consume far too much phosphorus. Higher dosage recommendations are not appropriate.

DIETARY SOURCES

Animal protein foods are the highest source of phosphorus for most people. Cola soft drinks also contain a large amount of phosphorus.

POTASSIUM

OVERVIEW

Drugs that deplete Potassium
✔ Albuterol
✔ Aminoglycosides
✔ Amphotericin B
✔ Aspirin
✔ Benzthiazide
✔ Bisacodyl
✔ Bumetanide
✔ Chlorothiazide
✔ Choline magnesium trisalicylate
✔ Choline salicylate
✔ Colchicine
✔ Corticosteroids
✔ Ethacrynic acid
✔ Foscarnet
✔ Furosemide
✔ Hydrochlorothiazide
✔ Hydroflumethiazide
✔ Indapamide
✔ L-Dopa
✔ Methyclothiazide
✔ Metolazone
✔ Nifedipine
✔ Penicillin antibiotics
✔ Polythiazide
✔ Quinethazone
✔ Ritodrine
✔ Sodium bicarbonate
✔ Terbutaline
✔ Torsemide
✔ Trichlormethiazide
✔ Verapamil

Potassium is one of the body's three major *electrolytes* (the other two being sodium and chloride). They exist as fully dissociated ions and are the main particles responsible for *osmotic pressure* in body fluids. Potassium is the primary electrolyte functioning inside cells throughout the body. Their ionic strength enables them to influence the solubility of proteins and other substances throughout the body.

Hormonal control of potassium and the other electrolytes is mediated through the hormones of the adrenal cortex and the pituitary gland. Potassium is absorbed readily through the intestinal tract, and the excess is excreted efficiently in the urine via the kidneys.

SYMPTOMS AND CAUSES OF DEFICIENCY

In addition to the above-mentioned drugs, diarrhea, kidney failure, diabetic acidosis, and prolonged malnutrition vomiting also can cause potassium deficiency. Other factors that can contribute to potassium depletion include use of alcohol or caffeine, excessive use of salt or sugar, and chronic stress. Symptoms associated with potassium deficiency include irregular heartbeat, poor reflexes, muscle weakness, fatigue, continuous thirst, edema (water retention), constipation, dizziness, mental confusion, and nervous disorders.

BIOLOGICAL FUNCTIONS AND EFFECTS

❑ Potassium plays essential roles in many of the body's most important functions, including nerve conduction, muscle contraction, and the beating of the heart.

❑ Potassium is the primary positively charged ion in *intracellular* fluids throughout the body. Approximately 98 percent of total body potassium resides inside cells.

❑ Potassium, along with sodium and chloride, helps to maintain normal osmotic equilibrium by controlling the distribution and balance of water throughout the body.

❑ Potassium controls the conduction of nerve impulses, maintenance of normal cardiac rhythm, and contraction of muscles.

❑ Potassium, in conjunction with other ions, helps to maintain the acid/alkaline balance throughout the body.

❑ Potassium has been shown to be effective in preventing *hypertension* and in some studies has shown that it can help to lower existing high blood pressure.

❑ Low levels of potassium are associated with an increased risk of stroke.

❑ One study reported that one serving of potassium-rich fruits or vegetables daily provided up to a 40 percent reduction in the risk of stroke.

SIDE EFFECTS AND TOXICITY

❑ *Hyperkalemia* (potassium toxicity) usually results from kidney failure, in which case blood levels rise because the kidneys cannot adequately excrete potassium.

❑ Malfunctioning adrenal glands can also cause hyperkalemia.

❑ Symptoms of hyperkalemia include mental confusion, numbness of the extremities, labored breathing, and deteriorating heart activity.

RDA AND DOSAGE

❑ No RDA has been established for potassium because it is so readily available.

❑ The estimated safe and adequate intake of potassium for adults is from 1.8 to 5.6 grams/day.

DIETARY SOURCES

❑ Potassium is plentiful in the diet. Potassium-rich foods include fresh fruits and vegetables, peanuts, meat, and milk.

❑ An average banana supplies over 600 mg of potassium; half a cantaloupe contains 885 mg; 3 to 4 ounces of raw spinach contains about 775 mg; 2 ounces of peanuts contain about 575 mg; and one large raw carrot contains about 330 mg.

S-ADENOSYL METHIONINE (SAMe)

OVERVIEW

Drugs that deplete SAMe
✔ Levodopa

SAMe is a metabolite of the essential amino acid methionine. It is a cofactor in three important biochemical pathways, and consequently SAMe is synthesized in cells throughout the body. Because of the important biochemical reactions that it regulates, studies are reporting that SAMe is beneficial for a wide variety of health and medical conditions.

SYMPTOMS AND CAUSES OF DEFICIENCY

Normally our bodies produce SAMe from the amino acid methionine. Since vitamin B_{12} and folic acid are necessary for the synthesis of SAMe, a deficiency of these vitamins can lead to a depletion of SAMe. Although there is no specific condition associated with a lack of SAMe, problems that would probably develop if a deficiency were to develop would include depression, poor liver detoxification, and elevated homocysteine.

BIOLOGICAL FUNCTIONS AND EFFECTS

❑ Methylation Reactions: SAMe functions as a methyl donor for the synthesis of nucleic acids (DNA and RNA), proteins, phospholipids, catecholamines, and various neurotransmitters.

❑ Transsulfuration: SAMe is the precursor in the sulfur metabolic pathways for the synthesis of cysteine, glutathione, and taurine.

❑ Polyamines: SAMe is also necessary for the synthesis of a group of compounds collectively referred to as polyamines, which are spermidine, puescine, and spermine. These polyamines are essential for cellular growth and differentialion, gene expression, protein phosphorylation, neuron regeneration, and the repair of DNA.

❑ Antioxidant production: Because SAMe is necessary for the synthesis of the antioxidant glutathione, it plays a role in protecting the body from free radical-induced aging damage.

❑ Detoxification: Glutathione is important for detoxification in the liver. Glutathione depletion is usually found in individuals with liver malfunction. SAMe supplementation promotes the synthesis of glutathione, which improves liver function and detoxification.

❑ Healthy Cellular Membranes: The ratio between phosphatidyl choline (PC) and cholesterol in cellular membranes determines their relative flexibility or stiffness. PC promotes flexibility whereas cholesterol promotes stiffness. Since SAMe is an important facilitator of phosphatidyl choline synthesis, it plays a role in promoting more pliant cellular membranes. Stiffer cell membranes are not able to transmit cellular signals as effectively and it is more difficult for neuropeptides and other messenger molecules to fit into receptor sites when cellular membranes are stiff.

❑ Nerve Protection: Protects against neuronal death caused by lack of oxygen (anoxia). It regenerates nerves and promotes remyelination of nerve fibers.

❑ Liver Protection: Protects the liver against alcohol, drugs, and cytokines. It protects against cholestasis (bile impairment or blockage) and it may protect against chronic active hepatitis. It also protects against liver damage caused by MAO inhibitors and anticonvulsants and it reverses hyperbilirubinaemia.

SIDE EFFECTS AND TOXICITY

SAMe has no reported toxicity. A few minor side effects have been occasionally reported, which include dry mouth, nausea, and restlessness. Individuals are urged to consult with their physician before combining SAMe with other anti-depressants, or with tryptophan or 5-HTP.

RDA AND DOSAGE

❑ No RDA has been set for SAMe.

❑ Dosages for SAMe range from 200 to 1,600 mg daily in divided doses.

AVAILABLE FORMS

S-adenosylmethionine (SAMe).

DIETARY SOURCES

SAMe does not occur in foods that we eat.

SELENIUM

OVERVIEW

Drugs that deplete Selenium
✔ Corticosteroids
✔ Oral contraceptives
✔ Valproic acid

Until the late 1950s, selenium was thought to be toxic. Although it can be toxic in high doses, it now is recognized as one of the most important nutritional *trace minerals*. Selenium plays important roles in *detoxification* and *antioxidant* defense mechanisms in the body. Recent research has shown that selenium is one of the most powerful anti-cancer agents ever tested.

SYMPTOMS AND CAUSES OF DEFICIENCY

The symptoms of selenium deficiency include destructive changes to the heart and pancreas, sore muscles, increased fragility of red blood cells, and a weakened immune system.

❑ The primary cause of selenium deficiency is insufficient dietary intake resulting from either poor food choices (as in junk foods and fast foods) or eating foods grown in selenium-depleted soils.

❑ Selenium is not an essential nutrient for plants and, therefore, many farmlands have become increasingly depleted of selenium because farmers see no need to add it to the soil.

❑ Food processing causes substantial loss of selenium. For example, whole-wheat bread has twice the selenium as white bread, and brown rice has 15 times more selenium than white rice.

❑ Human breast milk contains six times more selenium than cow's milk. A cow's milk diet for infants can contribute to low selenium levels and depressed immune systems in infants.

❑ Protein-calorie malnutrition can lead to selenium deficiency.

❑ The Keshan district in China had extremely high rates of childhood cardiomyopathies until it was discovered that the soil was deficient in selenium. Nutritional selenium supplementation has solved the problem.

❑ Increased rates of various types of cancer are associated with low dietary intake of selenium.

BIOLOGICAL FUNCTIONS AND EFFECTS

❑ Selenium is an indispensable *cofactor* for glutathione peroxidase, which is one of the most important *antioxidant enzymes* in the immune system.

❑ Selenium is a powerful anticancer nutrient. Numerous epidemiological studies have correlated low dietary selenium intakes with higher rates of cancer.

❑ The *antioxidant* activities of selenium enable it to protect against heart attacks and strokes.

❑ Selenium is important to the immune system. It has anti-viral activity, increases *T-lymphocytes*, and enhances natural killer cell activity.

❑ As an antioxidant, selenium helps to prevent lipid *peroxidation* and neutralizes destructive hydrogen peroxide. By neutralizing these types of *free radicals*, selenium works to prevent cancer and cardiovascular disease.

❑ Selenium is capable of detoxifying heavy metal toxins such as mercury and cadmium.

❑ Selenium greatly reduces the toxicity of the anticancer drug Adriamycin without reducing its antitumor activity.

❑ Selenium has significant anti-inflammatory properties.

❑ Recently it was discovered that the enzyme that converts thyroid hormone (T_4) to triiodothyronine (T_3, the active form) is a selenium-dependent enzyme.

❑ Selenium potentiates the antioxidant activity of vitamin E.

SIDE EFFECTS AND TOXICITY

❑ Selenium is a *trace mineral* that can be toxic. Although deaths from selenium toxicity have been reported in livestock, no deaths have been reported in humans.

❑ Symptoms of selenium toxicity include loss of hair and nails, sores on the skin, nervous system abnormalities, digestive dysfunction, and a garlicky breath odor.

RDA AND DOSAGE

❑ The RDA for selenium is 70 mcg/day for men and 55 mcg/day for women.

❑ Pharmacologic doses in the scientific literature range from 50 mcg to 500 mcg/day.

❑ Occasionally, physicians have used much higher doses in cancer therapy and to treat cases of acute inflammation.

❑ Available forms are sodium selenite, selenomethioine, and high-selenium yeast.

DIETARY SOURCES

❑ Whole grains are the best dietary source of selenium, followed by seafood, garlic, liver, eggs, dairy products, and some vegetables, including cabbage, celery, cucumbers, and radishes.

❑ The selenium content of foods is directly dependent on the selenium content of the soil. Foods grown on selenium-deficient soils in many areas of the United States have inadequate selenium content.

SILICON

OVERVIEW

<table>
<tr><td>Drugs that deplete Silicon

No studies that report drug-induced silicon depletion have been found.</td><td>Even though silicon is the most abundant mineral on earth, only recently was it discovered to be an essential trace mineral. The largest concentrations of silicon are found in the skin and cartilage, but it also occurs in connective tissue, bone, tendons, lymph nodes, trachea, aorta of the heart, and lungs.</td></tr>
</table>

Inhalation of silicon from the environment is partially responsible for its high occurrence in lung tissue.

Preliminary studies have shown an age-related decline in the silicon content of the skin, arteries, and thymus. At the same time, concentrations remain relatively stable in the heart, kidneys, muscles, and tendons.

SYMPTOMS AND CAUSES OF DEFICIENCY

❑ Silicon is so abundant in the environment that outright deficiencies do not exist. The discovery of silicon's role as an essential nutrient is quite recent, though, and very little work has been done regarding its metabolic activity and optimal dosage ranges.

❑ Silicon deficiency might be associated with the development of *osteoarthritis* and some aspects of *cardiovascular disease.*

❑ Laboratory animals fed silicon-deficient diets exhibit growth retardation and incomplete and deformed development of the skeleton.

BIOLOGICAL FUNCTIONS AND EFFECTS

❑ Silicon is an important component of the *mucopolysaccharides* and *collagen* of connective tissues. As such, it provides strength, rigidity, and flexibility to bones, teeth, tendons, ligaments, cell walls and membranes, nails, and skin.

❑ Silicon aids in building the organic matrix for proper mineralization of bones and teeth.

❑ Cell culture studies and work with chicks suggest that silicon somehow stimulates the production of mucopolysaccharides and collagen.

❑ There is some indication that adequate levels of silicon may be associated with lesser risk in the development of *atherosclerosis*.

❑ Silicon may help to limit or inhibit the absorption of aluminum.

SIDE EFFECTS AND TOXICITY

❑ Toxicity studies focus on silicosis, an occupational lung disease caused by inhaling silicon dioxide dust. This occurs in mining, sandblasting, and in the manufacture of glass, ceramics, abrasives, and petroleum products.

❑ Silicosis is characterized by a degenerative fibrosis of the lung tissue.

RDA AND DOSAGE

❑ Nutritional guidelines have not been determined.

❑ Daily intake of silicon is variously recommended at 5 to 10 mg/day. The estimated average daily dietary intake of silicon is from 20 to 50 mg/day, so most people apparently are getting sufficient silicon.

DIETARY SOURCES

❑ The best food sources of silicon are rice, bran, and brown rice.

❑ Dietary silicon is available in other unrefined grain products and in high-fiber vegetables.

❑ Beer contains a high concentration of easily absorbable silicon.

SODIUM

OVERVIEW

Drugs that deplete Sodium
✔ ACE Inhibitors
✔ Aminoglycosides
✔ Amphotericin B
✔ Aspirin and salicylates
✔ Choline magnesium trisalicylate
✔ Choline salicylate
✔ Colchicine
✔ Hydroflumethiazide
✔ Indapamide
✔ Loop diuretics
✔ Thiazide diuretics

Sodium is one of the body's three major *electrolytes* (the other two being potassium and chloride). They exist as fully dissociated *ions* and are the main particles responsible for *osmotic pressure* in body fluids. Sodium is the primary *extracellular* electrolyte in body fluids. Their ionic strength enables them to influence the solubility of proteins and other substances throughout the body.

Most Americans consume enormous amounts of sodium, from 10 to 35 times more than the recommended daily intake. Dietary sodium is easily absorbed from the intestine, carried by the blood to the kidneys, where it is either filtered out and returned to the blood or excreted.

SYMPTOMS AND CAUSES OF DEFICIENCY

Sodium deficiency is rare in humans. Conditions that could cause sodium deficiency include starvation, excessive vomiting, severe diarrhea, and excess perspiration, in conjunction with a lack of water. Symptoms of sodium deficiency are muscle weakness, poor concentration, memory loss, dehydration, and loss of appetite.

BIOLOGICAL FUNCTIONS AND EFFECTS

❑ In regulating body fluids, sodium has a major role in the regulation of blood pressure.

❑ Sodium ions play a critical role in the transmission of electrochemical impulses for nerve function and muscle contraction.

❑ Sodium helps regulate the acid/alkaline balance in the blood and lymph fluids.

❑ Sodium helps to control and operate the sodium/ potassium pump. This helps make the cell walls *permeable* and facilitates the transport of materials across cell membranes.

❑ Sodium helps regulate the transport and excretion of carbon dioxide.

SIDE EFFECTS AND TOXICITY

❑ High intake of sodium is associated with *edema* and elevated blood pressure.

RDA AND DOSAGE

❑ There is no RDA for sodium.

❑ A reasonable dietary intake is from 1 to 3 grams per day.

DIETARY SOURCES

Table salt is the most concentrated source of sodium. Enormous amounts of sodium are used in cooking and food processing. Often this "hidden salt" contributes more to an individual's daily diet than does the salt shaker. Protein foods generally contain more sodium than vegetables and grains. Fruits contain almost no sodium.

SULFUR

OVERVIEW

Drugs that deplete Sulfur
No studies that report drug-induced depletion of sulfur have been found.

Sulfur is found in the body primarily as a component of the four sulfur-containing amino acids cystine, cysteine, methionine, and taurine. Although all proteins contain sulfur, it is most prevalent in the *keratin* of skin and hair and in *insulin*. Tissues of the joints contain high levels of a sulfur-containing compound called chondroitin sulfate. Two B-vitamins, thiamin and biotin, contain sulfur, as does heparin, which is an *anticoagulant* synthesized primarily in the liver. Small amounts of sulfur exist in the body as organic sulfates and sulfites.

Sulfur plays an important role in determining the shape, structure, and functionality of proteins. The sulfur-containing amino acids in proteins can create crosslinks by forming disulfide bonds, which act to strengthen and stabilize proteins. Sulfur exists in its reduced form in cysteine and in an oxidized form as a double molecule in cystine.

Sulfur has a characteristic odor. The smell from burning feathers, hair, skin or nails is from its sulfur content, and "smelly" foods such as onions and garlic contain significant amounts of sulfur.

SYMPTOMS AND CAUSES OF DEFICIENCY

❑ Deficiency symptoms related to sulfur are unknown. A diet severely lacking in protein (such as in starvation) could cause a sulfur deficiency.

BIOLOGICAL FUNCTIONS AND EFFECTS

❑ The major role of sulfur, as part of *amino acids*, is to provide structure to proteins and *mucopolysaccharides* such as chondroitin sulfate and collagen.

❑ Sulfur, through disulfide (–S–S–) or sulfhydryl (–SH) bonds, gives proteins their characteristic different shapes. For example, hair curliness comes from the presence of disulfide bonds of cystine in hair.

❑ Sulfur plays an important metabolic role as a sulfhydryl group on the active site of co-enzyme A.

❑ Sulfur, in conjunction with magnesium, takes part in the metabolic detoxification of sulfuric acid in the body for excretion in the urine.

❑ Sulfur-containing *lipids* (sulfolipids) are found in the liver, kidneys, and brain.

❑ Sulfur is necessary for all of the biochemical processes involving thiamin, biotin, and lipoic acid.

❑ The hormone *insulin* consists of 51 amino acids in 2 polypeptide chains. The two parallel chains are joined by two disulfide bridges.

SIDE EFFECTS AND TOXICITY

No toxicity is associated with sulfur. Excesses are efficiently excreted in the urine.

RDA AND DOSAGE

❑ No RDA has been set for sulfur.

❑ The diets of most Americans are high in protein and provide more than adequate amounts of sulfur.

DIETARY SOURCES

❑ Protein-rich foods are good sources of sulfur.

VANADIUM

OVERVIEW

Drugs that deplete Vanadium
No studies that report drug-induced depletion of vanadium have been found.

How essential vanadium is in humans has yet to be established with certainty. In the late 1960s it was found to be an essential *trace mineral* for plant nutrition, and in the early 1970s it was discovered to be an essential nutrient for animals. It probably is essential for humans, too, but some debate still is waged on this issue. Nonetheless, interest in vanadium as a nutritional substance has been steadily building over the past twenty years or so.

Vanadium is a transition metal. As such, it has biochemical properties similar to chromium, molybdenum, manganese, and iron. Vanadium functions primarily as a *co-factor*, which enhances or inhibits various *enzymes*.

Vanadium accumulates primarily in organ tissues, with the highest concentrations in the liver, kidneys, and bone. Bone seems to be the long-term storage site for vanadium, and storage of accessible vanadium is primarily in fat and blood lipids.

SYMPTOMS AND CAUSES OF DEFICIENCY

No cases of vanadium deficiency are known.

BIOLOGICAL FUNCTIONS AND EFFECTS

❑ The most significant research on vanadium to date involves its insulin-like properties and its possible role in treating *diabetes*. Vanadium and vanadyl salts stimulate glucose metabolism. When given to patients with *Type II diabetes*, it markedly decreases blood glucose levels.

❑ Vanadium produces its insulin-like effects in the liver by a) decreasing the activity of the gluconeogenesis *enzyme*, glucose-6-phosphatase, b) increasing the activity of two glycolytic enzymes, glucokinase and phosphofructokinase, and c) increasing the production of glycogen.

❑ Vanadium may have a functional role as a building material in bones and teeth.

❑ The biochemical and physiological roles of vanadium are not yet fully understood. Nevertheless, it may be involved in the following processes: NADPH oxidation reactions, *lipoprotein* lipase activity, *amino acid* transport, and the growth of red blood cells.

❑ At higher dosage levels, vanadium seems to be able to assist in lowering elevated blood *cholesterol* and *triglyceride* levels.

❑ Vanadium is a potent inhibitor of Na+K+ ATPase *enzymes*.

SIDE EFFECTS AND TOXICITY

❑ Vanadium has no known toxicity as a dietary nutrient in humans.

❑ Vanadium also can be absorbed through inhalation, and excessive exposure could be toxic. Vanadium is used as a catalyst in a wide variety of industrial processes. Occasionally, in industrial accidents sufficient vanadium is inhaled so that it becomes toxic.

❑ Experimentally induced vanadium toxicity in animal studies produces reproductive and developmental abnormalities, including decreased fertility, birth defects, and death of the embryo.

RDA AND DOSAGE

❑ Dietary requirements for vanadium have not been established. To date, little is known about human nutritional needs for vanadium, or whether the amount or type Americans absorb is adequate.

❑ The daily requirement for vanadium is estimated to be in the order of 10 mcg/day. The average American diet contains from 15 to 30 mcg/day, which is more than enough to satisfy nutritional needs.

DIETARY SOURCES

Fats and vegetable oils are the richest food sources of vanadium. Vanadium also occurs in grains, meats, fish, and nuts. Other foods and spices that contain vanadium are dill seeds, parsley, black pepper, and mushrooms.

VITAMIN A (RETINOL)

OVERVIEW

Drugs that deplete Vitamin A (Retinol)
✔ Cholestyramine
✔ Colestipol
✔ Corticosteriods
✔ Neomycin
✔ Mineral oil

Vitamin A was the first fat-soluble vitamin to be recognized, in 1913. It was found to prevent night blindness and *xerophthalmia*. In 1932, beta-carotene (pro-vitamin A) was discovered to be the precursor to vitamin A. Vitamin A is necessary for vision, for the growth and maintenance of *epithelial* tissues, and for the growth and development of bones. It also regulates immunity and reproduction and has anticancer properties.

❑ Vitamin A belongs to a class of compounds called *retinoids*, which occur only in animal products. Retinoids with vitamin A activity are found in nature in three different forms: (a) the alcohol, retinol, (b) the aldehyde, retinal or retinaldehyde, and (c) the acid, retinoic acid.

❑ Beta-carotene consists of two molecules of vitamin A linked head to head. *Enzymes* in the intestinal tract split beta-carotene into two molecules of vitamin A whenever the body needs it.

❑ To be properly absorbed from the digestive tract, vitamin A requires fats as well as minerals.

❑ Substantial amounts of vitamin A are stored in the liver and, therefore, it does not have to be supplied in the diet daily.

SYMPTOMS AND CAUSES OF DEFICIENCY

❑ Vitamin A deficiency can be caused by inadequate dietary intake or bodily dysfunction that interferes with absorption, storage, or transport of vitamin A.

❑ Deficiency of vitamin A is associated with the development and promotion of epithelial cell cancers in various glands and organs in the body.

❑ Night blindness (*nyctalopia*) is the classic vision problem resulting from vitamin A deficiency. *Xerophthalmia* (drying and hardening of the membranes that line the eyes) also can develop. This condition causes blindness in hundreds of thousands of infants and children yearly worldwide but seldom occurs in the United States.

❑ Long-term vitamin A deficiency causes the skin to become dry, scaly, and rough, a condition called *keratinization,* in which small, hard bumps develop on the skin because hair follicles plug up with a hard protein called *keratin.*

❑ Vitamin A deficiency in infants and children hinders their growth and development. Bone deformities and dental problems often result.

BIOLOGICAL FUNCTIONS AND EFFECTS

❑ Vitamin A plays an essential role in vision. It interacts with a photosensitive pigment in the retina that facilitates night vision.

❑ Vitamin A plays an important role in maintaining the integrity of all *epithelial* tissue. Many studies show that adequate intake of vitamin A is associated with reduced risk to various epithelial-cell cancers (mouth, skin, lungs, bladder, breast, stomach, cervix).

❑ By maintaining healthy epithelial cells (surface cells of many glands, organs, and skin), vitamin A helps to create barriers to infections.

❑ Vitamin A is essential for the growth of bone and soft tissue. It also is necessary for the formation of tooth enamel in the development of teeth.

SIDE EFFECTS AND TOXICITY

❏ Because vitamin A is fat-soluble, excesses can accumulate to toxic levels in fatty tissues.

❏ Signs of vitamin A toxicity include dry itchy skin, brittle nails, hair loss, bone pain, gingivitis, headaches, muscle and joint pains, anorexia, fatigue, diarrhea, increased infections, and enlarged liver and abnormal liver function.

❏ Hypervitaminosis A has been reported in adults who have been taking in excess of 50,000 I.U. daily for several years, and in a case of taking a water-soluble synthetic vitamin A at 18,500 to 60,000 I.U. for several months.

❏ Doses greater than 10,000 I.U. can be toxic to a fetus. Therefore, women who are pregnant, and women of child-bearing age who can become pregnant should not take more than 10,000 I.U./day.

RDA AND DOSAGE

❏ The RDA for vitamin A is 5,000 I.U./day; No RDA has been set for beta-carotene.

❏ *Pharmacologic* doses in the scientific literature usually range from 10,000 I.U. to 35,000 I.U. Occasional applications can go much higher but should not be attempted without medical supervision.

❏ Dosages of vitamin A and beta-carotene sometimes are measured in terms of *retinol equivalents (R.E.)*. One R.E. (equal to 1 mcg) is equivalent to 5 I.U.

DIETARY SOURCES

❏ Good food sources of vitamin A are liver, kidney, butter, egg yolk, whole milk and cream, and fortified skim milk.

❑ Good food sources of pro-vitamin A (beta-carotene) are yellow and dark green leafy vegetables (carrots, sweet potatoes, squash, collards, spinach), and yellow fruit (apricots, peaches, cantaloupe).

❑ Cod liver oil and halibut fish oil contain high levels of vitamin A and have been used therapeutically.

VITAMIN B₁ (THIAMIN)

OVERVIEW

Drugs that deplete Vitamin B₁ (Thiamin)
✔ Aminoglycosides
✔ Bumetanide
✔ Cephalosporins
✔ Ethacrynic acid
✔ Fluoroquinolones
✔ Furosemide
✔ Macrolides
✔ Oral contraceptives
✔ Penicillins
✔ Phenytoin
✔ Sulfonamides
✔ Tetracyclines
✔ Torsemide
✔ Trimethoprim

Vitamin B₁, also known as thiamin, was the first of the B vitamins to be discovered. It was isolated in 1926 as a water-soluble, crystalline, yellowish-white powder with a salty, slightly nutty taste. In 1936, chemists accomplished the synthesis and determined its chemical formula.

Beriberi is the classic syndrome resulting from a vitamin B₁ deficiency. This disease is more prevalent in Asian countries where polished rice is the staple diet. When beriberi occurs in the United States, it is seen most commonly in severely malnourished infants and elderly people. In adults, chronic dieting, alcoholism, and diets consisting primarily of highly processed, refined foods are causes of vitamin B₁ deficiency.

SYMPTOMS AND CAUSES OF DEFICIENCY

Deficiencies of vitamin B₁ manifest primarily as disorders of the neuromuscular, intestinal, and cardiovascular systems. Deficiency symptoms include depression, irritability, memory loss, mental confusion, indigestion, weight loss, anorexia, muscular weakness, sore calf muscles, *edema*, rapid pulse rate, heart palpitations, fatigue, loss of reflexes in legs, defective muscular coordination, and nerve inflammation including "pins and needles" and numbness.

❑ A deficiency of thiamin is one of the most common nutritional deficiencies in the United States. One U.S. Department of Agriculture study reported that 45 percent of Americans consume less than the *RDA* of thiamin.

- ❏ Vitamin B$_1$ is easily destroyed or lost during cooking because it is heat-sensitive and water-soluble.
- ❏ Vitamin B$_1$ is depleted by *diuretic* drugs and intestinal conditions such as diarrhea, and malabsorption because of lactose intolerance and celiac disease (gliadin or wheat sensitivity).
- ❏ Alcohol interferes with the absorption of Vitamin B$_1$, and the vitamin also is necessary for the metabolism of alcohol. Severe deficiency associated with alcohol consumption produces a condition called Wernicke-Korsakoff syndrome, with symptoms ranging from mild confusion to severely impaired memory and cognitive function, and coma.

BIOLOGICAL FUNCTIONS AND EFFECTS

To be metabolically active, vitamin B$_1$ must combine with phosphoric acid to form the important *co-enzyme* thiamin pyrophosphate (TPP). Once converted to its active form, thiamin

- ❏ is required by every cell in the body to make *ATP*, the body's primary fuel and energy source.
- ❏ plays a major role in the conversion of glucose into biological energy.
- ❏ is necessary for the maintenance of nerve tissues, nerve function, and nerve transmissions.
- ❏ is important in the maintenance of muscular function, especially of the heart.
- ❏ is required for the synthesis of acetylcholine, which is the primary *neurotransmitter* involved in thought and memory processes.
- ❏ is necessary for maintenance and proper functioning of muscles, especially heart muscles.
- ❏ is involved in the synthesis of fatty acids.

SYMPTOMS OF TOXICITY

Because it is water-soluble, thiamin is not stored in the body. Accumulation to toxic levels is unlikely. Overdose and toxicity would require high doses (in the multiple gram range).

RDA AND DOSAGE

❏ The RDA for vitamin B_1 is 1.5 mg/day.

❏ Therapeutic dosage ranges in the scientific literature vary from 10 mg to 100 mg per day in divided doses, although some applications use even larger doses.

DIETARY SOURCES

All plant and animal foods contain vitamin B_1, but only in low concentrations. The richest sources are brewer's yeast and organ meats. Whole-grain cereals comprise the most important dietary source of vitamin B_1 in human diets.

VITAMIN B₂ (RIBOFLAVIN)

OVERVIEW

Drugs that deplete Vitamin B₂ (Riboflavin)

✔ Acetophenazine
✔ Aminoglycosides
✔ Amitriptyline
✔ Amoxapine
✔ Cephalosporins
✔ Chlorpromazine
✔ Clomipramine
✔ Desipramine
✔ Doxepin
✔ Fluoroquinolones
✔ Fluphenazine
✔ Imipramine
✔ Macrolides
✔ Mesoridazine
✔ Methdilazine
✔ Methotrimeprazine
✔ Nortriptyline
✔ Oral contraceptives
✔ Penicillins
✔ Perphenazine
✔ Prochlorperazine
✔ Promazine
✔ Promethazine
✔ Protriptyline
✔ Sulfonamides
✔ Tetracyclines
✔ Thioridazine
✔ Trifluoperazine
✔ Trimethoprim
✔ Trimipramine

Vitamin B₂ is water-soluble and, like other B vitamins, it is not stored in sufficient amounts in the body and therefore must be supplied daily. Vitamin B₂ is absorbed from the upper part of the small intestine and is absorbed better when taken with food. Only approximately 15 percent is absorbed if taken alone versus 60 percent absorption with food. Riboflavin belongs to a group of yellow fluorescent pigments called *flavins*. In its pure state, it is a yellow crystalline powder with a slight odor. When excreted, it gives the urine a characteristic bright yellow color.

SYMPTOMS AND CAUSES OF DEFICIENCY

Vitamin B₂ deficiencies affect primarily the skin, eyes, and mucous membranes of the intestinal tract. Deficiencies seldom occur alone but, rather, as a component of multiple-nutrient deficiencies. Additional symptoms include:

❑ *chelosis* (cracked corners of the mouth)
❑ inflamed mucous membranes
❑ soreness and burning of the lips, mouth, and tongue (possibly magenta-colored tongue)
❑ reddening, tearing, burning, and itching of the eyes
❑ eyes tiring easily
❑ eyes highly sensitive to light

❑ dry, itchy, scaly skin (seborrheic dermatitis)

❑ scaling *eczema* of the face and genitals.

❑ In severe long-term deficiency, damage to nerve tissue can cause depression and hysteria.

❑ Riboflavin is heat-stable but sensitive to destruction by light. Because it is water-soluble, substantial amounts are lost by leaching into water when cooking. The vitamin exists in the germ and bran of grains, so milling and processing of grains result in substantial losses.

❑ Individuals at greatest risk for riboflavin deficiency are alcoholics, infants, and elderly people on unbalanced, nutritionally deficient diets.

❑ A U.S. Department of Agriculture survey estimated that 34 percent of Americans get less than the *RDA* of vitamin B_2 daily.

BIOLOGICAL FUNCTIONS AND EFFECTS

❑ Facilitates the metabolism of carbohydrates, fats, and proteins.

❑ Combines with phosphoric acid to become part of two important flavin *co-enzymes*, FMN (flavin mononucleotide) and FAD (flavin adenine dinucleotide). FMN and FAD are known to bind to more than 100 flavoprotein enzymes, which catalyze oxidation-reduction reactions in cells. These enzymes include the *oxidases*, which function aerobically, and *dehydrogenases*, which function anaerobically.

❑ Plays a critical role in the conversion of carbohydrates to *ATP* in the production of energy. In energy production, flavoprotein enzymes function as hydrogen carriers in the electron transport system, resulting in the production of energy within the *mitochondria*.

❑ Contributes important *antioxidant* activity, both by itself and as part of the *enzyme* glutathione reductase.

❑ Is necessary for growth and reproduction.

❑ Is essential to the healthy growth of skin, hair, and nails.

SYMPTOMS OF TOXICITY

❑ There is no known toxicity for riboflavin. Its negligible storage and easy excretion make it a safe nutrient.

RDA AND DOSAGE

❑ The RDA for vitamin B$_2$ is 1.7 mg/day.

❑ Pregnant women, nursing mothers, and individuals who exercise heavily require somewhat higher intakes.

❑ High-potency vitamin formulations and therapeutic dosages are in the range of 15 mg to 50 mg daily in divided doses.

DIETARY SOURCES

The best sources of vitamin B$_2$ are liver, milk, and dairy products. Moderate sources include meats, dark green vegetables, eggs, avocados, oysters, mushrooms and fish (especially salmon and tuna).

VITAMIN B₃ (NIACIN)

OVERVIEW

Drugs that deplete Vitamin B₃ (Niacin)
✔ Aminglycosides
✔ Cephalosporins
✔ Estrogens, conjugated
✔ Estrogens, esterified
✔ Fluoroquinolones
✔ Isoniazid
✔ Macrolides
✔ Oral contraceptives
✔ Penicillins
✔ Sulfonamides
✔ Tetracyclines
✔ Trimethoprim

Niacin is a water-soluble B-vitamin that functions metabolically as a component of two important *co-enzymes*: nicotinamide adenine dinucleotide (NAD) and nicotinamide adenine dinucleotide phosphate (NADP), known as the pyridine nucleotides.

SYMPTOMS AND CAUSES OF DEFICIENCY

Severe deficiency of niacin is known as *pellagra*, which means "rough skin." Symptoms of pellagra are characterized by the "3 Ds": dermatitis, dementia, and diarrhea. Pellagra occurs in areas where nutrition is meager and corn is the dietary staple (tryptophan and niacin are poorly absorbed from corn.) In Mexico, however, where corn is treated with lye before use, deficiency is less common because the alkali increases absorption of tryptophan.

The parts of the body most affected by niacin deficiency are

❑ Skin: cracked pigmented scaly dermatitis, especially on parts exposed to the sun.

❑ Intestinal tract: inflammation of mucous membranes, causing many digestive abnormalities including swollen tongue and diarrhea.

❑ Nervous system: mental confusion and disorientation leading to psychosis or delirium.

BIOLOGICAL FUNCTIONS AND EFFECTS

❑ Niacin-containing *co-enzymes* NAD and NADP are involved in more than 200 reactions in the metabolism of carbohydrates, fatty acids, and amino acids, making it vital in supplying energy to, and maintaining the function of, every cell in the body.

❑ Niacin is especially important in the oxidation-reduction reactions in the *Krebs cycle*, involving the production of energy from carbohydrates.

❑ Niacin is useful in treating elevated blood *cholesterol* levels: it reduces *LDL* ("bad" cholesterol) and *triglycerides* and increases *HDL* ("good" cholesterol).

❑ Niacin reduced the recurrence rate of heart attacks by nearly 30 percent at dosages of about 2 grams per day and provided a 11 percent reduction in the overall mortality rate.

❑ Niacinamide has been shown to have anti-anxiety benefit resembling benzodiazepines, and Italian doctors report using it successfully to help addicted patients withdraw from benzodiazepines.

❑ Doses of nicotinic acid in the 75 mg range stimulate the release of *histamines*, which causes temporary *vasodilation* and the characteristic "niacin flush."

❑ Niacin has been identified as part of the *glucose tolerance factor* of yeast,which enhances the response to *insulin*.

SYMPTOMS OF TOXICITY

❑ Large doses of niacin cause transient side effects such as tingling sensations, flushing of the skin, and head throbbing because of its vasodilating action. These effects disappear within 20 to 30 minutes.

❑ The sustained-release form of niacin can be toxic to the liver and should not be used.

RDA AND DOSAGE

❑ The RDA for adult males is 18 mg/day and for adult females is 13 mg/day.

❑ Therapeutic dosage ranges in the scientific literature vary from 30 mg to 2,000 mg per day. Some studies, however, use dosages up to 6 grams per day. Dosages above 2 grams per day should be administered only under medical supervision.

❑ Available forms are nicotinic acid (niacin), niacinamide (nicotinamide), and inositol hexaniacinate.

DIETARY SOURCES

❑ Both niacin and its precursor, *tryptophan*, are included when determining the niacin content of foods.

❑ Lean meats, poultry, fish, and peanuts are good sources of both niacin and tryptophan.

❑ The best sources of niacin are organ meats, brewer's yeast, milk, legumes, peanuts and peanut butter.

❑ Intestinal bacteria also synthesize niacin.

VITAMIN B$_5$ (PANTOTHENIC ACID)

OVERVIEW

Drugs that deplete Vitamin B$_5$ (Pantothenic Acid)
✔ Aspirin and salicylates

Dr. Roger Williams discovered vitamin B$_5$ in 1933. Because it is present in all cells, he named it *pantothenic acid*, from the Greek word "panthothen," meaning "everywhere." Pantothenic acid is necessary for the production of some hormones and *neurotransmitters*, and it is involved in the metabolism of all carbohydrates, fats, and proteins.

Vitamin B$_5$ is most commonly available commercially as calcium pantothenate. After absorption, pantothenic acid is first converted to a sulfur-containing compound called pantotheine. Pantotheine then is converted into co-enzyme A, which is the only known biologically active form of pantothenic acid.

SYMPTOMS AND CAUSES OF DEFICIENCY

❑ Pantothenic acid is so widely available in foods that a deficiency in humans is virtually unknown.

❑ Experimentally induced deficiencies manifest as problems related to the skin, liver, thymus, and nerves.

BIOLOGICAL FUNCTIONS AND EFFECTS

❑ As a constituent of co-enzyme A (CoA), pantothenic acid participates in a wide variety of enzymatic reactions) within cells throughout the body.

❑ CoA is involved in the release of energy from carbohydrates in the *Krebs cycle*.

❑ Pantothenic acid can provide an anti-stress effect because CoA is necessary for the synthesis of steroid hormones and proper functioning of the adrenal glands.

- ❑ CoA functions in the production of fats, cholesterol, and bile acids.
- ❑ Pantothenic acid is necessary for the synthesis of acetylcholine, phospholipids, and porphyrin in the *hemoglobin* of red blood cells.
- ❑ Pantothenic acid may help to boost energy and athletic ability because of its role in the metabolism of carbohydrates.
- ❑ Pantothenic acid helps to detoxify alcohol by participating in the metabolism of acetaldehyde.
- ❑ Pantothenic acid has been reported to improve the stress reactions of well nourished individuals and to relieve "burning feet" syndrome.

Symptoms of Toxicity

- ❑ No known toxic effects arise from taking large doses of pantothenic acid.
- ❑ Ingestion of large amounts of panthothenic acid may cause diarrhea.

RDA and Dosage

- ❑ The RDA for pantothenic acid is 10 mg per day.
- ❑ *Pharmacologic* doses in the scientific literature range from 50 mg to 1000 mg per day.
- ❑ Available forms are calcium pantothenate and dexpanthenol.

Dietary Sources

- ❑ Pantothenic acid is present in all plant and animal tissues. Best sources of this vitamin include eggs, liver, fish, chicken, whole-grain breads and cereals, and legumes.
- ❑ Other good sources are cauliflower, broccoli, lean beef, white and sweet potatoes, and tomatoes.

VITAMIN B$_6$ (PYRIDOXINE)

OVERVIEW

Drugs that deplete Vitamin B$_6$ (Pyridoxine)
✔ Aminoglycosides
✔ Bumetanide
✔ Cephalosporins
✔ Diethylstilbesterol
✔ Estrogens, conjugated
✔ Estrogens, esterified
✔ Ethacrynic acid
✔ Fluoroquinolones
✔ Furosemide
✔ Hydralazine
✔ Isoniazid
✔ Levodopa
✔ Macrolides
✔ Oral contraceptives
✔ Penicillamine
✔ Penicillins
✔ Phenelzine
✔ Phenobarbital
✔ Quinestrol
✔ Sulfonamides
✔ Tetracyclines
✔ Theophylline
✔ Torsemide
✔ Trimethoprim

Vitamin B$_6$ is necessary for the proper functioning of more than 60 enzymes. Many of its activities are related to the metabolism of *amino acids* and other protein-related compounds such as *hemoglobin*, *serotonin*, various hormones, and the *prostaglandins*. After entering a cell, vitamin B$_6$ is phosphorylated, which converts it into its active form, pyridoxal phosphate (PLP).

SYMPTOMS AND CAUSES OF DEFICIENCY

Deficiencies of vitamin B$_6$ manifest primarily as dermatologic, circulatory, and neurologic changes. Because of its many metabolic roles, pyridoxine also produces a wide variety of deficiency symptoms. These include

❑ depression
❑ sleep disturbances
❑ nerve inflammation
❑ PMS
❑ lethargy
❑ decreased alertness
❑ anemia
❑ altered mobility
❑ elevated *homocysteine* levels
❑ nausea
❑ vomiting
❑ seborrheic dermatitis

The following B$_6$ deficiency conditions are explained in greater detail.

❑ **Depression from inhibition of serotonin synthesis**

Vitamin B$_6$ is essential for 5-hydroxytryptophan decarboxylase, an *enzyme* that catalyzes one of the steps in the conversion of *tryptophan* to *serotonin*. Thus, a vitamin B$_6$ deficiency can limit the brain's ability to synthesize serotonin. Low serotonin levels are associated with depression.

❑ **Insomnia from inhibition of melatonin synthesis**

Melatonin, which is our biochemical sleep trigger, is synthesized from serotonin in the brain. If a vitamin B$_6$ deficiency inhibits serotonin synthesis, there will be a corresponding decrease in the body's ability to synthesize melatonin, which may cause insomnia.

❑ **Elevated homocysteine**

Elevated *homocysteine* now is recognized as one of the most critical independent risk factors for *cardiovascular disease*. Homocysteine is a toxic intermediate metabolite in the metabolism of the *amino acid* methionine. It is capable of directly damaging the vascular system and initiating the process of *atherosclerosis*. Vitamin B$_6$ is one of the nutrients required to metabolize homocysteine so it doesn't build up in the blood and begin to damage the lining of the blood vessels.

❑ **PMS**

Vitamin B$_6$ seems to influence estrogen-induced gene expression. A B$_6$ deficiency results in a substantial increase in estrogen gene expression. Under these conditions, excess estrogen may be produced, which could cause symptoms such as heavy menstrual flow, tender breasts, irregular bleeding, and emotional mood swings.

In addition:

❑ Vitamin B$_6$ is one of the most commonly deficient nutrients in the United States. One U. S. Department of Agriculture study reported that approximately 80 percent of Americans consumed less than the RDA for vitamin B$_6$.

❑ Vitamin B$_6$ is water-soluble; substantial amounts are lost in cooking and food processing.

❑ In addition to the above-mentioned drugs that deplete vitamin B$_6$, numerous substances in the environment antagonize vitamin B$_6$. These include alcohol, tobacco smoke, yellow dye #5 (tartrazine), PCBs, rancid fats in fried foods, and the chemical used to accelerate the ripening process of fruits.

BIOLOGICAL FUNCTIONS AND EFFECTS

❑ Many pyridoxal phosphate enzymes are involved with amino acid metabolism, including: transamination (transfer of amino groups), deamination (removal of amino groups), desulfuration (transfer of sulfhydro groups), and decarboxylation (removal of COOH groups). In addition, Vitamin B$_6$

❑ Is necessary for the formation of hemoglobin and the growth of red blood cells.

❑ Is essential for the synthesis of *tryptophan*, and the conversion of tryptophan to niacin.

❑ Is required for the production of *neurotransmitters* derived from *amino acids* such as serotonin, GABA, *norepinephrine,* acetylcholine, and *histamine.*

❑ Facilitates conversion of *glycogen* to glucose for energy production.

❑ Is useful in treating depression. Vitamin B$_6$ is involved in the synthesis of serotonin, which elevates mood.

- ❏ Is useful in treating premenstrual syndrome (PMS) associated with oral contraceptives (estrogens inhibit the absorption of vitamin B_6).
- ❏ May be beneficial in preventing and treating repetitive motion injuries such as carpal tunnel syndrome.
- ❏ Helps to prevent *atherosclerosis* by metabolizing homocysteine.
- ❏ Some individuals with arthritis respond to pyridoxine. Because it is safe to use, it might be worth trying in all patients with arthritis.
- ❏ Many autistic infants respond to vitamin B_6.

SYMPTOMS OF TOXICITY

Vitamin B_6 can be toxic to the nerves when taken in large doses. Several cases have been reported in people taking 2 grams or more per day. Symptoms included tingling in the hands and feet, decreased muscle coordination, and a stumbling gait. All recovered without problems.

RDA AND DOSAGE

The RDA for vitamin B_6 is 2 mg/day.

- ❏ Therapeutic dosage ranges in the scientific literature vary from 10 mg to 100 mg per day, although some applications go higher.
- ❏ Available forms are pyridoxine hydrochloride, pyridoxal hydrochloride, and pyridoxal-5'-phpophate.

DIETARY SOURCES

- ❏ The best sources of pyridoxine are brewer's yeast, wheat germ, organ meats (especially liver), peanuts, legumes, potatoes, and bananas.
- ❏ The beneficial intestinal bacteria synthesize Vitamin B_6.

VITAMIN B$_{12}$ (CYANOCOBALAMIN)

OVERVIEW

Drugs that deplete Vitamin B$_{12}$ (Cyanocobalamin)
✔ Aminoglycosides
✔ Cephalosporins
✔ Chlorotrianisene
✔ Cholestyramine
✔ Cimetidine
✔ Clofibrate
✔ Colchicine
✔ Colestipol
✔ Co-trimoxazole
✔ Famotidine
✔ Fluoroquinolones
✔ Lansoprazole
✔ Macrolides
✔ Metformin
✔ Neomycin
✔ Nevirapine
✔ Nizatidine
✔ Omeprazole
✔ Oral contraceptives
✔ Penicillins
✔ Phenytoin
✔ Potassium chloride (timed release)
✔ Ranitidine
✔ Sulfonamides
✔ Tetracyclines
✔ Trimethoprim
✔ Zidovudine

Vitamin B$_{12}$ was isolated from liver extract in 1948 and has been shown to control *pernicious anemia* Cobalamin is the generic name for vitamin B$_{12}$, because it contains the heavy metal cobalt. Vitamin B$_{12}$ is an essential growth factor and plays a vital role in the metabolism of all cells, especially those of the intestinal tract, bone marrow, and nervous tissue.

Several different cobalamin compounds exhibit vitamin B$_{12}$ activity. Cyanocobalamin, the most stable and most active form of the vitamin, contains a cyanide group that is well below toxic levels and is totally safe. Vitamin B$_{12}$ is a water-soluble, red crystalline substance. Its red color comes from the presence of cobalt in the molecule.

A protein in gastric secretions called *intrinsic factor* binds to vitamin B$_{12}$ and facilitates its absorption. Without intrinsic factor, less than 1 percent of vitamin B$_{12}$ is absorbed. Relatively large amounts of vitamin B$_{12}$ can be stored in the liver.

SYMPTOMS AND CAUSES OF DEFICIENCY

Vitamin B$_{12}$ deficiencies manifest primarily as anemia and neurologic changes. Vitamin B$_{12}$ deficiency inhibits the synthesis of DNA, which affects the growth and repair of all cells. Symptoms of vitamin B$_{12}$ deficiency include fatigue, *peripheral neuropathy*, tongue and mouth irregularities, *macrocytic anemia* (abnormally enlarged red blood cells), depression, confusion and memory loss (especially in the elderly), poor blood clotting and easy bruising, dermatitis and skin sensitivity, loss of appetite, nausea and vomiting.

❑ Anemia is the first symptom of vitamin B_{12} deficiency. Pernicious anemia results from either inadequate vitamin B_{12} intake or reduced gastric (stomach) secretion of intrinsic factor, which reduces the absorption of B_{12}.

❑ Elderly people are most susceptible to vitamin B_{12} deficiency because their stomach cells lose the ability to produce intrinsic factor, which is necessary for B_{12} absorption.

❑ Deficiencies in elderly people often cause varying degrees of neuropsychiatric symptoms such as moodiness, confusion, abnormal gait, memory loss, agitation, delusions, dizziness, dementia, and hallucinations.

❑ Meatless diets are deficient in vitamin B_{12}. Strict vegetarians are urged to use a vitamin B_{12} supplement.

❑ Many drugs inhibit vitamin B_{12} absorption and, when taken over time, can lead to nutrient depletion.

BIOLOGICAL FUNCTIONS AND EFFECTS

Cobalamin *co-enzymes* are necessary for converting RNA to DNA. This means that B_{12} plays a central role in replicating the genetic code and makes it a critical growth factor in all cells of the body.

❑ Vitamin B_{12} aids in the synthesis of DNA.

❑ Vitamin B_{12} is required for the synthesis of *myelin*, which insulates the nerves, essential to the functioning and maintenance of the nervous system.

❑ Vitamin B_{12} aids in the synthesis of methionine and in the metabolism of folic acid.

❑ Vitamin B$_{12}$ is necessary for the maturation of red blood cells.

❑ Vitamin B$_{12}$ is involved in various aspects of protein, fat, and carbohydrate metabolism.

❑ Vitamin B$_{12}$ may help to prevent smokers from developing mouth and throat cancer.

❑ Many asthmatics are helped by vitamin B$_{12}$ therapy.

SYMPTOMS OF TOXICITY

There are no known symptoms of toxicity for vitamin B$_{12}$, even at doses 1000 times greater than the RDA.

RDA AND DOSAGE

❑ The RDA for vitamin B$_{12}$ is 6 mcg (micrograms).

❑ Pharmacologic dosages in the scientific literature range from 100 mcg up to 2,000 mcg.

❑ Intramuscular injection is the most effective route of administration, especially for the elderly.

❑ Studies now indicate that oral and sublingual B$_{12}$ is more effectively absorbed than previously thought.

❑ Available forms are cyanocobalamin and methylcobalamin.

DIETARY SOURCES

❑ Animal protein products are the source of this nutrient. It does not occur in fruits, vegetables, grain, or legumes.

❑ Organ meats are the best source of vitamin B$_{12}$, followed by clams, oysters, beef, eggs, milk, and chicken, and cheese.

VITAMIN C (ASCORBIC ACID)

OVERVIEW

Drugs that deplete Vitamin C (Ascorbic Acid)
✔ Aspirin
✔ Bumetanide
✔ Choline magnesium trisalicylate
✔ Choline salicylate
✔ Corticosteroids
✔ Ethacrynic acid
✔ Furosemide
✔ Indomethacin
✔ Oral contraceptives
✔ Tetracyclines
✔ Torsemide

Vitamin C is the vitamin that cures the world's oldest known nutritional deficiency disease, *scurvy*. In fact, its name is derived from Latin (*a* = not, *scorbutus* = scurvy, meaning without scurvy). It was first isolated by Albert Szent-Gyorgyi in 1928 from the adrenal glands of pigs, and called hexuronic acid. In 1933 it was successfully synthesized, and the name was changed to *ascorbic acid.*

Vitamin C is water-soluble and is easily absorbed from the small intestine. Although it is concentrated in many tissues throughout the body, the adrenal glands contain the highest concentration.

Humans are one of the few species who cannot manufacture vitamin C and must depend on the diet, or nutritional supplements, as the source of this vitamin. Vitamin C exists in nature in both its reduced form, L-ascorbic acid, and in its oxidized form, L-dehydroascorbic   acid. L-ascorbic acid is the most active form; however, they convert to each other back and forth in a reversible equilibrium, and both are antiscorbutic.

SYMPTOMS AND CAUSES OF DEFICIENCY

Although scurvy is rare in the United States, subclinical vitamin C deficiencies are common. Deficiency symptoms include capillary fragility, hemorrhage, muscular weakness, easy bruising, gums that bleed easily, poor healing of wounds, anemia, poor appetite and growth, and tender and swollen joints.

❑ Stressful situations (both physical and emotional) tend to deplete the body's stores of vitamin C quickly.

❑ Individuals most likely to have deficiencies include elderly people on poor diets, alcoholics, people who are severely ill or under chronic stress, and infants who are fed only cow's milk.

❑ Studies have shown that:

   a) up to 95 percent of institutionalized elderly people are deficient

   b) 75 percent of cancer patients are deficient

   c) 20 percent of healthy elderly people are deficient.

BIOLOGICAL FUNCTIONS AND EFFECTS

Vitamin C participates in oxidation-reduction reactions, energy production, metabolism of *tyrosine*, reduction and storage of iron, and activation of folic acid. It is essential in the formation or synthesis of *collagen, serotonin, norepinephrine, thyroxine,* and some of the *corticosteroids.*

❑ In his 1972 book *The Healing Factor: Vitamin C Against Disease*, Irwin Stone, M.D., discussed more than 500 studies that reported the value of high doses of vitamin C in preventing and treating about 100 diseases. Research since then has continued to support the vast importance of this nutrient.

❑ Vitamin C plays a major role in the synthesis of *collagen* and *elastin* (the major structural components of skin), tendons, bone matrix, tooth dentin, blood vessels, and connective tissues between cells. Collectively, collagen is the most abundant protein in the body, comprising 25 to 30 percent of total body protein.

❑ Vitamin C is one of the body's most powerful *antioxidants*. Being water-soluble, it protects all body fluids, within every cell in the body, and is highly concentrated in the brain to protect against brain aging.

❑ Vitamin C helps the body handle all types of stress. It is required for the synthesis of the body's main stress response hormones in the adrenal glands, including *adrenalin, noradrenalin, cortisol,* and *histamine.* Stresses, such as fever, burns, exposure to cold, physical trauma, fractures, high altitude, and radiation, all require larger doses of vitamin C.

❑ Vitamin C prevents the formation of *nitrosamines* and dramatically reduces *cervical dysplasia,* as well as intestinal and cervical cancers. Vitamin C is claimed to prevent formation of bladder tumors, inhibit hyaluronidase (an enzyme found in malignant tumors), slow the degradation of cellular tissue and decrease the invasion of cancerous growth, stimulate production of *leukocytes* that engulf and destroy cancer cells, and prevent damage from *free radicals,* which can cause cancer.

❑ In preventing *cardiovascular disease,* vitamin C

a) increases *HDL (good) cholesterol*

b) decreases elevated *LDL* and total cholesterol by conversion to bile acids for excretion

c) is necessary for synthesis of collagen and elastin, which maintain strength and elasticity of blood vessels

d) decreases free radical oxidation of cholesterol

e) decreases levels of lipoprotein(a) or Lp(a), which are known to produce atherosclerosis.

❑ Plaque in the arteries is an insoluble complex made up of calcium-phospholipid-cholesterol. Sodium ascorbate can convert insoluble plaque to sodium calcium-phospholipid-cholesterol which is soluble. This conversion helps to reduce atherosclerotic plaque build-up.

❑ Vitamin C boosts immunity by:

    a) increasing production of disease-fighting white blood cells (neurtophils, lymphocytes, and natural killer cells).

    b) increasing levels of the *antibodies* that fight infections

    c) increasing the body's production of *interferon*

    d) modulates *prostaglandin* synthesis

❑ Vitamin C functions as an *antihistamine,* and as a phosphodiesterase inhibitor (the same action as some asthma medications). Vitamin C reduces the frequency and intensity of bronchial spasms in individuals who have asthma.

❑ Ascorbic acid is effective in treating most viruses (if enough is used) including herpes, shingles, viral hepatitis, and polio, by stimulating the production of interferons.

❑ An analysis of 14 placebo-controlled trials shows a 35 percent average reduction in the duration of the common cold when treated with vitamin C, and a decrease in the severity of symptoms.

❑ Vitamin C increases the healing of scars, broken bones, burns, and other conditions.

❑ Vitamin C detoxifies heavy metal toxins such as mercury, lead, cadmium, and nickel.

❑ Vitamin C is capable of regenerating the antioxidant form of vitamin E.

SIDE EFFECTS AND TOXICITY

❑ Vitamin C is nontoxic; excesses are excreted in the urine.

❑ Diarrhea is the only significant side effect from an overdose of vitamin C.

❑ Approximately 15 percent of people taking moderately high doses of vitamin C experience abdominal gas, bloating, and cramping. The mineral ascorbates, such as calcium or magnesium ascorbate, are much less acidic and usually solve this problem.

❑ Although vitamin C has not been proven to cause kidney stones, in some individuals its metabolic pathway produces a high amount of oxalic acid, which could be a problem. Therefore, people with a history of gout, kidney stones, or kidney disease should not take high dosages of vitamin C without medical supervision.

❑ Vitamin C does not destroy vitamin B_{12} and cause pernicious anemia.

❑ Large doses of vitamin C will interfere with:

a) tests to determine occult blood in the stool

b) tests to monitor blood glucose levels in diabetics

RDA AND DOSAGE

❑ The RDA for vitamin C is 60 mg per day.

❑ *Pharmacologic* doses in the scientific literature range from 500 mg up to 20 grams. Higher doses of vitamin C should be taken in three or four divided doses throughout the day.

❑ Any kind of physical or emotional stress calls for higher vitamin C intake.

❑ Taking vitamin C to bowel tolerance (just below the diarrhea point) is a therapeutic technique that has gained some acceptance. The intake necessary to reach bowel tolerance varies from person to person.

❑ Available forms are ascorbic acid, calcium ascorbate, magnesium ascorbate, sodium ascorbate, Ester C, and ascorbyl palmitate

DIETARY SOURCES

❑ Fresh fruits, especially citrus fruits, strawberries, cantaloupe, and currants.

❑ Fresh vegetables, especially Brussels sprouts, collard greens, lettuce, cabbage, peas, and asparagus.

VITAMIN D (CALCIFEROL)

OVERVIEW

Drugs that deplete Vitamin D (Calciferol)
✔ Barbiturates
✔ Carbamazepine
✔ Cholestyramine
✔ Cimetidine
✔ Colestipol
✔ Corticosteroids
✔ Famotidine
✔ Fosphenytoin
✔ Isoniazid
✔ Mineral oil
✔ Nizatidine
✔ Phenobartibal
✔ Phenytoin
✔ Ranitidine
✔ Rifampin

Vitamin D was isolated in 1930 and named calciferol. Since then, more *metabolites* have been found, and the two major forms of this vitamin are now known to be vitamin D_2 (ergocalciferol) and vitamin D_3 (cholecalciferol). Vitamin D is actually a hormone precursor, which can be manufactured by the body. Therefore, in a classical sense, it is not actually an essential nutrient. Because rickets is related to vitamin D deficiency, however, vitamin D has been traditionally classified as a vitamin.

Vitamin D is known as the "sunshine vitamin." It is formed in the body by the action of the sun's ultraviolet rays on the skin, converting the biological precursor into vitamin D. Vitamin D is a fat-soluble nutrient that is stored in body fats, principally the liver.

SYMPTOMS AND CAUSES OF DEFICIENCY

Rickets is the classic childhood vitamin D deficiency disease. Insufficient vitamin D limits calcium absorption, which can create bones that are not strong enough to withstand the ordinary stresses and strains of weight bearing. In adults, vitamin D deficiency can result in *osteomalacia* and *osteoporosis*. Symptoms of vitamin D deficiency include:

❑ In children: knock-knees, bowed legs, spinal curvature, pigeon breast, disfiguring of the skull, and tooth decay and dental problems.

❑ In adults: rheumatic pains, muscle weakness, increased the likelihood of fractures of the hip and pelvis, gradual loss of hearing.

❑ Causes of Vitamin D deficiency include:

a) inadequate dietary intake

b) limited exposure to sunlight, which reduces the body's synthesis of vitamin D

c) kidney or liver malfunctions that inhibit the conversion of vitamin D to its metabolically active forms.

❑ Vitamin D deficiency increases the risk for osteoporosis by reducing bone mass and bone density. There is no evidence, however, that vitamin D supplementation is effective in treating osteoporosis.

❑ Osteomalacia is the adult equivalent of rickets, wherein vitamin D deficiency causes softening of the bones, which can lead to deformities. This condition occurs more frequently in elderly people. It can cause rheumatic pain and muscle weakness and increases the likelihood of fractures of the hip and pelvis.

❑ Vitamin D deficiency can cause a gradual hearing loss because demineralization of the bones in the middle ear inhibits the transmission of vibrations to the nerves that communicate with the brain.

❑ Vitamin D deficiency causes muscle weakness, severe tooth decay, and phosphorus retention in the kidneys.

BIOLOGICAL FUNCTIONS AND EFFECTS

Vitamin D promotes the absorption of calcium and phosphorus for the growth of bones and teeth. For this reason, it is an essential growth nutrient for infants and children.

❑ The active form of vitamin D is called calcitrol. Because calcitrol is produced in the kidneys and functions elsewhere in the body, it is considered a hormone, with the intestines and bone as its targets.

❑ Calcitrol is the most active form of vitamin D, acting in the intestines to promote absorption of calcium and phosphorus.

❑ Vitamin D is involved in the formation (*mineralization*) of bone, as well as in the mobilization (demineralization) of bone mineral.

❑ Vitamin D might be helpful in preventing and treating some cancers. Geographical areas with the least amount of sunlight have the highest rates of colorectal and breast cancer. The active form of vitamin D, calcitrol, inhibits the growth of human melanoma, leukemia, and breast, lymphoma, and colon cancer cells.

❑ Calcitrol regulates serum levels of calcium and phosphorus.

❑ Vitamin D may help to prevent osteoporosis, as it facilitates absorption of calcium from the intestines. Low calcium levels stimulate the parathyroid gland, which initiates pulling calcium out of the bone.

❑ Some individuals with *psoriasis* respond to therapy with the active form of vitamin D. Supporting this is the fact that sunlight and ultraviolet light are also often helpful for psoriasis.

❑ The active form of vitamin D enhances the *immune system* by stimulating the activity of *macrophages*.

SIDE EFFECTS AND TOXICITY

❑ Vitamin D can be toxic. Excessive intake of this nutrient causes hypercalcemia, calcium deposits in soft tissues such as kidneys, arteries, heart, ear, and lungs.

❑ Signs of vitamin D toxicity include headache, weakness, nausea and vomiting, and constipation.

RDA AND DOSAGE

❑ The RDA for vitamin D is 400 I.U. per day.

❑ Pharmacologic doses in the scientific literature range from 400 I.U. up to 1,000 I.U. daily.

VITAMIN E (ALPHA TOCOPHEROL)

OVERVIEW

Drugs that deplete Vitamin E (Alpha Tocopherol)
✔ Cholestyramine
✔ Clofibrate
✔ Colestipol
✔ Fenofibrate
✔ Gemfibrozil
✔ Haloperidol
✔ Mineral oil

In 1932, Evans and Bishop discovered that something in vegetable oils was necessary for reproduction in rats, and they named it vitamin E. They referred to it as the "anti-sterility vitamin," which turned out to be an unfortunate designation, as it subsequently was found not to cause this activity in humans. The same researchers isolated the pure substance from wheat germ oil in 1936 and gave it the chemical name of tocopherol (after the Greek word "tokos," meaning "offspring," and "phero," meaning "to bring forth").

Vitamin E actually is a group of eight compounds including four tocopherols (alpha, beta, gamma, and delta) and four additional tocotrienol derivatives. Alpha tocopherol is the most common and the most potent form and is what usually is meant by the term vitamin E. Pure vitamin E compounds are easily oxidized, so they are manufactured as acetate or succinate esters.

Natural vitamin E is d-alpha tocopherol, whereas synthetically produced vitamin E is a mixture consisting of both the d- and l- isomers as dl-alpha tocopherol. Different studies report that natural vitamin E has from 34 to 50 percent greater bioavailability than synthetic vitamin E.

SYMPTOMS AND CAUSES OF DEFICIENCY

❑ Vitamin E is destroyed by heat and oxidation during cooking and food processing. Therefore, reliance on processed foods and fast foods can contribute to depletion. Low levels of selenium and a high intake of polyunsaturated fatty acids both contribute to depletion of vitamin E.

❑ Symptoms of vitamin E deficiency include dry skin, dull dry hair, rupturing of red blood cells resulting in anemia, easy bruising, PMS, fibrocystic breasts, hot flashes, *eczema, psoriasis,* cataracts, *benign prostatic hyperplaysia (BPH),* poor wound healing, muscle weakness, and sterility.

❑ Premature infants are likely to be deficient because very little vitamin E is transferred across the placenta. Breast milk, however, contains enough vitamin E to meet the infant's needs.

BIOLOGICAL FUNCTIONS AND EFFECTS

❑ Vitamin E is the body's most important fat-soluble *antioxidant.* As such, it ensures the stability and integrity of cellular tissues and membranes throughout the body by preventing *free radical* damage.

❑ Vitamin E (100 I.U./day) causes up to a 40 percent reduction in the risk to the nation's number-one killer, *cardiovascular disease.* It accomplishes this by decreasing platelet stickiness, protecting blood vessels against developing atherosclerotic lesions, and protecting *LDL*-cholesterol against oxidation.

❑ Low levels of vitamin E are associated with a greater risk for developing various forms of cancer, including lung, oral, colon, rectal, cervical, pancreatic, and liver. This also may be because of its ability to protect tissues against free radical damage. In most cases, however, the amount necessary to protect against cancer is substantially greater than the amount provided in the average American diet.

❑ Vitamin E supplementation has been shown to enhance *immune system* function and increase resistance to infection.

❑ During heavy exercise, vitamin E markedly reduces the amount of exercise-induced free radical damage to the blood and tissues, and also decreases the incidence of exercise-induced injury to muscles.

❑ Vitamin E protects the eyes against cataracts and macular degeneration.

❑ Some studies have shown that vitamin E supplementation (from 150 I.U. to 600 I.U. daily) helps many women alleviate the symptoms of PMS.

SIDE EFFECTS AND TOXICITY

❑ Although it is fat-soluble, vitamin E is a relatively nontoxic nutrient. Approximately 60 to 70 percent of the daily dose is excreted in the feces.

❑ Vitamin E can increase blood-clotting time and, therefore, high-level supplementation is not advised for individuals who are taking *anticoagulant* drugs without medical supervision.

❑ Most individuals studied while taking large doses of vitamin E have not shown toxic effects. But symptoms reported from isolated cases in which people were taking more than 1000 I.U. daily included headache, fatigue, nausea, double vision, muscular weakness, and intestinal distress.

RDA AND DOSAGE

❑ The RDA for vitamin E is 30 I.U. per day.

Pharmacological doses in the scientific literature range from 100 I.U. to 1000 I.U. daily.

❑ Natural vitamin E (d-alpha tocopherol) is more bioavailable and, therefore, better than synthetic vitamin E (dl-alpha tocopherol).

DIETARY SOURCES

❑ Vitamin E is one of the most widely available nutrients in commonly available foods. Sources of vitamin E include vegetable oils, wheat germ oil, seeds, nuts, and soy beans.

❑ Other adequate sources are leafy greens, Brussels sprouts, whole-wheat products, whole-grain breads and cereals, avocados, spinach, and asparagus.

VITAMIN K

OVERVIEW

Drugs that deplete Vitamin K
✔ Aminoglycosides
✔ Barbiturates
✔ Cephalosporins
✔ Cholestyramine
✔ Fluoroquinolones
✔ Fosphenytoin
✔ Macrolides
✔ Mineral oil
✔ Penicillins
✔ Phenobartibal
✔ Phenytoin
✔ Sulfonamides
✔ Tetracyclines
✔ Trimethoprim

In 1935, a scientist in Copenhagen observed that newly hatched chicks receiving a diet containing all of the known essential nutrients were developing a hemorrhagic (bleeding) disease. The problem was thought to be related to a decline of *prothrombin*, a substance necessary for normal clotting of blood. The Danish scientist named this newly discovered anti-hemmorrhagic factor vitamin K or "Koagulationsvitamin."

Vitamin K refers to a group of three vitamins called the quinones: (a) phylloquinone (K1), which occurs in green plants, (b) menaquinone (K2), which is synthesized by intestinal bacteria, and (c) menadione (K3), manufactured synthetically. The vitamin Ks are fat-soluble nutrients. Bile and pancreatic juice are necessary for their absorption from the upper small intestine, where they are then carried to the liver.

SYMPTOMS AND CAUSES OF DEFICIENCY

Vitamin K deficiency is rare except in newborn infants. When it does occur, it can cause hemorrhaging and death. Deficiency symptoms include easy bleeding, as well as skeletal disorders such as *rickets, osteoporosis,* and *osteomalacia.*

BIOLOGICAL FUNCTIONS AND EFFECTS

❑ Vitamin K is an enzymatic *co-factor* that is necessary for the production of a number of blood-clotting factors, including *prothrombin,* and factors VII, IX, and X.

- ❏ Vitamin K also is necessary for the synthesis of osteocalcin, a unique protein in bone that attracts calcium to bone tissue. Osteocalcin modulates the deposition of calcium into bone matrix.
- ❏ Because vitamin K plays a significant role in the calcification of bone, it may play a role in the prevention and treatment of osteoporosis.
- ❏ Laboratory experiments show that vitamin K inhibits the growth of several forms of cancer, including breast, ovary, colon, stomach, kidney, liver and lung.

SIDE EFFECTS AND TOXICITY

- ❏ Large doses of vitamin K can be toxic. Consequently, it is available only by prescription.
- ❏ Vitamin K can cause a fatal form of jaundice in infants.

RDA AND DOSAGE

- ❏ The RDA for vitamin K is 65 mcg for women and 80 mcg for men.
- ❏ Pharmacologic doses in the scientific literature range from 30 to 100 mcg.

DIETARY SOURCES

- ❏ Best sources of vitamin K are liver, green leafy vegetables, and members of the cabbage family.
- ❏ Because intestinal bacteria synthesize vitamin K, we are not dependent upon food for this nutrient.

ZINC

OVERVIEW

Drugs that deplete Zinc
✔ Benazepril
✔ Benzthiazide
✔ Bumetanide
✔ Captopril
✔ Chlorothiazide
✔ Chlorthalidone
✔ Cholestyramine
✔ Cimetidine
✔ Clofibrate
✔ Corticosteroids
✔ Enalapril
✔ Ethacrynic acid
✔ Ethambutol
✔ Famotidine
✔ Fenofibrate
✔ Fosinopril
✔ Furosemide
✔ Hydrochlorothiazide
✔ Hydroflumethiazide
✔ Indapamide
✔ Lisinopril
✔ Methyclothiazide
✔ Metolazone
✔ Moexipril
✔ Nevirapine
✔ Nizatidine
✔ Oral contraceptives
✔ Penicillamine
✔ Polythiazide
✔ Quionapril
✔ Quinethazone
✔ Ramipril
✔ Ranitidine
✔ Tetracycline
✔ Torsemide
✔ Trandolapril
✔ Triamterene
✔ Trichlomethiazide
✔ Valproic acid
✔ Zidovudine

Zinc is necessary for the functioning of well over 300 different enzymes and, as such, it plays a vital role in an enormous number of biological processes. Zinc is widely distributed in microorganisms, plants and animals. In humans, the highest concentrations of zinc are found in the liver, pancreas, kidneys, bone, and voluntary muscles. Zinc is highly concentrated in parts of the eye, prostate gland, sperm, skin, hair, and nails.

SYMPTOMS AND CAUSES OF DEFICIENCY

Marginal zinc deficiencies are thought to be quite common in the United States, and, because of its extensive range of biological activities, zinc deficiency can cause a wide range of deficiency symptoms. Symptoms of zinc deficiency are acne, impaired sense of smell and taste, delayed healing of wounds, anorexia, lowered immunity, frequent infections, depression, photophobia, night blindness, problems with skin, hair and nails, menstrual problems, joint pain, and nystagmus.

Zinc deficiency conditions were first reported in the 1960s in growing children and adolescent males from Egypt, Iran, and Turkey. Diets low in animal protein and high in phytate-containing grains produced symptoms of dwarfism, hypogonadism (inadequate development of sex organs), and failure to mature sexually.

❑ Pregnant women have greater needs for zinc. Deficiency can cause impaired fetal development, infants with low birthweight, and birth defects. Stretch marks during pregnancy also are partially a result of zinc deficiency.

❑ Zinc deficiency can be caused by inadequate dietary intake due to foods grown on zinc-depleted soils. Food processing also removes zinc, so fast foods and processed foods also are zinc-depleted. Protein- or calorie-restricted diets can also lead to zinc deficiency.

❑ Zinc depletion is frequently seen in the following medical conditions: alcoholism, macular degeneration, diabetes, malignant melanoma, liver and kidney diseases, malabsorption syndromes such as celiac sprue, and inflammatory bowel diseases such as Crohn's disease.

BIOLOGICAL FUNCTIONS AND EFFECTS

❑ A few of the important enzymatic activities of zinc are:

a) alcohol dehydrogenase, which works in the liver to detoxify alcohol

b) alkaline phosphatase, which frees inorganic phosphates to be used in bone metabolism

c) carbonic anhydrase, which helps excrete carbon dioxide

d) zinc/copper-containing superoxide dismutase

e) cytochrome C, which is important in electron transport and energy production

f) carboxypeptidase, which is necessary for the digestion of dietary proteins.

❑ Zinc is necessary in the synthesis of DNA and RNA, protein synthesis, cellular division, and gene expression. Zinc protects DNA from damage.

- ❑ Zinc helps regulate a wide variety of *immune system* activities, including *T-lymphocytes*, CD4s, natural killer cells, interleukin II, and zinc/copper superoxide dismutase.

- ❑ Zinc facilitates healing of wounds, especially in burns, surgical incisions, and other types of scars.

- ❑ Zinc enhances immune function which makes it especially important for AIDS patients.

- ❑ Zinc gluconate lozenges reduce the length and severity of the common cold.

- ❑ Zinc is necessary for the maturation of sperm, for ovulation, and for fertilization.

- ❑ Zinc is required for normal growth and maturation.

- ❑ Zinc often is useful in treating acne and eczema.

- ❑ Zinc is a critical regulator of the sensory perceptions of taste, smell, and vision. It controls salt-taste perception and is necessary for visual adaptation to dark and night vision.

- ❑ Zinc regulates vitamin A levels in the blood by controlling the release of stored vitamin A from the liver.

- ❑ Although zinc is a component of *insulin*, it does not seem to be a regulator of insulin activity.

- ❑ Zinc promotes the conversion of thyroxine to triiodothyronine.

- ❑ Because of its anti-inflammatory properties, zinc has been used successfully to treat some types of arthritis.

- ❑ Zinc is necessary for a healthy prostate gland and helps to prevent *benign prostatic hyperplasia (BPH)*.

SIDE EFFECTS AND TOXICITY

❑ Zinc is relatively nontoxic, and although toxicity has been reported in humans, it is uncommon.

❑ Ingestion of high levels of zinc can induce a copper deficiency. Doses of 45 mg/day are safe, but regular intakes greater than 150 mg/day could pose a problem.

❑ Zinc toxicity can cause diarrhea, dizziness, drowsiness, vomiting, muscle incoordination, and lethargy.

❑ Inhalation of zinc oxide in certain industrial environments can also be a source of excess exposure.

❑ Cooking acidic foods in galvanized cookware used to be a possible source of excess zinc intake. Widespread use of stainless steel and plastic materials to prepare and store foods has largely eliminated this problem.

❑ Galvanized pipes in older plumbing systems used to leach zinc into drinking water supplies, but modern plumbing has phased out the use of galvanized pipes.

RDA AND DOSAGE

❑ The RDA for zinc is 15 mg/day.

❑ Pharmacologic doses in the scientific literature range from 50 to 150 mg/day.

DIETARY SOURCES

❑ The best dietary sources of zinc are lean meats, liver, eggs, and seafood (especially oysters).

❑ Whole-grain breads and cereals are good sources of zinc.

INDEX

Note: *This index uses the generic names of drugs. If you are using a brand name drug and do not know its generic name, you can look it up in the Brand Names/Generic Names list that follows this index. It lists the generic name for each brand name drug.*

BRAND NAMES / GENERIC NAMES

Abelcet® Injection, *see* Amphotericin B
Abitrate®, *see* Clofibrate
Accupril®, *see* Quinapril
Aceon®, *see* Perindopril Erbumine
Aches-N-Pain® (OTC), *see* NSAIDs
Achromycin® Ophthalmic, *see* Tetracyclines
Achromycin® Topical, *see* Tetracyclines
Acticort 100®, *see* Corticosteroids
Actron® (OTC), *see* NSAIDs
Acular® Ophthalmic, *see* NSAIDs
Adalat®, *see* Nifedipine
Adalat® CC, *see* Nifedipine
Adapin® Oral, *see* Doxepin
Adlone® Injection, *see* Corticosteroids
Adriamycin PFS™, *see* Chemotherapy
Adriamycin RDF®, *see* Chemotherapy
Adrucil® Injection, *see* Chemotherapy
Adprin-B®, Extra Strength (OTC), *see* Aspirin
Advil® (OTC), *see* NSAIDs
Advil®, Children's, Oral Suspension, *see* NSAIDs
AeroBid®-M Oral Aerosol Inhaler, *see* Corticosteroids
AeroBid® Oral Aerosol Inhaler, *see* Corticosteroids
Aerolate III®, *see* Theophylline
Aerolate JR®, *see* Theophylline
Aerolate SR®, *see* Theophylline
Aeroseb-Dex®, *see* Corticosteroids
Aeroseb-HC®, *see* Corticosteroids
Agoral Plain® (OTC), *see* Mineral Oil
A-hydroCort®, *see* Corticosteroids
AK-Dex®, *see* Corticosteroids
AK-Pred® Ophthalmic, *see* Corticosteroids
AKTob® Ophthalmic, *see* Aminoglycosides
Ala-Cort®, *see* Corticosteroids
Ala-Scalp®, *see* Corticosteroids
Alba-Dex®, *see* Corticosteroids
Albert® Glyburide, *see* Glyburide
Aldomet®, *see* Methyldopa
Alesse™, *see* Oral Contraceptives
Aleve® (OTC), *see* NSAIDs
Alkaban-AQ®, *see* Chemotherapy
Alkeran®, *see* Chemotherapy
Alphatrex®, *see* Corticosteroids
Alphatrex®, *see* Corticosteroids
Altace®, *see* Ramipril
ALternaGEL® (OTC), *see* Aluminum Hydroxide
Alu-Cap® (OTC), *see* Aluminum Hydroxide
Aludrox® (OTC), *see* Aluminum Hydroxide and Magnesium Hydroxide
Alu-Tab® (OTC), *see* Aluminum Hydroxide
Amaryl®, *see* Glimepiride
AmBisome®, *see* Amphotericin B
Amcort®, *see* Corticosteroids

A-methaPred® Injection, *see* Corticosteroids
Amikin® Injection, *see* Aminoglycosides
Amoxil®, *see* Penicillins
Amphocin®, *see* Amphotericin B
Amphojel® (OTC), *see* Aluminum Hydroxide
Ampicin® sodium, *see* Penicillins
Amytal®, *see* Barbiturates
Anacin® (OTC), *see* Aspirin
Anafranil®, *see* Clomipramine
Anaprox®, *see* NSAIDs
Ancef®, *see* Cephalosporins
Anergan®, *see* Promethazine
Anucort-HC® Suppository, *see* Corticosteroids
Anuprep HC® Suppository, *see* Corticosteroids
Anusol® HC-1 (OTC), *see* Corticosteroids
Anusol® HC-2.5% (OTC), *see* Corticosteroids
Anusol-HC® Suppository, *see* Corticosteroids
Apo®-Amitriptyline, *see* Amitriptyline
Apo®-Amoxi, *see* Penicillins
Apo®-Ampi Trihydrate, *see* Penicillins
Apo®-ASA, *see* Aspirin
Apo®-Atenol, *see* Beta-Blockers
Apo®-Capto, *see* Captopril
Apo®-Carbamazepine, *see* Carbamazepine
Apo®-Cefaclor, *see* Cephalosporins
Apo®-Chlorpromazine, *see* Chlorpromazine
Apo®-Chlorpropamide, *see* Chlorpropamide
Apo®-Chlorthalidone, *see* Chlorthalidone
Apo®-Cimetidine, *see* Cimetidine
Apo®-Clomipramine, *see* Clomipramine
Apo®-Clonidine, *see* Clonidine
Apo®-Diclo, *see* NSAIDs
Apo®-Diflunisal, *see* NSAIDs
Apo®-Doxepin, *see* Doxepin
Apo®-Doxy, *see* Doxycycline
Apo®-Doxy Tabs, *see* Doxycycline
Apo®-Enalapril, *see* Enalapril
Apo®-Erythro E-C, *see* Macrolides
Apo®-Famotidine, *see* Famotidine
Apo®-Fenofibrate, *see* Clofibrate
Apo®-Fluphenazine, *see* Fluphenazine
Apo®-Furosemide, *see* Furosemide
Apo®-Glyburide, *see* Glyburide
Apo®-Hydralazine, *see* Hydralazine
Apo®-Hydro, *see* Hydrochlorothiazide
Apo®-Imipramine, *see* Imipramine
Apo®-Indapadmide, *see* Indapamide
Apo®-Indomethacin, *see* Indomethacin
Apo®-Indomethacin, *see* NSAIDs
Apo®-Keto, *see* NSAIDs
Apo®-Keto-E, *see* NSAIDs
Apo®-Lisinopril, *see* Lisinopril
Apo®-Lovastatin, *see* Lovastatin
Apo®-Methyldopa, *see* Methyldopa
Apo®-Metoprolol (Type L), *see* Beta-Blockers
Apo®-Minocycline, *see* Minocycline

Apo®-Nadol, *see* Beta-Blockers
Apo®-Naproxen, *see* NSAIDs
Apo®-Nizatidine, *see* Nizatidine
Apo®-Nortriptyline, *see* Nortriptyline
Apo®-Pen VK, *see* Penicillins
Apo®-Perphenazine, *see* Perphenazine
Apo®-Pindol, *see* Beta-Blockers
Apo®-Piroxicam, *see* NSAIDs
Apo®-Prednisone, *see* Corticosteroids
Apo®-Primidone, *see* Primidone
Apo®-Propranolol, *see* Beta-Blockers
Apo®-Ranitidine, *see* Ranitidine Hydrochloride
Apo®-Sulfamethoxazole, *see* Sulfonamides
Apo®-Sulfasalazine, *see* Sulfasalazine
Apo®-Sulfatrim, *see* Co-Trimoxazole
Apo®-Sulfatrim, *see* Sulfonamides
Apo®-Sulin, *see* NSAIDs
Apo®-Tetra, *see* Tetracyclines
Apo®-Thioridazine, *see* Thioridazine
Apo®-Timol, *see* Beta-Blockers
Apo®-Timop, *see* Beta-Blockers
Apo®-Tolbutamide, *see* Tolbutamide
Apo®-Triazide, *see* Hydrochlorothiazide and
    Triamterene
Apo®-Trimip, *see* Trimipramine
Apo®-Zidovudine, *see* Zidovudine
Apresazide®, *see* Hydralazine and
    Hydrochlorothiazide
Apresoline®, *see* Hydralazine
Aquaphyllin®, *see* Theophylline
Aquatag®, *see* Benzthiazide
Aquatensen®, *see* Methyclothiazide
Argesic®-SA, *see* Salsalate
Aristocort®, *see* Corticosteroids
Aristocort® A, *see* Corticosteroids
Aristocort® Forte, *see* Corticosteroids
Aristocort® Intralesional, *see* Corticosteroids
Aristospan® Intra-Articular, *see* Corticosteroids
Aristospan® Intralesional, *see* Corticosteroids
Artha-G®, *see* Salsalate
Arthritis Foundation® Pain Reliever (OTC), *see*
    Aspirin
Arthropan® (OTC), *see* Choline Salicylate
Articulose-50® Injection, *see* Corticosteroids
Ascriptin® (OTC), *see* Aspirin
Asendin®, *see* Amoxapine
Asmalix®, *see* Theophylline
Aspergum® (OTC), *see* Salicylates
Asprimox® (OTC), *see* Aspirin
Atarax®, *see* Hydroxyzine
Atolone®, *see* Corticosteroids
Atridox™, *see* Doxycycline
Atromid-S®, *see* Clofibrate
Augmentin®, *see* Penicillins
Aureomycin®, *see* Chlortetracycline
Aventyl® Hydrochloride Nortriptyline
Axid®, *see* Nizatidine
Axid® AR (OTC), *see* Nizatidine
Ayercillin®, *see* Penicillins
Azmacort™, *see* Corticosteroids

Azulfidine®, *see* Sulfasalazine
Azulfidine® EN tabs, *see* Sulfasalazine
Bactocill®, *see* Penicillins
Bactrim™, *see* Co-Trimoxazole
Bactrim™ DS, *see* Co-Trimoxazole
Baldex®, *see* Corticosteroids
Barbilixir®, *see* Barbiturates
Barbita®, *see* Barbiturates
Baycol™, *see* Cerivastatin
Bayer® Aspirin (OTC), *see* Aspirin
Bayer® Buffered Aspirin (OTC), *see* Aspirin
Bayer® Enteric 500, Extra Strength, Aspirin
    (OTC), *see* Aspirin
Bayer® Enteric 500, Regular Strength, Aspirin
    (OTC), *see* Aspirin
Bayer® Low Adult Strength (OTC), *see* Aspirin
Bayer® Plus, Extra Strength (OTC), *see* Aspirin
Beepen-VK®, *see* Penicillins
Betaloc®, *see* Beta-Blockers
Betaloc® Durules®, *see* Beta-Blockers
Betapace®, *see* Beta-Blockers
Betapen®-VK, *see* Penicillins
Betatrex®, *see* Corticosteroids
Beta-Val®, *see* Corticosteroids
Betaxin®, *see* Vitamin B_1
Betimol® Ophthalmic Beta-Blockers
Betnesol® (Disodium Phosphate), *see*
    Corticosteroids
Betoptic® Ophthalmic, *see* Beta-Blockers
Betoptic® S Ophthalmic, *see* Beta-Blockers
Bewon®, *see* Vitamin B_1
Biaxin™, *see* Macrolides
Bicillin® C-R, *see* Penicillins
Bicillin® C-R 900/300, *see* Penicillins
Bicillin® L-A, *see* Penicillins
BiCNU®, *see* Chemotherapy
Biomox®, *see* Penicillins
Bio-Tab®, *see* Doxycycline
Bisac-Evac® (OTC), *see* Bisacodyl
Bisacodyl Uniserts®, *see* Bisacodyl
Bisco-Lax®, *see* Bisacodyl
Blocadren® Oral, *see* Beta-Blockers
Brethaire® Inhalation Aerosol, *see* Terbutaline
Brethine® Injection, *see* Terbutaline
Brethine® Oral, *see* Terbutaline
Brevibloc® Injection, *see* Beta-Blockers
Brevicon®, *see* Oral Contraceptives
Brevital®, *see* Barbiturates
Bronalide®, *see* Corticosteroids
Bricanyl® Injection, *see* Terbutaline
Bricanyl® Oral, *see* Terbutaline
Bronkodyl®, *see* Theophylline
Bufferin® (OTC), *see* Aspirin
Buffex® (OTC), *see* Aspirin
Bumex®, *see* Bumetanide
Burinex®, *see* Bumetanide
Butalan®, *see* Barbiturates
Buticaps®, *see* Barbiturates
Butisol Sodium®, *see* Barbiturates
Calan®, *see* Verapamil

Calan® SR, *see* Verapamil
CaldeCORT®, *see* Corticosteroids
CaldeCORT® Anti-Itch Spray, *see*
  Corticosteroids
Cama® Arthritis Pain Reliever, *see* Aspirin
Camptosar®, *see* Chemotherapy
Capoten®, *see* Captopril
Carbatrol®, *see* Carbamazepine
Carter's Little Pills® (OTC), *see* Bisacodyl
Cartrol® Oral, *see* Beta-Blockers
Cataflam® Oral, *see* NSAIDs
Catapres® Oral, *see* Clonidine
Catapres-TTS® Transdermal, *see* Clonidine
Ceclor®, *see* Cephalosporins
Ceclor® CD, *see* Cephalosporins
Cedax®, *see* Cephalosporins
CeeNU®, *see* Chemotherapy
Cefobid®, *see* Cephalosporins
Cefotan®, *see* Cephalosporins
Ceftin® Oral, *see* Cephalosporins
Cefzil®, *see* Cephalosporins
Celebrex™, *see* Celecoxib
Celestone®, *see* Corticosteroids
Celestone® Soluspan, *see* Corticosteroids
Celontin®, *see* Methsuximide
Cel-U-Jec®, *see* Corticosteroids
Cena-K®, *see* Potassium Chloride (TR)
Ceptaz™, *see* Cephalosporins
Cerebyx®, *see* Fosphenytoin
C.E.S.™, *see* Estrogens, Conjugated
Cetacort®, *see* Corticosteroids
Chibroxin™ Ophthalmic, *see* Fluoroquinolones
Chlorprom®, *see* Chlorpromazine
Chlorpromanyl®, *see* Chlorpromazine
Ciloxan™ Ophthalmic, *see* Fluoroquinolones
Cipro™, *see* Fluoroquinolones
Cipro™ I.V., *see* Fluoroquinolones
Claforan®, *see* Cephalosporins
Claripex®, *see* clofibrate
Clavulin®, *see* Penicillins
Clinoril®, *see* NSAIDs
Clocort® Maximum Strength, *see*
  Corticosteroids
Clysodrast®, *see* Bisacodyl
Colestid®, *see* Colestipol
CombiPatch®, *see* Oral Contraceptives
Compazine®, *see* Prochlorperazine
Congest, see Estrogens, Conjugated
Coptin®, *see* Sulfonamides
Coreg®, *see* Beta-Blockers
Corgard®, *see* Beta-Blockers
CortaGel® (OTC), *see* Corticosteroids
Cortaid® Maximum Strength (OTC)
  Corticosteroids
Cortaid® With Aloe, *see* Corticosteroids
Cort-Dome®, *see* Corticosteroids
Cortef®, *see* Corticosteroids
Cortef® Feminine Itch, *see* Corticosteroids
Cortenema®, *see* Corticosteroids
Cortifoam®, *see* Corticosteroids

Cortizone®-5 (OTC), *see* Corticosteroids
Cortizone®-10 (OTC), *see* Corticosteroids
Cortone® Acetate, *see* Corticosteroids
Cosmegen®, *see* Chemotherapy
Cotrim®, *see* Co-Trimoxazole
Cotrim® DS, *see* Co-Trimoxazole
Covera-HS®, *see* Verapamil
Crysticillin® A.S., *see* Penicillins
Cuprimine®, *see* Penicillamine
Cutivate™, *see* Corticosteroids
Cytosar-U®, *see* Chemotherapy
Cytoxan® Oral, *see* Chemotherapy
Cytoxan® Injection, *see* Chemotherapy
Dacodyl® (OTC), *see* Bisacodyl
Dalalone L.A.®, *see* Corticosteroids
DaunoXome®, *see* Chemotherapy
Decaderm®, *see* Corticosteroids
Decadron®, *see* Corticosteroids
Decadron® LA, *see* Corticosteroids
Decadron® Turbinaire, *see* Corticosteroids
Decaject-L.A.®, *see* Corticosteroids
Decaspray®, *see* Corticosteroids
Declomycin®, *see* Demeclocycline Deficol, *see*
  Bisacodyl
Deficol® (OTC), *see* Bisacodyl
Dekasol-L.A.®, *see* Corticosteroids
Delcort®, *see* Corticosteroids
Delta-Cortef ® Oral, *see* Corticosteroids
Deltasone®, *see* Corticosteroids
Delta-Tritex®, *see* Corticosteroids
Demadex®, *see* Torsemide
Demulen®, *see* Oral Contraceptives
Depacon®, *see* Valproic Acid
Depakene®, *see* Valproic Acid
Depakote®, *see* Valproic Acid
Depen®, *see* Penicillamine
depMedalone®, *see* Corticosteroids
Depoject® Injection, *see* Corticosteroids
Depo-Medrol® Injection, *see* Corticosteroids
Depopred® Injection, *see* Corticosteroids
Deproic, *see* Valproic acid
Dermacort®, *see* Corticosteroids
Dermarest Dricort®, *see* Corticosteroids
DermiCort®, *see* Corticosteroids
Dermolate® (OTC), *see* Corticosteroids
Dermtex®, *see* Corticosteroids
Desogen®, *see* Oral Contraceptives
Detensol®, *see* Beta-Blockers
Dexair®, *see* Corticosteroids
Dexasone L.A.®, *see* Corticosteroids
Dexone®, *see* Corticosteroids
Dexone L.A.®, *see* Corticosteroids
Dezone®, *see* Corticosteroids
Diabeta®, *see* Glyburide
Dialume®, *see* Aluminum Hydroxide
Di-Gel® (OTC), *see* Aluminum Hydroxide,
  Magnesium Hydroxide, and Simethicone
Dilantin®, *see* Phenytoin
Diomycin, see Macrolides
Diphenylan Sodium®, *see* Phenytoin

Diprolene®, *see* Corticosteroids
Diprolene® AF, *see* Corticosteroids
Diprosone®, *see* Corticosteroids
Disalcid®, *see* Salsalate
Diucardin®, *see* Hydroflumethiazide
Diuchlor®, *see* Hydroflumethiazide
Diurigen®, *see* Chlorothiazide
Diuril®, *see* Chlorothiazide
Dixarit®, *see* Clonidine
D-Med® Injection, *see* Corticosteroids
Dolobid®, *see* NSAIDs
Dopamet®, *see* Methyldopa
Dopar®, *see* Levodopa
Doryx®, *see* Doxycycline
Doxy®, *see* Doxycycline
Doxychel®, *see* Doxycycline
Doxycin, see Doxycycline
Doxytec, see Doxycycline
Droxia™, *see* Chemotherapy
DTIC-Dome®, *see* Chemotherapy
Dulcolax® (OTC), *see* Bisacodyl
Duraclon®, *see* Clonidine
Duralone® Injection, *see* Corticosteroids
Duricef®, *see* Cephalosporins
Dyazide®, *see* Hydrochlorothiazide and
  Triamterene
Dycill®, *see* Penicillins
Dymelor®, *see* Acetohexamide
Dynabac®, *see* Macrolides
Dynacin® Oral, *see* Minocycline
Dynapen®, *see* Penicillins
Dyrenium®, *see* Triamterene
Easprin®, *see* Aspirin
E-Base®, *see* Macrolides
Econopred® Ophthalmic, *see* Corticosteroids
Econopred® Plus Ophthalmic, *see*
  Corticosteroids
Ecotrin® (OTC), *see* Aspirin
Ecotrin® Low Adult Strength (OTC), *see*
  Aspirin
Edecrin®, *see* Ethacrynic Acid
E.E.S.®, *see* Macrolides
Efudex® Topical, *see* Chemotherapy
Elavil®, *see* Amitriptyline
Eldecort®, *see* Corticosteroids
Elixomin®, *see* Theophylline
Elixophyllin®, *see* Theophylline
Elocom, see Corticosteroids
Elocon® Topical, *see* Corticosteroids
Elspar®, *see* Chemotherapy
Eltroxin®, *see* Levothyroxine
Empirin® (OTC), *see* Aspirin
E-Mycin®, *see* Macrolides
Enduron®, *see* Methyclothiazide
Enovil®, *see* Amitriptyline
Entocort®, *see* Corticosteroids
Entrophen®, *see* Aspirin
Epitol®, *see* Carbamazepine
Epivir®, *see* Lamivudine
Epivir® HBV, *see* Lamivudine

Eramycin®, *see* Macrolides
Erybid™, *see* Macrolides
Eryc®, *see* Macrolides
EryPed®, *see* Macrolides
Ery-Tab®, *see* Macrolides
Erythro-Base®, *see* Macrolides
Erythrocin®, *see* Macrolides
Esidrix®, *see* Hydrochlorothiazide
Eskalith®, *see* Lithium
Eskalith® CR, *see* Lithium
Estratab®, *see* Estrogens, Esterified
Estrostep®, *see* Oral Contraceptives
Estrostep® Fe, *see* Oral Contraceptives
Estrovis®, *see* Quinestrol
Etibi®, *see* Ethambutol
Euglucon®, *see* Glyburide
Evista®, *see* Raloxifene
Excedrin® IB (OTC), *see* NSAIDs
Exna®, *see* Benzthiazide
Ezide®, *see* Hydrochlorothiazide
Feldene®, *see* NSAIDs
Fleet® Laxative (OTC), *see* Bisacodyl
Fleet® Mineral Oil Enema (OTC), *see*
  Mineral Oil
Flonase®, *see* Corticosteroids
Flovent®, *see* Corticosteroids
Floxin®, *see* Fluoroquinolones
Fludara®, *see* Chemotherapy
Fluoroplex® Topical, *see* Chemotherapy
Flutex®, *see* Corticosteroids
Folex® PFS, *see* Methotrexate
Fortaz®, *see* Cephalosporins
Foscavir® Injection, *see* Foscarnet
FUDR®, *see* Chemotherapy
Fungizone®, *see* amphotericin B
Gantanol®, *see* Sulfonamides
Garamycin®, *see* Aminoglycosides
Gas-Ban DS® (OTC), *see* Aluminum
  Hydroxide, Magnesium Hydroxide, and
  Simethicone
Gaviscon®-2 Tablet (OTC), *see* Aluminum
  Hydroxide and Magnesium Trisilicate
Gaviscon® Liquid (OTC), *see* Aluminum
  Hydroxide and Magnesium Carbonate
Gaviscon® Tablet (OTC), *see* Aluminum
  Hydroxide and Magnesium Trisilicate
Gelusil® (OTC), *see* Aluminum Hydroxide,
  Magnesium Hydroxide, and Simethicone
Gemcor®, *see* Gemfibrozil
Gemzar®, *see* Chemotherapy
Gen-Blybe, see Glyburide
Gen-K®, *see* Potassium Chloride (TR)
Gen-Pindolol, see Beta-Blockers
Gen-Timolol, see Beta-Blockers
Genoptic® Ophthalmic, *see* Aminoglycosides
Genoptic® S.O.P. Ophthalmic, *see*
  Aminoglycosides
Genora®, *see* Oral Contraceptives
Genora® 1/35, *see* Oral Contraceptives
Genora® 1/50, *see* Oral Contraceptives

Genpril

Genpril® (OTC), *see* NSAIDs

Genpril® (OTC), *see* NSAIDs
Gentacidin® Ophthalmic, *see* Aminoglycosides
Gentafair®, *see* Aminoglycosides
Gentak® Ophthalmic, *see* Aminoglycosides
Gentrasul®, *see* Aminoglycosides
Geocillin®, *see* Penicillins
Glucophage®, *see* Metformin
Glynase™® PresTab™, *see* Glyburide
G-myticin® Topical, *see* Aminoglycosides
Gynecort® (OTC), *see* Corticosteroids
Haldol®, *see* Haloperidol
Haldol® Decanoate, *see* Haloperidol
Halfprin® 81 (OTC), *see* Aspirin
Haltran® (OTC), *see* NSAIDs
Hemril-HC® Uniserts®, *see* Corticosteroids
Hexadrol®, *see* Corticosteroids
Hi-Cor-1.0®, *see* Corticosteroids
Hi-Cor-2.5®, *see* Corticosteroids
Hivid®, *see* Zalcitabine
Honvol®, *see* Diethylstilbestrol
Hycamtin™, *see* Chemotherapy
Hycort®, *see* Corticosteroids
Hydrap-ES®, *see* Hydralazine, Hydrochlorothiazide, and Reserpine
Hydrea®, *see* Chemotherapy
Hydrex®, *see* Benzthiazide
Hydrocort®, *see* Corticosteroids
Hydrocortone® Acetate, *see* Corticosteroids
Hydrocortone® Phosphate, *see* Corticosteroids
HydroDIURIL®, *see* Hydrochlorothiazide
Hydromox®, *see* Quinethazone
Hydro-Par®, *see* Hydrochlorothiazide
HydroSKIN®, *see* Corticosteroids
Hydro-Tex® (OTC), *see* Corticosteroids
Hygroton®, *see* Chlorthalidone
Hytone®, *see* Corticosteroids
Ibuprin® (OTC) NSAIDs
Ibuprohm®, *see* NSAIDs
Ibu-Tab®, *see* NSAIDs
Idamycin®, *see* Chemotherapy
Ifex®, *see* Chemotherapy
I-Gent®, *see* Aminoglycosides
Ilosone®, *see* Macrolides
I-Methasone®, *see* Corticosteroids
Indochron E-R®, *see* Indomethacin
Indocid, *see* Indomethacin
Indocid SR, *see* Indomethacin
Indocin®, *see* Indomethacin
Indocin® I.V., *see* Indomethacin
Indocin® SR, *see* Indomethacin
Inflamase® Forte Ophthalmic, *see* Corticosteroids
Inflamase® Mild Ophthalmic, *see* Corticosteroids
Isoptin®, *see* Verapamil
Isoptin® SR, *see* Verapamil
Jaa Amp® Trihydrate, *see* Penicillins
Jaa-Prednisone®, *see* Corticosteroids
Janimine®, *see* Imipramine
Jenamicin® Injection, *see* Aminoglycosides

Jenest-28™, *see* Oral Contraceptives
K+ 10®, *see* Potassium Chloride (TR)
Kantrex®, *see* Aminoglycosides
Kaochlor®, *see* Potassium Chloride (TR)
Kaochlor® SF, *see* Potassium Chloride (TR)
Kaon-Cl®, *see* Potassium Chloride (TR)
Kaon Cl-10®, *see* Potassium Chloride (TR)
Kay Ciel®, *see* Potassium Chloride (TR)
K+ Care®, *see* Potassium Chloride (TR)
K-Dur® 10, *see* Potassium Chloride (TR)
K-Dur® 20 Potassium Chloride (TR)
Keflex®, *see* Cephalosporins
Keftab®, *see* Cephalosporins
Kefurox® Injection, *see* Cephalosporins
Kefzol®, *see* Cephalosporins
Kenacort®, *see* Corticosteroids
Kenaject-40®, *see* Corticosteroids
Kenalog®, *see* Corticosteroids
Kenalog-10®, *see* Corticosteroids
Kenalog-40®, *see* Corticosteroids
Kenalog® H, *see* Corticosteroids
Kenalog® in Orabase®, *see* Corticosteroids
Kenonel®, *see* Corticosteroids
Kerlone® Oral, *see* Beta-Blockers
Key-Pred® Injection Corticosteroids
Key-Pred-SP® Injection, *see* Corticosteroids
K-Lease®, *see* Potassium Chloride (TR)
K-Lor™, *see* Potassium Chloride (TR)
Klor-Con®, *see* Potassium Chloride (TR)
Klor-Con® 8, *see* Potassium Chloride (TR)
Klor-Con® 10 Potassium Chloride (TR)
Klor-Con/25®, *see* Potassium Chloride (TR)
Klorvess®, *see* Potassium Chloride (TR)
Klotrix®, *see* Potassium Chloride (TR)
K-Lyte/Cl®, *see* Potassium Chloride (TR)
K-Norm®, *see* Potassium Chloride (TR)
Kondremul® (OTC), *see* Mineral Oil
K-Tab®, *see* Potassium Chloride (TR)
LactiCare-HC®, *see* Corticosteroids
Lanacort® (OTC), *see* Corticosteroids
Laniazid® Oral, *see* Isoniazid
Lanophyllin®, *see* Theophylline
Lanoxicaps®, *see* Digoxin
Lanoxin®, *see* Digoxin
Largactil®, *see* Chlorpromazine
Larodopa®, *see* Levodopa
Lasix®, *see* Furosemide
L-Dopa®, *see* Levodopa
Lescol®, *see* Fluvastatin
Leustatin®, *see* Chemotherapy
Levaquin™, *see* Fluoroquinolones
Levate®, *see* Amitriptyline
Levlen®, *see* Oral Contraceptives
Levoprome®, *see* Methotrimeprazine
Levora®, *see* Oral Contraceptives
Levo-T™, *see* Levothyroxine
Levothroid®, *see* Levothyroxine
Levoxyl®, *see* Levothyroxine
Lipitor®, *see* Atorvastatin
Liquid Pred®, *see* Corticosteroids

Lithane®, *see* Lithium
Lithobid®, *see* Lithium
Lithonate®, *see* Lithium
Locoid®, *see* Corticosteroids
Lodine®, *see* NSAIDs
Lodine® XL, *see* NSAIDs
Loestrin®, *see* Oral Contraceptives
Loestrin® Fe, *see* Oral Contraceptives
Lo/Ovral®, *see* Oral Contraceptives
Lopid®, *see* Gemfibrozil
Lopressor®, *see* Beta-Blockers
Lorabid®, *see* Cephalosporins
Losec®, *see* Omeprazole
Lotensin®, *see* Benazepril
Lozide®, *see* Indapamide
Lozol®, *see* Indapamide
Lukeran®, *see* Chemotherapy
Luminal®, *see* Barbiturates
Lysodren®, *see* Chemotherapy
Maalox® (OTC), *see* Aluminum Hydroxide and Magnesium Hydroxide
Maalox® Plus (OTC), *see* Aluminum Hydroxide, Magnesium Hydroxide, and Simethicone
Maalox® Therapeutic Concentrate (OTC) Aluminum Hydroxide and Magnesium Hydroxide
Magalox Plus® (OTC), *see* Aluminum Hydroxide, Magnesium Hydroxide, and Simethicone
Mandol®, *see* Cephalosporins
Maox®, *see* Magnesium Oxide
Marazide®, *see* Benzthiazide
Marcillin®, *see* Penicillins
Marpres®, *see* Hydralazine, Hydrochlorothiazide, and Reserpine
Marthritic®, *see* Salsalate
Mavik®, *see* Trandolapril
Maxaquin®, *see* Fluoroquinolones
Maxidex®, *see* Corticosteroids
Maxipime®, *see* Cephalosporins
Maxivate®, *see* Corticosteroids
Maxzide®, *see* Hydrochlorothiazide and Triamterene
Mazepine®, *see* Carbamazepine
Mebaral®, *see* Barbiturates
Meclomen®, *see* NSAIDs
Medimet®, *see* Methyldopa
Medipren®, *see* NSAIDs
Medralone®, *see* Corticosteroids
Medrol®, *see* Corticosteroids
Mefoxin®, *see* Cephalosporins
Mellaril®, *see* Thioridazine
Mellaril-S®, *see* Thioridazine
Menadol® (OTC), *see* NSAIDs
Menest®, *see* Estrogens, Esterified
Metahydrin®, *see* Trichlormethiazide
Methylone®, *see* Corticosteroids
Meticorten®, *see* Corticosteroids
Metreton® Ophthalmic, *see* Corticosteroids

Mevacor®, *see* Lovastatin
Mezlin®, *see* Penicillins
Micro-K® 10, *see* Potassium Chloride (TR)
Micro-K® Extencaps®, *see* Potassium Chloride (TR)
Micro-K® LS®, *see* Potassium Chloride (TR)
Micronase®, *see* Glyburide
Microsulfon®, *see* Sulfonamides
Microzide™, *see* Hydrochlorothiazide
Midol® 200 (OTC), *see* NSAIDs
Milkinol® (OTC), *see* Mineral Oil
Minocin® IV Injection, *see* Minocycline
Minocin® Oral, *see* Minocycline
Mircette™, *see* Oral Contraceptives
Mithracin®, *see* Chemotherapy
Mobenol®, *see* Tolbutamine
Modecate® Enanthate, *see* Fluphenazine
Modicon™, *see* Oral Contraceptives
Moditen® Hydrochloride, *see* Fluphenazine
Monitan®, *see* Beta-Blockers
Mono-Gesic®, *see* Salsalate
Monopril®, *see* Fosinopril
Motrin®, *see* NSAIDs
Motrin®, Children's, Oral Suspension, *see* NSAIDs
Motrin® IB (OTC), *see* NSAIDs
Motrin®, Junior Strength, (OTC), *see* NSAIDs
M-Prednisol® Injection, *see* Corticosteroids
MSD® Enteric Coated ASA, *see* Aspirin
Mustargen®, *see* Chemotherapy
Mutamycin®, *see* Chemotherapy
Myambutol®, *see* Ethambutol
Mycifradin® Sulfate Oral, *see* Neomycin
Mycifradin® Sulfate Topical Neomycin
Mykrox®, *see* Metolazone
Mylanta® (OTC), *see* Aluminum Hydroxide, Magnesium Hydroxide, and Simethicone
Mylanta®-II (OTC), *see* Aluminum Hydroxide, Magnesium Hydroxide, and Simethicone
Myleran®, *see* Chemotherapy
Mysoline®, *see* Primidone
Nadopen-V®, *see* Penicillins
Nafcil™ Injection, *see* Penicillins
Nalfon®, *see* NSAIDs
Nallpen® Injection, *see* Penicillins
Naprelan®, *see* NSAIDs
Naprosyn®, *see* NSAIDs
Naqua®, *see* Trichlormethiazide
Nardil®, *see* Phenelzine
Nasacort®, *see* Corticosteroids
Nasacort® AQ, *see* Corticosteroids
Nasalide® Nasal Aerosol, *see* Corticosteroids
Nasarel™, *see* Corticosteroids
Navelbine®, *see* Chemotherapy
Naxen®, *see* NSAIDs
Nebcin® Injection, *see* Aminoglycosides
NebuPent® Inhalation, *see* Pentamidine
N.E.E.® 1/35, *see* Oral Contraceptives
Nelova™ 0.5/35E, *see* Oral Contraceptives
Nelova™ 1/35E, *see* Oral Contraceptives

Nelova™ 1/50M, *see* Oral Contraceptives
Nelova™ 10/11, *see* Oral Contraceptives
Nembutal®, *see* Barbiturates
Neo-Codema®, *see* Hydrochlorothiazide
Neo-Cultol® (OTC), *see* Mineral Oil
Neo-Estrone®, *see* Estrogens, Esterified
Neo-fradin® Oral, *see* Neomycin
Neosar® Injection, *see* Chemotherapy
Neo-Tabs® Oral, *see* Neomycin
Neut® Injection, *see* Sodium Bicarbonate
Nordette®, *see* Oral Contraceptives
Norethin™ 1/35E, *see* Oral Contraceptives
Norethin™ 1/50M, *see* Oral Contraceptives
Norinyl® 1+35, *see* Oral Contraceptives
Norinyl® 1+50, *see* Oral Contraceptives
Normodyne®, *see* Beta-Blockers
Noroxin® Oral, *see* Fluoroquinolones
Norpramin®, *see* Desipramine
Nor-tet® Oral, *see* Tetracyclines
Norzine®, *see* Thiethylperazine
Novambarb®, *see* Barbiturates
Novamoxin®, *see* Penicillins
Novantrone®, *see* Chemotherapy
Novasen, *see* Aspirin
Novo-Atenol, *see* Beta-Blockers
Novo-AZT, *see* Zidovudine
Novo-Butamide, *see* Tolbutamide
Novo-Captopril, *see* Captopril
Novo-Carbamaz, *see* Carbamazepine
Novo-Chlorpromazine, *see* Chlorpromazine
Novo-Cimetine, *see* Cimetidine
Novo-Clonidine, *see* Clonidine
Novo-Difenac®, *see* NSAIDs
Novo-Difenac®-SR, *see* NSAIDs
Novo-Diflunisal, *see* NSAIDs
Novo-Digoxin, *see* Digoxin
Novo-Doxepin, *see* Doxepin
Novo-Doxylin, *see* Doxycycline
Novo-Famotidine, *see* Famotidine
Novo-Fibrate, *see* clofibrate
Novo-Glyburide, *see* Glyburide
Novo-Hydrazide, *see* Hydrochlorothiazide
Novo-Hylazin, *see* Hydralazine
Novo-Keto-EC, *see* NSAIDs
Novo-Medopa®, *see* Methyldopa
Novo-Metformin, *see* Metformin
Novo-Methacin, *see* Indomethacin
Novo-Methacin, *see* NSAIDs
Novo-Metoprolol, *see* Beta-Blockers
Novo-Naprox, *see* NSAIDs
Novo-Pen-VK®, *see* Penicillins
Novo-Pindol, *see* Beta-Blockers
Novo-Piroxicam, *see* NSAIDs
Novo-Pramine, *see* Imipramine
Novo-Prednisolone, *see* Corticosteroids
Novo-Prednisone, *see* Corticosteroids
Novo-Propamide, *see* Chlorpropamide
Novo-Ranidine, *see* Ranitidine Hydrochloride
Novo-Ridazine, *see* Thioridazine
Novo-Rythro Encap, *see* Macrolides

Novo-Secobarb, *see* Barbiturates
Novo-Semide, *see* Furosemide
Novo-Soxazole, *see* Sulfonamides
Novo-Sundac, *see* NSAIDs
Novo-Tetra, *see* Tetracyclines
Novo-Thalidone, *see* Chlorthalidone
Novo-Timol, *see* Beta-Blockers
Novo-Tolmetin, *see* NSAIDs
Novo-Triamzide, *see* Hydrochlorothiazide and Triamterene
Novo-Trimel, *see* Co-Trimoxazole
Novo-Trimel, *see* Sulfonamides
Novo-Tripramine, *see* Trimipramine
Novo-Tryptin, *see* Amitriptyline
Nozinan®, *see* Methotrimeprazine
Nu-Amoxi, *see* Penicillins
Nu-Ampi Trihydrate, *see* Penicillins
Nu-Atenol, *see* Beta-Blockers
Nu-Capto, *see* Captopril
Nu-Carbamazepine, *see* Carbamazepine
Nu-Cimet, *see* Cimetidine
Nu-Clonidine, *see* Clonidine
Nu-Cotrimox, *see* Co-Trimoxazole
Nu-Cotrimox, *see* Sulfonamides
Nu-Diclo, *see* NSAIDs
Nu-Diflunisal, *see* NSAIDs
Nu-Doxycycline, *see* Doxycycline
Nu-Famotidine, *see* Famotidine
Nu-Glyburide, *see* Glyburide
Nu-Hydral, *see* Hydralazine
Nu-Indo, *see* Indomethacin
Nu-Indo, *see* NSAIDs
Nu-Ketoprofen, *see* NSAIDs
Nu-Ketoprofen-E, *see* NSAIDs
Nu-Medopa, *see* Methyldopa
Nu-Metop, *see* Beta-Blockers
Nu-Naprox, *see* NSAIDs
Nu-Pen-VK, *see* Penicillins
Nu-Pindol, *see* Beta-Blockers
Nu-Pirox, *see* NSAIDs
Nu-Prochlor, *see* Prochlorperazine
Nu-Propranolol, *see* Beta-Blockers
Nu-Ranit, *see* Ranitidine Hydrochloride
Nu-Tetra, *see* Tetracyclines
Nu-Timolol, *see* Beta-Blockers
Nu-Triazide, *see* Hydrochlorothiazide and Triamterene
Nu-Trimipramine, *see* Trimipramine
Nuprin® (OTC), *see* NSAIDs
Nutracort®, *see* Corticosteroids
Nydrazid® Injection, *see* Isoniazid
Occlucort®, *see* Corticosteroids
Ocu-Dex®, *see* Corticosteroids
Ocuflox™ Ophthalmic, *see* Fluoroquinolones
Ocumycin®, *see* Aminoglycosides
Ocupress®, *see* Beta-Blockers
Omnipen®, *see* Penicillins
Omnipen®-N, *see* Penicillins
Orabase® HCA, *see* Corticosteroids
Orafen, *see* NSAIDs

Orasone®, *see* Corticosteroids
Oretic®, *see* Hydrochlorothiazide
Orinase® Diagnostic Injection, *see* Tolbutamide
Orinase® Oral, *see* Tolbutamide
Oncovin® Injection, *see* Chemotherapy
Ortho® 0.5/35, *see* Oral Contraceptives
Ortho-Cept®, *see* Oral Contraceptives
Ortho-Cyclen®, *see* Oral Contraceptives
Ortho-Novum® 1/35, *see* Oral Contraceptives
Ortho-Novum® 1/50, *see* Oral Contraceptives
Ortho-Novum® 7/7/7, *see* Oral Contraceptives
Ortho-Novum® 10/11, *see* Oral Contraceptives
Ortho Tri-Cyclen®, *see* Oral Contraceptives
Orudis®, *see* NSAIDs
Orudis® KT (OTC), *see* NSAIDs
Oruvail®, *see* NSAIDs
Ovcon® 35, *see* Oral Contraceptives
Ovcon® 50, *see* Oral Contraceptives
Ovral®, *see* Oral Contraceptives
Ovrette®, *see* Oral Contraceptives
Pamelor®, *see* Nortriptyline
Pamprin IB® (OTC), *see* NSAIDs
Pandel®, *see* Corticosteroids
Panmycin® Oral, *see* Tetracyclines
Paraplatin®, *see* Chemotherapy
Pathocil®, *see* Penicillins
Paxene®, *see* Chemotherapy
PCE®, *see* Macrolides
Pediapred® Oral, *see* Corticosteroids
PediaProfen™, *see* NSAIDs
Penecort®, *see* Corticosteroids
Pentacarinat®, *see* Pentamidine
Pentam-300® Injection, *see* Pentamidine
Pentothal®, *see* Barbiturates
Pen.Vee K®, *see* Penicillins
Pepcid®, *see* Famotidine
Pepcid® AC Acid Controller, *see* Famotidine
Peptol®, *see* Cimetidine
Periostat™, *see* Doxycycline
Permapen®, *see* Penicillins
Permitil® Oral, *see* Fluphenazine
Pfizerpen®, *see* Penicillins
Phenazine®, *see* Promethazine
Phenergan®, *see* Promethazine
Phillips'® Milk of Magnesia (OTC), *see*
  Magnesium Hydroxide
Pipracil®, *see* Penicillins
Platinol®, *see* Chemotherapy
Platinol®-AQ, *see* Chemotherapy
PMS-Carbamazepine, *see* Carbamazepine
PMS-Cholestyramine, *see* Cholestyramine
  Resin
PMS-Desipramine, *see* Desipramine
PMS-Erythromycin, *see* Macrolides
PMS-Fluphenazine, *see* Fluphenazine
PMS-Imipramine, *see* Imipramine
PMS-Ketoprofen, *see* NSAIDs
PMS-Levothyroxine Sodium, *see*
  Levothyroxine
PMS-Perphenazine, *see* Perphenazine

PMS-Prochlorperazine, *see* Prochlorperazine
PMS-Sulfasalazine, *see* Sulfasalazine
PMS-Thioridazine, *see* Thioridazine
Polycillin®, *see* Penicillins
Polycillin-N®, *see* Penicillins
Polymox®, *see* Penicillins
Ponstel®, *see* NSAIDs
Potasalan®, *see* Potassium Chloride (TR)
Pravachol®, *see* Pravastatin
Predair®, *see* Corticosteroids
Predaject®, *see* Corticosteroids
Predalone T.B.A.®, *see* Corticosteroids
Predcor®, *see* Corticosteroids
Predcor-TBA®, *see* Corticosteroids
Pred Forte® Ophthalmic, *see* Corticosteroids
Pred Mild® Ophthalmic, *see* Corticosteroids
Prednicen-M®, *see* Corticosteroids
Prednisol® TBA Injection, *see* Corticosteroids
Prelone® Oral, *see* Corticosteroids
Premarin®, *see* Estrogens, Conjugated
Premphase™, *see* Estrogen and
  Medroxyprogesterone
Prempro™, *see* Estrogen and
  Medroxyprogesterone
Pre-Par®, *see* Ritodrine
Prevacid®, *see* Lansoprazole
Prevalite®, *see* Cholestyramine Resin
Prilosec™, *see* Omeprazole
Principen®, *see* Penicillins
Prinivil®, *see* Lisinopril
Pro-amox®, *see* Penicillins
Pro-Ampi® Trihydrate, *see* Penicillins
Proaqua®, *see* Benzthiazide
Procardia®, *see* Nifedipine
Procardia® XL, *see* Nifedipine
Procort® (OTC), *see* Corticosteroids
Proctocort™, *see* Corticosteroids
Procytox®, *see* Chemotherapy
Pro-Indo®, *see* Indomethacin
Prolixin Decanoate® Injection, *see*
  Fluphenazine
Prolixin Enanthate® Injection, *see* Fluphenazine
Prolixin® Injection, *see* Fluphenazine
Prolixin® Oral, *see* Fluphenazine
Proloprim®, *see* Trimethoprim
Pro-Piroxicam®, *see* NSAIDs
Prorazin®, *see* Prochlorperazine
Prorex®, *see* Promethazine
Prostaphlin®, *see* Penicillins
Pro-Trin®, *see* Sulfonamides
Psorion® Cream Corticosteroids
Pulmicort, *see* Corticosteroids
Pulmicort Turbuhaler®, *see* Corticosteroids
Purinethol®, *see* Chemotherapy
PVF® K, *see* Penicillins
Questran®, *see* Cholestyramine Resin
Questran® Light, *see* Cholestyramine Resin
Quibron®-T, *see* Theophylline
Quibron®-T/SR, *see* Theophylline
Raxar®, *see* Fluoroquinolones

Relafen®, *see* NSAIDs
Renese®, *see* Polythiazide
Rescriptor®, *see* Delavirdine
Respbid®, *see* Theophylline
Retrovir®, *see* Zidovudine
Rheumatrex®, *see* Methotrexate
Rhinalar®, *see* Corticosteroids
Rhinaris®F, *see* Corticosteroids
Rhinocort®, *see* Corticosteroids
Rhodis™, *see* NSAIDs
Rhodis-EC™, *see* NSAIDs
Rhoprolene, *see* Corticosteroids
Rhoprosone, *see* Corticosteroids
Rhotral, *see* Beta-Blockers
Rifadin®, *see* Rifampin
Rifadin® Injection, *see* Rifampin
Rifadin® Oral, *see* Rifampin
Rimactane®, *see* Rifampin
Rimactane® Oral, *see* Rifampin
Robicillin® VK, *see* Penicillins
Rocephin®, *see* Cephalosporins
Rofact™, *see* Rifampon
Roubac®, *see* Sulfonamides
Rubex®, *see* Chemotherapy
Rubramin®, *see* Vitamin B_{12}
Rum-K®, *see* Potassium Chloride (TR)
Salazopyrin®, *see* Suylfasalazine
Salazopyrin EN-Tabs®, *see* Sulfasalazine
Saleto-200® (OTC), *see* NSAIDs
Saleto-400®, *see* NSAIDs
Salflex®, *see* Salsalate
Salgesic®, *see* Salsalate
Salsitab®, *see* Salsalate
Saluron®, *see* Hydroflumethiazide
S.A.S.™, *see* Sulfasalazine
Scalpicin®, *see* Corticosteroids
Seconal™, *see* Barbiturates
Sectral®, *see* Beta-Blockers
Septra®, *see* Sulfonamides
Septra® DS, *see* Sulfonamides
Ser-Ap-Es®, *see* Hydralazine,
     Hydrochlorothiazide, and Reserpine
Serentil®, *see* Mesoridazine
Sertan®, *see* Primidone
Sinequan® Oral, *see* Doxepin
Slo-bid™, *see* Theophylline
Slo-Phyllin®, *see* Theophylline
Slow-K®, *see* Potassium Chloride (TR)
Solfoton®, *see* Barbiturates
Solu-Cortef®, *see* Corticosteroids
Solu-Medrol® Injection, *see* Corticosteroids
Solurex L.A.®, *see* Corticosteroids
Sotacor®, *see* Beta-Blockers
Sotalol®, *see* Beta-Blockers
Sparine®, *see* Promazine
Spectrobid®, *see* Penicillins
S-T Cort®, *see* Corticosteroids
Stelazine®, *see* Trifluoperazine
Stemetil®, *see* Prochlorperazine
Sterapred®, *see* Corticosteroids

Stilphostrol®, *see* Diethylstilbestrol
St Joseph® Adult Chewable Aspirin (OTC), *see* Aspirin
Sulfatrim®, *see* Co-Trimoxazole
Sumycin® Oral, *see* Tetracyclines
Suprax®, *see* Cephalosporins
Surmontil®, *see* Trimipramine
Sustaire®, *see* Theophylline
Syn-Captopril, *see* Captopril
Syn-Flunisolide, *see* Cortcosteroids
Syn-Minocycline, *see* Minocycline
Syn-Nadolol, *see* Beta-Blockers
Synacort®, *see* Corticosteroids
Synphasic®, *see* Oral Contraceptives
Syn-Pindol®, *see* Beta-Blockers
Synthroid®, *see* Levothyroxine
Tac™-3, *see* Corticosteroids
Tac™-40, *see* Corticosteroids
Tacaryl®, *see* Methdilazine
TACE®, *see* Chlorotrianisene
Tagamet®, *see* Cimetidine
Tagamet® HB (OTC), *see* Cimetidine
Taro-Ampicillin® Trihydrate, *see* Penicillins
Taro-Atenol®, *see* Beta-Blockers
Taro-Sone®, *see* Corticosteroids
Taxol®, *see* Chemotherapy
Taxotere®, *see* Chemotherapy
Tazicef®, *see* Cephalosporins
Tazidime®, *see* Cephalosporins
Teejel®, *see* Choline Salicylate
Tegretol®, *see* Carbamazepine
Tegretol®-XR, *see* Carbamazepine
Tegrin®-HC (OTC), *see* Corticosteroids
Teladar®, *see* Corticosteroids
Ten-K®, *see* Potassium Chloride (TR)
Tenormin®, *see* Beta-Blockers
Terramycin® I.M. Injection, *see*
     Oxytetracycline
Terramycin® Oral, *see* Oxytetracycline
Tetracap® Oral, *see* Tetracyclines
Thalitone®, *see* Chlorthalidone
Theo-24®, *see* Theophylline
Theobid®, *see* Theophylline
Theochron®, *see* Theophylline
Theoclear-80®, *see* Theophylline
Theoclear L.A.®, *see* Theophylline
Theo-Dur®, *see* Theophylline
Theolair™, *see* Theophylline
Theo-Sav®, *see* Theophylline
Theospan-SR®, *see* Theophylline
Theostat-80®, *see* Theophylline
Theovent®, *see* Theophylline
Theo-X®, *see* Theophylline
Thorazine®, *see* Chlorpromazine
Ticar®, *see* Penicillins
Timoptic® OcuDose®, *see* Beta-Blockers
Timoptic® Ophthalmic, *see* Beta-Blockers
Timoptic-XE® Ophthalmic, *see* Beta-Blockers

Tindal®, *see* Acetophenazine
TOBI™ Inhalation Solution, *see* Aminoglycosides
Tobrex® Ophthalmic, *see* Aminoglycosides
Tofranil®, *see* Imipramine
Tofranil-PM®, *see* Imipramine
Tolectin®, *see* NSAIDs
Tolectin® DS, *see* NSAIDs
Tolinase®, *see* Tolazamide
Topicycline® Topical Tetracyclines
Topilene, *see* Corticosteroids
Topisone, *see* Corticosteroids
Toposar® Injection, *see* Chemotherapy
Toprol XL®, *see* Beta-Blockers
Toradol® Injection, *see* NSAIDs
Toradol® Oral NSAIDs
Torecan®, *see* Thiethylperazine
Totacillin®, *see* Penicillins
Totacillin®-N, *see* Penicillins
T-Phyl®, *see* Theophylline
Trandate®, *see* Beta-Blockers
Tremytoine®, *see* Phenytoin
Trendar® (OTC), *see* NSAIDs
Triacet™, *see* Corticosteroids
Triadapin®, *see* Doxepin
Triam-A®, *see* Corticosteroids
Triam Forte®, *see* Corticosteroids
Tricosal®, *see* Choline Magnesium Trisalicylate
Triderm®, *see* Corticosteroids
Tri-Kort®, *see* Corticosteroids
Trilafon®, *see* Perphenazine
Tri-Levlen®, *see* Oral Contraceptives
Trilisate®, *see* Choline Magnesium Trisalicylate
Trilog®, *see* Corticosteroids
Trilone®, *see* Corticosteroids
Trimox®, *see* Penicillins
Trimpex®, *see* Trimethoprim
Tri-Norinyl®, *see* Oral Contraceptives
Triphasil®, *see* Oral Contraceptives
Triptil®, *see* Protriptyline
Tristoject®, *see* Corticosteroids
Trisulfa®, *see* Sulfonamides
Trisulfa-S®, *see* Sulfonamides
Tritec®, *see* Ranitidine Bismuth Citrate
Trovan™, *see* Fluoroquinolones
Tuinal®, *see* Barbiturates
U-Cort™, *see* Corticosteroids
Ultracef®, *see* Cephalosporins
Unasyn®, *see* Penicillins
Uni-Dur®, *see* Theophylline
Unipen® Injection, *see* Penicillins
Unipen® Oral, *see* Penicillins
Uniphyl®, *see* Theophylline
Uni-Pro® (OTC), *see* NSAIDs
Univasc®, *see* Moexipril

Uridon®, *see* Chlorthalidone
Uri-Tet® Oral, *see* Oxytetracycline
Uritol®, *see* Furosemide
Urobak®, *see* Sulfonamides
Urozide®, *see* Hydrochlorothiazide
Valisone®, *see* Corticosteroids
Valium®, *see* Diazepam
Vantin®, *see* Cephalosporins
Vasotec®, *see* Enalapril
Vasotec® I.V., *see* Enalapril
V-Cillin K®, *see* Penicillins
Veban®, *see* Chemotherapy
Veetids®, *see* Penicillins
Velosef®, *see* Cephalosporins
VePesid® Injection, *see* Chemotherapy
VePesid® Oral, *see* Chemotherapy
Verelan®, *see* Verapamil
Vibramycin®, *see* Doxycycline
Vibramycin® IV, *see* Doxycycline
Vibra-Tabs®, *see* Doxycycline
Videx®, *see* Didanosine
Vincasar® PFS™ Injection, *see* Chemotherapy
Viramune®, *see* Nevirapine
Vistaril®, *see* Hydroxyzine
Vivactil®, *see* Protriptyline
Voltaren® Ophthalmic, *see* NSAIDs
Voltaren® Oral, *see* NSAIDs
Voltaren Rapide®, *see* NSAIDs
Voltaren®-XR Oral, *see* NSAIDs
Westcort®, *see* Corticosteroids
Wimpred, *see* Corticosteroids
Winstrol®, *see* Stanozolol
Wycillin®, *see* Penicillins
Wymox®, *see* Penicillins
Xanax®, *see* Alprazolam
Yutopar®, *see* Ritodrine
Zagam®, *see* Fluoroquinolones
Zanosar®, *see* Chemotherapy
Zantac®, *see* Ranitidine Hydrochloride
Zantac® 75 (OTC), *see* Ranitidine Hydrochloride
Zarontin®, *see* Ethosuximide
Zaroxolyn®, *see* Metolazone
Zebeta®, *see* Beta-Blockers
Zerit®, *see* Stavudine
Zestril®, *see* Lisinopril
Zinacef® Injection, *see* Cephalosporins
Zithromax™, *see* Macrolides
Zocor®, *see* Simvastatin
Zolicef®, *see* Cephalosporins
Zonalon® Topical Cream, *see* Doxepin
ZORprin®, *see* Aspirin
Zosyn™, *see* Penicillins
Zovia®, *see* Oral Contraceptives
Zymenol® (OTC), *see* Mineral Oil

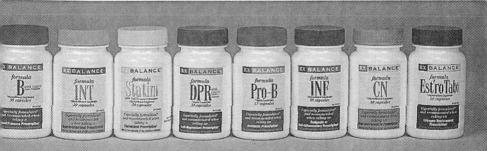